THE PASTOR'S ROLE IN EDUCATIONAL MINISTRY

Edited with Introductions by
RICHARD ALLAN OLSON

YEARBOOKS IN CHRISTIAN EDUCATION · V
Fortress Press Philadelphia

YEARBOOKS IN CHRISTIAN EDUCATION • V

This yearbook is the fifth in a series of volumes produced jointly by the Division for Life and Mission in the Congregation of The American Lutheran Church and the Division for Parish Services of the Lutheran Church in America.

The Age-Sex Pyramid, p. 164, from the United States Census Bureau; The Grid figure, p.210, from: *The Managerial Grid* by Robert Blake and Jane Srygley Mouton (Houston: Gulf Publishing Company, 1964), used with permission; Congregational Goal Sheet, p. 207, from the Joint ALC/LCA Parish Life and Ministry Pilot Test Project; Participation of the Pastor in the Decision-making Process, p. 233, from "How to Choose a Leadership Pattern" by Robert Tannenbaum and Warren H. Schmidt in *Harvard Business Review*, March-April, 1958; The Teacher Growth Pyramid, p. 239, is adapted from Dale's Cone of Experience, p. 267 in this book; Hoag's Ladder of Learning, p. 268, from *The Ladder of Learning* by Victor Hoag. Used by permission of the Seabury Press, New York. The Shannon-Weaver communication model, p. 251, from *The Process and Effects of Mass Communication*, ed. Wilbur Schramm (Urbana, Illinois: University of Illinois Press, 1954), p. 4; Dale's Cone of Experience, p. 267, from *Audio Visual Methods in Teaching*, Third Edition, by Edgar Dale. Copyright © 1946, 1954, 1969, by Holt, Rinehart and Winston, Inc. Reprinted by permission of The Dryden Press.

Quotations on p. 12, Ralph Daniel Heim, *Leading a Church School* (Philadelphia: Fortress Press, 1968), p. 79; p. 64, Ronald Goldman, *Readiness for Religion* (New York: The Seabury Press, 1970) p. 222; p. 180, Gilbert Highet, *The Art of Teaching* (New York: Alfred A. Knopf, 1950), p. 15.

5235F75 Printed in U.S.A. 1-1046

NEW DIMENSIONS FOR THE PASTOR-EDUCATOR

Pastors, directors of educational ministry, theological students, and other leaders concerned with educational ministry in the church are searching for—and sometimes finding—ideas, resources, and experiences which offer possibilities for viable forms of educational ministry today.

Many look at the church's educational efforts these days with disdain or at best with a jaundiced eye. Some will blame the confusion (or is it new insight?) of the theologies of liberation, hope, or play. Some suggest that planners in Philadelphia or Minneapolis merely don't have their heads screwed on tight and the evolving concepts of educational ministry are less than adequate. Pluralism and secularization in American society are blamed by others for the bad days in the church's educational program, whatever its dimensions. Ambivalence about the authority of the Bible in the church divides some congregations and frightens others. Changing value patterns in the youth culture, such as the increasing appreciation for diversity and the social and political challenges of a post-War on Poverty, post-Watergate America, are among the factors influencing the sometimes indecisive, sometimes negative, oft-times frustrated reactions of pastors and critics to educational ministry.

Yet pastors involved in educational ministries in widely differing places are visualizing and experiencing educational efforts which transform people. In those efforts, the pastor's role remains a crucial one. The pastor's role in our socio-cultural-political milieu will clearly not be identical to last year's model. New demands have brought new configurations.

For example, pastors and professional church educators will be conscious of their presuppositions about education per se, and especially about education in the church. "What was good enough for me is good enough for you" will probably not work many places.

Education increasingly will have to be the opportunity where people are helped to critique the world and to build new ways of viewing the world which are theologically appropriate and ethically sensitive. This book is designed to help the readers reflect on their views of educational ministry and perhaps on their own education and assumptions.

Almost every pastor is very humble about one thing—being a theologian! Whatever the connotations of the word *theologian* for you and me, we who are the leaders must begin to see our unique role as being theological educators in the parishes of our world. This means simply helping people recall the theologies of the past and write (live) new theological perspectives for the present and future which are consonant with the faith delivered to the saints. Living faith needs nurturing through the use of our minds as well as our hearts. At many points this yearbook is a testimony to the importance of this dimension. Richard Simon Hanson, Dick Luecke, and Jack White especially focus on this aspect.

Often I find myself so tied up in my own pursuits that I hardly can think of alternatives to my present practice or picture of the world. Cal Kuder, Richard Rehfeldt, John Lundin, Dick Preis, and John Cochran, writing out of their parish bases, provide some new looks at perennial problems. They provide evidence that good things are happening in congregations, sometimes serendipitously but always meaningfully. Personal crises, youth activities, and sermons all provide opportunities for education. Cochran, White, and Luecke try to interest us in new kinds of involvement in the socio-cultural-political sphere in order to help people survive in an altogether difficult and demanding time. Whether the issue is upper echelon government scandal, conservation, broken Indian treaties, or continuing racial injustice, we need ways to begin to deal with the stuff of these areas theologically and ethically. No blue ribbon panels will write finis to the issues; local programs of caring and interpretation will be necessary and essential to the mission of the church. Whatever might be the necessity for structure and function alterations with the churchwide agencies or congregational committees, ventures of action and reflection will test our mettle and provide clues to fresh interpretation. The action will be rich material for educational reflection and clarification of the faith in our time. We have so often professed that education occurs only in classrooms, yet increasingly we are admitting that classrooms can be in strange places and education can take place in the midst of live issues to which the Word speaks.

One of the places where issues of Christian life and ministry are sharpened is in the emerging efforts at congregation development.

Pastors are finding new opportunities to expand their facilitator roles in helping people communicate with one another about gospel and mission. Like those in the traditional priestly role, they are bridge-builders enabling new energy and ideas to surface and come to fruition. Certainly pastors and educators have seen the educational dimensions of parish practice for ages, but the holistic, systematic, intentional emphases of the current programs seem hopeful and exciting.

Robert Bacher and Norm Wegmeyer as co-directors of the field-centered Parish Life and Ministry Development Project give the most complete description of theory and rationale for the project to date. Let's hope the organization development movement in the church takes the educational task seriously and helps people think and act in new ways, and does not succumb to furniture-arranging and window-dressing. It has such great potential to be a servant of the gospel. Pastors are seeing the potentials and problems in many situations.

Whenever or wherever pastors or church educators have an opportunity to do educational ministry, they can rely on the recent developments in the areas of media, planning, psychology of learning, and communication. More and more we are seeing these insights coming to bear as Frank Klos describes them in his chapter. Klos does not merely give us quick recipes for instant success; he presents theoretical perspectives which need to be tested and modified. As these new modes interface with the theological methodology and education to which we are accustomed, the Spirit will have plenty of work helping us decipher the exciting future.

The title of this yearbook has a presumptuous air about it—as though someone knows precisely what every pastor ought to do or even more incredulous, that we know what all pastors are doing. Some may be expecting a sociological report or a theological treatise on the pastor's role. The editor and advisory group had a different, but no less important, goal. In the face of cynicism and despair in some quarters about educational ministry, this yearbook tries to give examples of work in the parish which 1) suggest the dynamic of contemporary educational ministry; 2) take seriously differential approaches to people and situations; 3) show the importance of central avenues of insight and faithful witness like biblical scholarship and theological studies to the everyday task of educational ministry; 4) discuss directions for seeing educational ministry in and outside the congregation; and 5) put it together in communities.

The yearbook can be viewed as an attempt to encourage new alternatives, more self-awareness of the role of the professional in church education, and meaningful ministries which make the gospel available to increasing numbers of people with increasing commitment and understanding.

Thanks to Frank Klos for teaching me much about editing, and to the writers who worked hard to meet deadlines. Especial thanks to the families, congregations, agencies, and schools who gave us time to put together this volume.

Richard Allan Olson

CONTENTS

1

PASTORS LOOK AT EDUCATIONAL MINISTRY

Many earnest persons, who have found direct education for themselves fruitless and unprofitable, declare that they first began to learn when they began to teach, and that in the education of others they discovered the secret of their own.

—Gamaliel Bradford

The true aim of every one
who aspires to be a teacher
should be, not to impart his own opinions,
but to kindle minds.

—F. W. Robertson

Homines, dum docent, discunt.
Men, while teaching, learn.

—Seneca

Clearly, the pastor, to no small degree is "it" in education. In this connection it is worthwhile noticing that thought and effort for church renewal today is highlighting the pastor's educational role. Always, recognizing the basic importance of the teaching office in his ministry, he can be expected to keep an ardent educational commitment fresh and informed.

—Ralph Daniel Heim

ON VISIONING

In an attempt to get some feel for the state of educational ministry in the church today, five pastors were selected to write their perceptions of the problems and possibilities growing out of their experiences in congregations. They were asked to describe how they understand their call to educational ministry in the light of the gospel, how their particular situation affects their responses, how their work in educational ministry is related to the priesthood of all believers, how their participation in educational efforts is meaningful in personal and professional ways, how they evaluate their work in educational ministry, and what skills, resources, and organizational models have been helpful. The pastors' visioning give us reason for hope rather than despair.

The diversity of pastoral styles and different understandings of the pastor's educational role comes across clearly in the following five articles. Calvin Kuder notes the priority of educational ministry in a large congregation. Pursuing the example of Jesus' command to "feed my sheep," he suggests that finding the appropriate diet (matching response to need) for contemporary Lutherans is not easily done, but the opportunity is too great to pass up. He describes three such opportunities: small group Bible study, the confirmation-first Communion issue, and confirmation classes. Lay involvement in leadership and decision-making and flexible scheduling provided opportunities for new insights and responsibility to emerge. Kuder emphasizes the value of planning, goal identification, and evaluation for furthering the work in educational ministry.

Richard Rehfeldt outlines his "travels" in the development of his educational ministry stance. He sees educational opportunities at a variety of points of contact, and sees a listening, personalizing, participating, thinking, acting, enabling style as best able to help people find relevant answers to their questions about their life and faith.

He probes his own attitudes to show how the pastor's role can develop. His examples of the encouraging results of lay ministry are solid reasons to expand an understanding of educational ministry beyond traditional classrooms.

Richard I. Preis describes his experiences with sermon preparation groups and the energizing effect they have had on parish life. In vivid detail he portrays the struggles and results which can be produced when participation in worship planning is encouraged and programmed. Not only is corporate life enhanced, but individuals gain insight and courage to face life in faithful ways.

In similar ways, small groups have enabled people to search for new understandings in the midst of fellow searchers. Preis leaves the theorizing to others and lets us look at these experiences for what they are—the serious efforts of one congregation to do educational ministry. The familiar theme of the benefits for pastors in these experiences is reiterated. This should be encouraging news for pastors who are groping for new approaches to ministry.

John Lundin focuses his view of educational ministry on adult education. He sees his role as equipper of the saints, and describes his efforts to develop a lay-centered program through The American Lutheran Church *P*rogram of *A*dult *C*hristian *E*ducation (PACE). His emerging program is characterized by searching out needs, setting priorities for concerns, and developing a holistic, interconnected series of events filled with variety. Lundin emphasizes adult education as the program behind the program to help people think theologically about their concerns in rural South Dakota and to help them structure their congregational life in more viable forms. He concludes with his experience of growth through involvement in continuing education stimulated by adult education in the parish.

John Cochran completes this section by putting his ministry in a black, urban community directly in front of us. He writes with the same enthusiasm that characterizes his ministry. Centered in Word and sacrament, his ministry shows the necessity of entering the local culture with eyes wide open to new forms and disciplines. The use of deacons is particularly suggestive for broadening the base of ministry and entering more fully into the life of the people. The whole ministry can be conceptualized as a teaching-learning situation. In no way can Cochran's ministry be sloughed off as not applicable to a wide range of settings—urban or suburban, white or black. He helps us envision hope in the midst of changing circumstances and changing opportunities.

ME–A PASTOR-EDUCATOR

Calvin D. Kuder

In the past year, I spent 124 hours in the classroom! My annual report to the congregation I serve itemized those hours as follows:

Sunday church school (a group of 30 adults)	30 hours
Confirmation ministry classes	40 hours
A weekly women's Bible study group	19 hours
A weekly men's Bible study group	15 hours
Pastor's classes (preparation for membership)	11 hours
School of Religion (a course in sex education for teenagers)	5 hours
Preparation for first Communion	4 hours
Total	124 hours

A Lot of Time

The magnitude of this total didn't particularly impress me until I got to comparing notes with a college professor friend and discovered that 120 classroom hours is his typical semester's work load. In short, what is only one of many responsibilities for me is equivalent to a half year's work for a professional educator.

To press the analogy a bit further, my professor friend is relatively free of the administrative chores which attach themselves to teaching. He does not have to recruit his own students, attend to their registration, procure his own supplies, arrange schedules and classrooms (and maybe set them up), or perform all the other myriad chores which devolve upon me as pastor-educator. Rather, the professor has the whole administrative machinery of the college to rely on, to say nothing of the professional support of colleagues or considerable research and library facilities at his finger tips. While I am fortunate to have a co-pastor who not only shares the teaching load but also helps in such areas as course design, administration, and evaluation, I know that most pastors must go it alone.

Of all the teaching situations listed in my report, only the pastor's class for church membership involves repeated use of the same curriculum materials and resources. While some of my teaching makes use of the prepared curriculum materials of the church, I find an old rule of thumb that says two hours of out-of-class preparation for every hour in class still holds true for me. And further, a significant part of my teaching involves "do-it-yourself" course design as well as classroom leadership.

The Christian education that occupies a large place in my ministry I conceive of in professional terms. Including administration, preparation, and classroom time, I estimate that I spend about 480 hours a year in educational ministry, or about twelve 40-hour work weeks. Granted, no pastor works only a 40-hour week, but somewhere between one-sixth and one-fourth of my time goes to education. Anything which takes up that much time has to be a major concern. That means that as a pastor I am also a professional educator.

Not everyone who is busy, however, is automatically a professional. To me, operating professionally as an educator means giving serious attention to the teaching-learning process; becoming increasingly knowledgeable about how persons learn; devising new and varied approaches and resources to enable the growth and change of learning to take place; and becoming more informed and knowledgeable about the content which is to be taught.

To whatever degree I have achieved this sort of professionalism as a pastor-educator it has come about largely through on-the-job training and continuing education programs over the years. While my seminary training did provide a sort of minimal foundation in Christian education, it was less than adequate. Conversations with contemporary seminarians and observation of seminary curricula would lead me to believe that this situation has not improved much. Seminaries now require much concentrated work in clinical pastoral education, a recognition of the need which today's pastors have for refined skills in many diverse counseling situations. It strikes me as somewhat strange that while most parish pastors will spend as much, and probably more, time in teaching as they will in counseling, the seminaries have yet to respond to this reality with the kind of intense and required preparation in Christian education that would compare to the CPE program.

Go and Teach; Feed My Sheep

I teach because I have been commanded to. Jesus commanded his followers to go and teach. There's nothing in the history of the intervening years between Jesus and me to indicate that the command has been revoked. As one to whom the gospel has been entrusted by the church, there is no question about my mandate to teach. However, that ancient injunction with the dogmatic and evangelistic encrustations which have gathered around it seems rather too narrow a base for me. Undergirding my self-image as pastor-educator, I prefer to hear another command of Jesus', "Feed my sheep." Not only does it suggest a wider pastoral role, it invites us to focus on those to whom we minister.

"Go and teach" suggests a magisterial role for pastors as educators. They teach because they are ordained to do so. People sit under pastors' tutelage and (presumably) learn from them because of their teaching authority. Without meaning to caricature, that is precisely the image many pastors once had, and perhaps still have. To be sure, the word of God is self-authenticating, and those who teach it derive certain authority by so doing, but too often both pastors and pupils get confused about where the authority really rests.

"Feed my sheep" offers a biblical-theological base that invites a kind of creative dialogue or tension between leader and learner. Moreover, it describes the way things are in the 1970s in the congregation. The people—God's people—the body of Christ—are as much in need of being fed as ever they were. Conscientious shepherds (pastors) must struggle to find the kind of diet those sheep need. Moreover, they have to devise an adequate delivery system for their product. Having readied the pasture, they have to get balky sheep into it!

The people in today's churches may be as balky as the sheep in our Lord's parables, but they are not stupid. They are better educated, more sophisticated, and a great deal busier than members of the last generation. They are not necessarily less faithful or less pious than their forebears, but their piety and faith are being expressed in different forms. Faced with a multitude of conflicting demands and pressures, they are not likely to attend a class or join a Bible study group just because it's a nice, religious thing to do. Whether one gets his data from *The Reader's Digest* or the latest footnoted sociological tome, the evidence is abundant that people, including the people of our churches, are alienated from God and from each other, laden with guilt, full of doubt, and torn between loyalties. The need for the proclamation release of the gospel, with its forgiving, healing power, into the midst of life has never been greater.

While I'll not put down preaching and the role it can and should play in a total pastoral ministry for one minute, I surely don't want to limit myself to it. I don't believe people want to be ministered to by preaching alone, any more than they want to be cared for by a doctor who pretends the medical discoveries of the last 30 years never happened! I'm willing to devote one-sixth or one-fourth or one-half of my time to Christian education because I believe that's where the needs are exhibited and where the greatest opportunities lie for relating the gospel to people's lives.

The Priesthood of All Believers—450 Years Later

One of the most cherished and least honored parts of our Lutheran heritage is the concept of the priesthood of all believers. My own recent attempts (and reports of others' attempts) to democratize the leadership of worship convince me that many Lutherans are more Catholic than the Pope! They have become accustomed to a clergy-dominated church, and any attempts to move toward making the priesthood of all believers an operating principle rather than merely a polemical slogan are too threatening to cope with. Something of the same phenomenon is true in education. While we have a long tradition of lay teachers in our Sunday church schools, we also have a parallel tradition in which the really important teaching is reserved to the clergy, e.g., catechetics and adult Bible study. While this is not universally the case, insofar as it exists, it is symptomatic of a situation ripe for change.

One recent experience suggests a way this might be done. The 1972 Parish Education Month theme "And Now the Good News," with its emphasis on Bible reading and Bible study, provided the occasion for change. Through the generosity of two parishioners, 500 copies of the special Lutheran edition of *Good News for Modern Man* were purchased. It was widely ballyhooed that a copy would be given away to every man, woman, and child who committed himself or herself to any of several educational programs, including Sunday church school, the men's and women's mid-week Bible study groups, and a new program which was billed simply as Home Bible Study Groups. The give-away made a good start for the new Sunday church school year, rekindled interest in the established Bible study groups, and served as an attention-getter for the new program. The goals of program were to help adults:

- Engage in Bible study in small groups in an informal setting;
- Gain some skills for their own personal study of the Bible;
- Examine in depth a particular portion of Scripture, in this case the letter to the Philippians.

Twenty-five groups were organized to meet in natural neighborhood zones throughout the city and surrounding fringe areas. A host family was recruited from within each zone and supplied with printed invitations, which they were asked to mail to the persons within their zone after having added their own names, address of the meeting place, and time. The invitation was to spend four consecutive Thursday nights in informal Bible study with a small group of fellow church members who happen to be neighbors. At the same time, a leader was recruited from within each zone. These leaders were asked to come together for a one-time training session the week before the program began. The Book of Philippians was chosen as the basis for the study because it was short enough to be handled in the time available and included some basic theological concepts. I prepared detailed guides for the leaders to use in each session. These were similar in style and approach to the leader's guide for an adult Sunday church school course, with great emphasis on suggested learning experiences which would require the active participation of all who were present.

For the one-time training session, I simply led the group of leaders through the first session of the proposed series of Bible studies. This session was held in the parlor of the church, which approximates a home-like setting, to simulate as nearly as possible the situation in which the leaders would be functioning. Instead of using a chalkboard or overhead projector, I relied on a piece of poster board and a felt-tip marker so that the leaders could see that it is possible to adapt teaching tools to the setting one expects to be in. The training session proved to be very lively and the discussion could well have continued far into the night. However, at the end of one hour I simply pointed out that the time we had agreed upon had elapsed. As leaders, they would have to keep the same kind of covenant with their groups.

The following Thursday evening I sat in my study biting my fingernails, wondering what, if anything, was happening. Here was a major educational program in operation and I, as "big chief" teacher, was not even part of the action! A quick round of telephone calls revealed that something indeed was happening. Two of the groups never happened. No one except the host family and the leader showed up. In a couple of other cases the attendance was very small. But most of the groups had not only come together around a study of the Word of God, but they had done so with real excitement and enthusiasm. A total of 150 persons participated, and every last one had a chance to express personal opinions, test new ideas, and incidentally build some new friendships. In succeeding weeks, the weaker groups were consolidated so that we finished with 20 functioning groups, each with an average of seven or eight participants.

By far the most significant aspect of the whole venture was the role played by the 20 group leaders. In a way that most people had not experienced before, participants and leaders alike discovered that serious Bible study can be engaged in by concerned Christians without the direct leadership of the chief guru.

The idea of the pastor as teacher of teachers surely is not a new one. However, it seems to me that most past efforts have been aimed at someone pumping enough skills and confidence into a batch of recruits to keep the Sunday church school rolling another year. Surely leadership education must take many forms, but I think there is a difference between equipping and motivating persons to work together in discovering and sharing the faith and those efforts which aim merely at keeping programs in operation.

The Pastor As Plotter and Schemer

More than ever the pastor-educator needs to be plotter and a schemer. Surely he or she will continue to be a teacher. As I indicated at the outset of this essay, I do a great deal of teaching. But more and more of that teaching does not fit traditional patterns. Increasingly I see my teaching being directed to helping the people of God discover, design, and implement their teaching ministry.

To achieve this requires what I call plotting and scheming. By tradition, many of the church's most faithful people expect the pastor to do whatever teaching is done. Shifting toward a more collegial style, with the teaching ministry more widely shared, involves some education in self-changing attitudes, overcoming biases, giving up old patterns. It also involves some motivation. Today's church people are fantastically busy with a multitude of concerns. Few are standing by waiting to have new responsibilities thrust on them. Drawing people into leadership roles in education sometimes can be done directly; sometimes it can be done indirectly through a little plotting and scheming. Three diverse examples will serve as partial illustrations.

The congregation I serve is fortunate to have excellent facilities. A relatively new building includes 26 classrooms, each complete with properly sized furniture, teaching equipment, and audio-visual paraphernalia. A generous budget provides ample quantities of curriculum materials in their latest revisions. Despite all these fine things, and although the congregation has been growing, attendance in Sunday church school has been declining. While the birth rate and sociological changes have something to do with this, a half-hearted attitude on the part of many Sunday church school teachers also has been a factor. Recently we have gone to a team teaching system (hardly a new idea) to enhance the quality of teaching, and also to say in a highly visible, symbolic way that Sunday church school *is* important. I am not so naïve as to think that this one step by itself will stem the tide of declining attendance. I do think that the process of analyzing the church's educational ministry and spreading responsibility for its implementation is a healthy one.

The confirmation-first Communion study made by the church-at-large provides a second illustration. The study process itself and numerous articles in *The Lutheran* aroused considerable interest. By the time the LCA adopted the study commission's report, it probably would have been possible for me as pastor to make whatever recommendations I thought best, have them approved by the church council, and proceed to implement any changes that were called for. That would have been easy and it also would have bypassed a tremendous educational opportunity.

Instead of asking the church council to approve our ideas, my co-pastor and I asked them to appoint a task force to study the whole matter of confirmation and first Communion and to prepare recommendations for the council's consideration. A group of 12 persons from teenagers to grandmothers, life-long Lutherans to recent converts, was appointed. Our first step was to arrange a three-session seminar on confirmation and first Communion in which members of the task force (as well as any others who might be interested) were asked to participate to gain some necessary backgrounds for carrying out their assignment. Once the seminar was completed we envisioned one or two quick sessions from which we expected a fairly simple set of recommendations. But that was not the way it was to be. Given the ball, that task force was not about to be told what to do with it until they were satisfied that they had done their job. This could have been perceived as a serious threat to pastoral prerogatives, which may be why we have so many patriarchal pastors around.

About 20 hours of meetings later, the task force had produced a 12-page report including its own definition of confirmation ministry and a design for detailed educational programs relating to Baptism, first Communion and confirmation, together with a suggested plan of transition from former patterns to new ones and a thoroughgoing rationale for the whole business. Throughout this process the two pastors functioned in a team teaching fashion, alternating leadership functions and trying hard to enable a process rather than to dictate a course of action. One healthy by-product was the opportunity afforded a few people to see pastors disagreeing with each other (a shock to some) and to discover that God's truth and will for our times is a living process, not a series of canned pronouncements from on high.

The completed task force report was submitted to the church council a month in advance of the time it was to be considered.

An hour in a council meeting was set aside to consider the report with task force members on hand to interpret it. The report was adopted unanimously, and a year later the first dissenting voice has yet to be heard! This seems amazing when we consider that we were dealing with fundamental issues, such as Baptism, Holy Communion, and the nature of the church, and that we were tampering with 400-year-old traditions. The absence of dissent is a direct result of the thoroughgoing educational process which enabled everyone to see and understand what was being done and why.

In the past year we have completed special instructional programs for all young people presently in confirmation classes, and they have begun receiving Holy Communion. A regular schedule of preparatory classes for 10- and 11-year-olds has been started to enable them to begin receiving Holy Communion. Interestingly, this program has been designed so that parents must participate with their children and share the leadership responsibility. So far this new venture has met with enthusiastic and grateful response.

A third illustration of my own scheming and plotting arises out of experiences with confirmation classes. Up until two years ago, I routinely followed the familiar pattern of 30 or so weekly Saturday morning class sessions from fall to spring each year, noticing always a growing sense of ennui and restlessness, both in myself and in the students, as the year wore on.

The simple expedient of developing a new schedule has helped reduce the boredom and now provides some exciting opportunities for a better teaching-learning situation. Eight one-hour weekly sessions are held in the fall on Tuesday evening from 6:30 to 7:30 P.M. On the first Saturday in December we have an all-day session. Pupils bring their lunches, and we have the equivalent in time of four weekly sessions or more. No classes are held during the balance of December, avoiding inevitable conflicts with the Christmas season and giving pupils a break in routine. Beginning in January, twelve more weekly class sessions are held. Following Easter, another extended session is held, either an all-day Saturday affair or a 24-hour retreat. The extended time sessions provide the chance to engage in learning experiences, which just won't fit into one-hour periods, and the weekly sessions provide for the cumulative kinds of learning experiences and reinforcement which are important, giving the students the best of both approaches without working either to death.

Measuring Successes and Failures

The only way to determine whether you have reached a goal is to have that goal clearly identified. I'd venture to say that goal identification is a process most pastors have not dealt with in relationship to their roles as educators, unless perhaps they have had some implicit goals in institutional terms, i.e., a growing Sunday church school or more pupils in confirmation classes. Perhaps they measure success in terms of the number of innovations introduced and new programs established. Unless one is willing to settle for a series of "Hawthorne effects," change for the sake of change is a risky goal to pursue. More adequate than any of these kinds of goals is a process of goal-setting and evaluation with the people of the congregation jointly determining what is hoped for, devising ways to achieve it, and measuring successes and failures in the process. This process, of course, applies to all areas of congregational life, not only to educational ministry. I only can report some modest efforts in this direction to date. The task force approach to a specific concern (e.g., confirmation-first Communion) is a step in this direction. While it is easy to be critical of prepackaged and ready-made educational programs which issue from denominational headquarters, most of us have not yet become skillful enough to adapt prepared resources creatively to local situations, much less to design our own. Perhaps my crystal ball is unusually hazy, but I have great difficulty envisioning a time when every pastor and every parish will be "doing its own thing" in Christian education. But I think the time already is here when every pastor and congregation need to develop the kind of self-evaluation apparatus to be able to set goals for their educational ministries, devise appropriate means of implementation, and provide for periodic measurement of what is happening.

How crucial this is can be illustrated by the struggle I have experienced in helping to develop a totally new kind of educational resource. The day I took up my duties in my present parish, a congregational meeting was held at which action was taken to purchase 41 acres of land for development as a congregational retreat and conference center. The site was only six miles from town and included some heavily forested and hilly land with a small stream traversing the property. A small house and a decrepit barn were the only buildings. Glowing reports were offered about the potential for individual and group camping, outdoor educational and recreational opportunities, and much more. The impetus to take this step had come out of the congregation's efforts at programs of this kind using rented facilities. As we undertook the development of this site, we experienced considerable frustration because no one was quite sure where to begin. It became increasingly clear that the fundamental problem was not how many and what kind of physical improvements needed to be made, as some of our eager-beaver people saw it, but what goals we hoped to achieve through this new resource. Working our way around to the development of a simple statement of goals and purposes took a good many months, but now we are able to proceed with some coherence and sense of direction. Since the development of this facility is envisioned on a pay-as-you-go basis over several years, the need for continual re-evaluation is paramount. Programming and facilities need to be developed hand-in-hand. While it is true that we cannot have overnight retreats without a place to have them, the mere existence of such a place does not guarantee an instant program of retreats.

Obviously I have much to learn about developing adequate evaluative structures for my educational ministry. Doing it is going to take more time, not less. However, the time is here for pastors to see themselves as professionals in their educational ministry.

GETTING PEOPLE INVOLVED

Richard I. Preis

"That was another good camel, Pastor."

That comment from Mary as she was leaving the worship service startled me. "What is she talking about?" I thought. And then it dawned on me. She was referring to the sermon series that had been developed for the Lenten season. Tradition says that a camel is a horse put together by a committee. And, during that Lenten season at Trinity, we were having sermons put together by a committee.

Mary's comment was really a compliment, first of all, because she appreciated the sermon of that day and gained something from it, and second, because she had grasped the idea of what we were trying to do with that series.

Camel Sermons

I had attended several conferences in which the leaders had encouraged each pastor to select a group of members who would meet with him sometime following the services of the day and discuss the sermon. This would provide the pastor with some feedback so that he could discover whether what he was trying to communicate was really getting through to the people. We had tried this at Trinity and found it helpful. This was a good experience for the pastors, and was beneficial for future sermon planning. It was good for the people who had been selected to give the feedback because it made them think about and express what they had heard that day in the message.

The thought occurred to me one day, though, "It is a fine idea to have that feedback, but why not give the members the opportunity for some input to the sermon of the day as well?" I decided to invite a group of six members to meet with me one evening a week for eight weeks during the Lenten season and assist me in the preparation of the Lenten sermon series. This would be helpful for me in my preparation of the sermon. And it would also be a good educational experience for the people who would be involved.

I chose the Lord's Prayer as the theme for the Lenten series. It had been ten years since that had been the theme of a series at Trinity, and I needed to refresh myself in my thinking about the prayer. It could be easily divided for the Sundays in the Lenten season.

As I made the selection of the people on the sermon committee, I considered age, sex, occupation, and years of membership in the congregation. I wanted a representative group. I wanted the whole congregation to feel that it was involved in the project. Those selected were a husband and wife in their forties who had been members of the congregation for about a year—he was a businessman and she was a housewife; a young man who had grown up in the congregation—single, a second year law student at the University of Michigan; a woman in her forties, employed by a local bank, who had been a member of Trinity all her life—she had married here, her children had been baptized, confirmed, and married in the church, and now she had grandchildren who had been baptized in the church; a young woman in her twenties who had recently had her first child—she was a social worker by profession; and finally, a former vice-chairman of the congregation who had been a member for eight years—a retired air force colonel who now taught high school mathematics.

All of these persons were enthusiastic about the venture and agreed to commit themselves to attend the eight weekly sessions and the Sunday worship services, and to do outside reading. I gave each of the members a different book on the Lord's Prayer, including Thielicke's *Our Heavenly Father*, Buttrick's *Prayer*, Spurgeon's *Sermons on the Lord's Prayer*, Girgensohn's *Teaching Luther's Catechism*, and Meyer's *This Faith Is Mine: Meditations for Youth on Luther's Catechism*.

It was announced to the congregation through the monthly *Trinity News Tidings* and the Sunday bulletin and at the worship service, as well as in the brochure for the Lenten season, that a committee of six members would be meeting with the pastor to prepare the Lenten sermon series on the Lord's Prayer. The names of the members of the committee were listed, and the congregation was invited to give comments and suggestions to the committee members. I felt it important that the church members be aware of this project so that they might feel a bit involved. The congregation was asked to pray for the committee and its work. The prayer committee of the congregation included committee members on the daily prayer list. An item appeared in the monthly intercessory prayer calendar requesting the prayers of the congregation for the committee.

The assigned books were distributed to the members before our first session. We gathered that first Monday in the church lounge; none of us was really sure what was going to happen, but we all were excited at the prospect before us. We began with prayer asking God to send his Spirit to guide us in leading the congregation to a deeper understanding and appreciation of the model prayer given to us.

The first sermon was to be on the meaning of prayer itself, and the introduction to the Lord's Prayer. I asked a few leading questions, and then sat back and let the committee members converse with each other. I must admit that it was not easy for me to do that. Like many preachers, I have a tendency to dominate discussion groups. In this one it was essential that I hold back. Instead, I sat with a clipboard and paper and wrote notes as fast as I could, attempting to record the major ideas and concepts coming from the group. Periodically someone would comment, "Say, Pastor, what do you think? You're not saying much. That's not like you," and I would enter into the discussion. Occasionally I would ask for clarification of a point someone was making.

The discussion was far more lively and productive than I had hoped for. These people really opened up to one another. Two hours later we stopped. Someone exclaimed, "How will you ever compose a sermon from this discussion?" All I could say was, "Let's see what happens."

We decided that the First Petition would be our theme for the next Monday, and we would all do our reading for our homework.

I had enough material for several sermons on prayer, but I was able to glean from it a major theme and concept that kept running through the discussion. By Friday the manuscript had been completed. The secretary ran off copies for the members of the committee. On Sunday the sermon was delivered at both services. Again, an announcement was made concerning the nature of the sermon series. It was a delight to look into the faces of the members of the committee as I preached their sermon. I could see the expressions on their faces change as some phrase or comment that had been made at the meeting appeared in the sermon.

Following the service the committee members picked up their copies of the manuscript to take home and read before the next session. Each of them made a comment expressing excitement as he walked out the door where I was greeting.

The format of the remaining sessions was different from the first. For the first half hour the members of the committee commented on the sermon of the previous Sunday. Did the message come through? Was it clear? Was it valid? Did the sermon reflect the thinking of the group, and did it reflect good Lutheran theology and good Bible study? I was thrilled that these were the criteria that the group established. And, believe me, it was quite an experience to sit and listen to their comments and suggestions on how things could be improved and ideas expressed more clearly.

Following the discussion of Sunday's sermon, we moved onto digging into the theme for the next week. Again, the ideas flowed forth each week. The one evening discussion which left an indelible impression in my memory concerned the petition, "And forgive us our trespasses, as we forgive those who trespass against us." The young law student had been given Thielicke's book, which deals with the matter of individual and corporate guilt in the realm of war. The idealistic law student and the retired air force colonel, who had been a navigator on a bomber during the Second World War, engaged in an intense dialogue. The rest of us said very little that night. Occasionally we entered the discussion with a question or an attempt to clarify. Each of us was moved that night. Five of us had lived through the Second World War. The two members in their twenties knew little of Korea and much of Vietnam. Genuine Christian love and concern for each other's feelings and position came through in the conversation that evening. And the sermon that resulted was powerful.

At the third session Lucille, the woman who had been a life-long member of the church, told us that she was having a coffee hour at her home after the early service. Her four sisters and their families are members of the congregation, and she was inviting them to her home after The Service to discuss the sermon. She was bringing us not only her reactions, but the reactions of her whole family. One evening she told us that her teen-age daughter really "dug" the introduction to one sermon, and said it really spoke to her where she was, and made her want to listen all the way through. Then Lucille's college-age son responded that the introduction was so "Father Knows Best-y" that it really turned him off, and he had trouble getting back on the track. This provided for interesting discussion in our committee, and the members concluded that it is a difficult task to prepare a message that is going to come through to a whole congregation of diverse personalities and ages.

One evening Marillyn, the housewife, said, "Pastor, why did you have to put in that last paragraph? You ended the one before with a question, a good question; one to make us think, and then you had to go on and resolve it for us. Why not just stop sometime and let us think? You preachers always seem to feel that you have to give all the answers." Did that set me back! She was right, and the following week the discussion of the petition worked around to a key question, and I ended the sermon with that question—really ended it, and said, "Amen." On her way out that Sunday, Marillyn winked at me and said, "Pastor, right on!" That was one of the best compliments I had ever had.

As the weeks progressed, each member of the committee began adding to the discussion not only his or her ideas, but also the ideas and comments of members of their own families and members of the congregation who had said things to them about the sermon. Lucille was not the only one who was getting feedback and input from others. Many more people than just the seven of us were involved in the sermon preparation.

At the final session we only discussed the sermon of the previous Sunday. We had completed the series, and there was no new petition to discuss. Everyone was a bit disappointed that the series had come to an end. However, we did more that evening than discuss the final sermon. Each of us shared what had happened to him or her during the past weeks. A new understanding and appreciation for the Sunday sermon and The Service had developed, a feeling of gratitude for being able to be involved with fellow believers in studying the Bible, grappling with doctrine, and communicating it to others. One of the tremendous benefits was the openness in sharing with each other that had taken place. As our final activity we shared together in a service of Holy Communion around a table in the lounge with bread that Marillyn had baked, wine that Rus had brought, cake that Lucille had made, and coffee that Ted had brought. At the end we prayed together our Lord's Prayer with a deeper understanding of those words than any of us had ever experienced before.

One of the conclusions reached by the group was that more members of the congregation should be involved in this type of parish education. They were able to see the various means of education that had taken place during those weeks, and the involvement that not just they, but others in the parish, had experienced. They commented on the fact that it was probably more work for me. And I assured them that I had never had more joy in sermon preparation in my 14 years in the ministry.

The sermon committee process has not ended at Trinity. Last summer a group of six individuals met with me for a series of sermons on the parables. We used the same format. And I made sure that one of Lucille's sisters was in the group so that we could get the feedback from that after-church coffee group. Plans are being made for future sermon committees on the Ten Commandments, the Beatitudes, and other sections of Matthew 5—7.

Worship Opportunities

One of the most obvious places in the life of a congregation for parish education is the worship service. And yet, so often this is the one place where the clergy and other professionals do all the planning. A greater appreciation for our liturgy and our hymnody and a greater understanding of Scripture can come into the lives of the people of God when they are involved in the planning for that which is the gathering of the family of God.

In the past four years we have discovered that one of the most meaningful parts of the catechism program occurs in the final weeks of the third year. The members of the confirmation class begin sorting through what has happened to them in their Christian education growth, especially during the three years of catechism. They then prepare their own services of confirmation. The basics that are part of the confirmation service in the *Service Book and Hymnal* are always in their service, but the language and format and the music and the mode of expression are different. Confirmation is the students' expression. It is their confirmation of faith, and they feel so much more a part of it when they do the planning of the service. This past year the members of the class added a simple action which spoke so much to the congregation. The young people said that they were a class, yet they were individuals. Underneath those robes they were individual persons, but they were also part of a fellowship and part of each other. Therefore, they requested that they participate in the blessing. Confirmands on either side of the kneeling person receiving the blessing would stand. Then they, along with the pastors, would place their hands on his head. What an impact that act had on the congregation. Many people commented that a wonderful lesson had been given to the congregation that morning by that simple action.

Each Sunday at 8:15 we have two services. One is the traditional service in the sanctuary. The other is a folk worship service in our youth room. The pastor who is not preaching that Sunday is involved in the folk worship service. Members of the congregation assist in the planning of that service, and when one of us is out of town at a meeting or conducting one of our catechism class retreats, the members plan and conduct the entire service.

Our worship committee prepares litanies and prayers for special services. These members have gained a keener appreciation for what is involved in the whole worship experience. Pastors are available for assistance, and we welcome the opportunity to be involved. In fact, we have gained a closer relationship with our people as we share with them in the planning of worship.

Small Group Programs

Another phase of the congregation's education program which has brought members closer to one another, to the pastors, and to the Lord has been our small group program. This developed as a result of some experiences I had at Chicago Theological Seminary with Ross Snyder.

My co-pastor and I each conduct small groups, but we have different approaches. I invite a group of nine people to make a commitment to meet with me for one evening a week for eight weeks. As with the sermon preparation group, I feel it is important to have a cross section of ages. I invite five women and four men ranging in age from teens or early twenties to over sixty. I feel it is essential to have one of our senior members in the group—someone who has lived as an adult through the depression of the 1930s. I feel it is also important to have a senior member and a teenager or college student dialoguing with each other. These two persons have often added the greatest delight to our study groups. At our first session each of us makes a "me collage," and then we share them with one another as a means of introducing ourselves to one another. We then study the passages in Paul's letters which speak of the Body of Christ and the differences of gifts. At the close of each session I give an assigned reading. Our readings include excerpts from Thielicke, Tillich, Kierkegaard, Ross Snyder, and plays by Arthur Miller and Tennessee Williams. As the sessions progress, the members become more and more willing to open up to one another and share ideas with one another. I must admit that I have often used these groups for sermon material. One evening a member of the group commented, "Hey, did you notice we got honorable mention in last Sunday's sermon?" During the sessions, members of the group find out that there are other people in their congregation who are struggling with the same questions about the Christian faith as they are, and that here is an opportunity to share with one another and search for help and answers.

At the final session we gather at a table for a shared meal. Each one brings something, including bread and wine, and we receive the Sacrament with one another. One of the exciting benefits occurs when a member comes to me and asks, "Will you invite my husband (sister or son) to be in your next group?"

My co-pastor conducts his small groups for couples only. He and his wife invite five other couples to meet an evening a week for seven weeks. They meet in each other's homes. Sometimes they use a study book or individual writings. They usually adopt a group project. One such group conducted an ecology in-gathering at a worship service at which the members of the congregation were invited to bring materials to the church that could be taken to our recycling station. They also have a meal as their final session, and share with each other what has happened to them during the past seven weeks. A number of these groups have continued to meet with one another on a semi-regular basis.

These small groups are beneficial for the people of our congregation, and the positive results have been seen in the life of our parish. However, the persons who benefit most are the pastors. This has been a marvelous way for us to become more closely involved with other people. It just is not possible to get into the homes of all our members as frequently as we would like, to assist them in their struggles with the faith and the problems they face. And, in many ways, this should not be our responsibility and task alone. It should be a shared task with the priesthood of believers. And this is what happens in our small groups. Men, women, and young people are sharing the faith with one another. They are studying with one another. They are learning more about each other as Christian believers, they are learning more about themselves, and they are learning more about their relationship with their Lord.

It is a marvelous experience and opportunity to be a pastor involved in learning with your people what it means to be a member of the household of faith.

THE ROAD TO EDUCATIONAL MINISTRY

Richard Rehfeldt

In less than ten years in the parish ministry, I have traveled a great distance both literally and figuratively. After five and a half years in the parish ministry at Waverly, Iowa, I and my family went to Scotland where I would have two years of study at the University of St. Andrews in the Department of Practical Theology. In addition to traveling on the Continent, I also served as interim pastor of a Lutheran congregation in the midlands of England during one of the summers. Then I returned to the full-time parish ministry in Des Moines, Iowa.

During this time, I also traveled a great distance in my understanding of the pastor's role in educational ministry. It is these travel experiences which have helped shape my current view.

Before I retrace my journey, I shall discuss some of the views regarding the pastor's role in educational ministry which have remained constant for me up to this point.

Constant Views

One of these views is this: I have always felt that the pastor of a congregation is teaching all the time through words, actions, and his challenges to people to think creatively. In a sense, every ministerial function can be a teaching function. Of course, there is specific teaching involved in the pastor's leading confirmation classes, adult groups, and teacher training sessions. Then too, there ought to be a great deal of teaching involved in one's preaching. For the distinction between *kerygma* and *didache* can not be pressed too far since proclamation of the truth needs some interpretation, some teaching, some constant hammering away at that truth.

Also, I believe that there can be a large element of teaching in the priestly functions of ministering in Baptisms, weddings, and funerals.

Therefore over the years, I have made a practice of meeting with parents prior to the Baptism of their children. In these meetings we discuss the Lutheran view of Baptism and the roles of parents and the congregation in a shared responsibility. Through three to four hours of premarital counseling, special six-week sessions for persons, and through four- to six-week sessions for high school students, I attempt to allow sufficient opportunity to discuss with fellow members of the congregation the meaning and purpose of weddings and marriage. I also seek to assist persons prior to, during, and following death in arriving at a Christian understanding of death and funeral services. The teaching involved in these situations is the setting forth of the emphases of the Lutheran tradition and the challenge to people to respond to the gospel of Jesus Christ.

Beyond these more or less obvious areas for teaching, I have always viewed working with church councils, committees, and lay leaders as an area of educational ministry. In all of these situations, I try to involve these persons in examining their responsibilities and specific roles in worship, evangelism, stewardship, youth work, and other areas of congregational service. Through retreats, books, articles, films, tape recordings, and discussions I strive with them to explore the mission and purpose of the church as seen from their particular leadership capacity. The teaching involved in these instances may be described as enabling people to think creatively.

For example, the resolutions committee of our congregation engages in educational activity as a routine part of its procedure. Before any specific topics for resolutions are proposed, we read and discuss together such books as Wallace E. Fisher's *From Tradition to Mission*, Mark Gibbs and T. Ralph Norton's *God's Frozen People* and *God's Lively People*. We then outline the make-up of our congregation, its various organizations and functions. Then we spend several meetings trying to formulate a description of the church's role in today's world. It is only after this preparation that we attempt to suggest topics for resolutions. Thus, this vital task becomes a learning experience for a new group of men and women each year.

Two other views regarding the pastor's role in educational ministry have remained somewhat constant in my thinking and acting. The first is my belief that pastors need to exhibit enthusiasm in their total ministry, particularly in those areas which relate most obviously to their teaching ministry. This enthusiasm reveals better than words that pastors really believe in their task. I'm enthusiastic about my task because I am involved with people of all ages in exploring our relationship to each other, to all of God's people, and to our living Lord. Then too, it is exciting for me to dig into God's Word with others where we find power for living and where we are constantly surprised by joy, strength, and forgiveness.

Pastors' enthusiasm also sets an example for others in their teaching ministry. This in turn helps free people from inhibitions, opens them up to the experience at hand and to each other, while providing an effervescent type of leadership. A Sunday school teacher said to me after one of our in-service training sessions, "I wish I had your enthusiasm." Several months after she made this remark, I had the opportunity of observing this teacher in a classroom situation. From all appearances, both she and her students were indeed enthusiastic about their learning tasks.

Closely related to the need for enthusiasm is the element of joy in learning. Some people have the mistaken idea that if students are enjoying themselves, they are not learning properly. To the contrary: I sense we learn best when we participate in an experience with joy. Throughout my ministry, I have felt that it is a teacher's job to maximize good feelings, friendliness, and joy in every learning situation. Now to be sure, there are times of confrontation, hard work, and frustration. Yes, these also are times of learning. Then too, when a teacher and student struggle together through these difficult times, the resulting experience often is joyful.

These, then, are my constant views regarding the pastor's role in educational ministry: pastors are teaching in every aspect of their ministry; they should strive to be enthusiastic about their task and aim to lead others to experience joy in the process of learning. Now, I would like to balance these views with the areas in which my mind has changed.

From Lecturing to Listening

Fresh from the seminary, excited about the gospel of Jesus Christ, and eager to share what I had learned, I entered into a teaching ministry in a congregation of more than twenty-seven hundred baptized persons. Within a matter of months, I had initiated several classes of adult Bible study, and studies in doctrine and the history of the Lutheran church. I found great personal satisfaction in sharing with the congregation what I had learned in seminary and in preparation for these classes. Further, I was greatly pleased that I could hold an audience for fifty to sixty minutes through my lecturing method.

This lecturing method, complete with a good deal of humor (which I later came to see as a device which keeps people at a distance), I used in confirmation instruction classes, in-service teacher training sessions, and even in my home visits regarding forthcoming Baptisms.

Then, through small group meetings and more and more listening, I began to realize that I was often speaking on questions, issues, and subjects which were not vital to the persons involved. Slowly, I began to see that one of the pastor's main functions in educational ministry is to listen and to help people listen to each other. Through listening, I began to find out where people hurt. That is, through listening to people individually and in groups, I discovered what their real questions and problems were at that time. Further, by listening for the feelings expressed, I began to learn about their real struggles in life and with Christianity. It was then that I felt that my leading groups and preaching became more relevant. Indeed, people began to tell me, "That sermon, that discussion, really spoke to me."

As I began to turn more and more from total lecturing to listening, I saw my role as pastor to be one of humanizing a learning situation. I began to see that Christian education is person-centered. Thus, I began to concern myself with both halves of the situation: with the person as well as with the subject. I began to see that the whole person—not just his mind—must be engaged in meaningful experiences.

All of this meant that I would have to try to create a climate of acceptance and openness in my total educational ministry. It meant that I would have to allow persons to engage others, and not just me, in dialogue. It was at this time that I reread Reuel Howe's *The Miracle of Dialogue* and read for the first time his *Partners in Preaching,* both of which helped me become open to the element of dialogue in my total ministry.

The results of this change from constant lecturing to a greater amount of listening can best be seen in my change of approach to confirmation instruction. In the early years of my parish ministry, I relied almost entirely on the lecture method and a question and answer period to see if the young people remembered what I had told them. From this method I turned more and more to having the students seek out their own answers by providing them with workbooks and worksheets. I began to ask more and more probing questions of the students while following material furnished by our denominational publishing house. Finally, I have arrived at a method which creates a situation or involves the students in examining their feelings and ideas on a subject. All of this is done after deliberately revealing to the students that I want to help them discover the answers to *their* questions. Now they often spend almost the entire class session asking sincere and vital questions. This did not happen overnight. It took weeks and months of being with the young people in classrooms, at small group meetings in their homes, and on weekend retreats where we really learned to know each other. As we built mutual trust, it became easier to share deeper feelings.

The listening method has more loose ends than does the lecturing approach. Yet I feel if people are wrestling with issues and subjects long after a particular class or discussion is over, learning is still going on in their lives. Further, I believe that when a leader listens more than he lectures, he still has the task of answering the questions people have and then, in Paul Tillich's words, "leading them to ask questions which only the Gospel can answer." This often has forced me to deviate from my original class outline so that the group may spend several weeks in systematic study. Just recently, one group which was discussing "The Jesus People" raised questions about the Baptism of the Holy Spirit and judgment. These questions prompted the group to study Scripture and a book on doctrine.

From Propounding to Personalizing

By turning more and more from lecturing to listening, I changed my view of my role in concrete teaching situations. Formerly, I felt my job was to propound the great number of facts which I had tucked away during my seminary years. Currently, I see my task as personalizing the gospel of our Lord Jesus. So as I push aside the tables and the lectern and sit on a chair in a circle with my students (whom I refer to as friends), as I eat popcorn and drink Pepsi in their living rooms or around the fireplace at a retreat center, as we go off on field trips to the funeral home and other places, we interact with each other, as persons, in a learning community. Here the emphasis is on helping persons apply the facts of their faith.

I also carry this approach over into my adult education classes. Rather than expounding on the various doctrines of Lutheran tradition, I spend a lot of time listening to people. Then we explore together the teachings of the Lutheran heritage. Together we discover how these teachings apply to our lives and our world.

Therefore, I see the pastor's role in specific teaching situations to be one in which he does not say through word and action, "Listen and learn," but rather, "Strive with me to apply the truths of our faith to our daily lives."

From Attending to Participating

Early in my ministry, I was very concerned with the total number of people who would attend Sunday worship, adult classes, and the other opportunities in Christian education. But as I began to listen to and strive with persons in learning situations, I became more concerned with the quality of participation by people in these situations than with the number of people in attendance.

At first I wanted the group to interact solely with me as their leader. Then I started to break groups in smaller groups where they could interact with each other. Although I had learned long ago the statement of Paul Tillich that "there is no communication without participation," it took me years to put it into practice.

Two concerns still arise when I strive for the goal of participation with my fellow learners. First, my pride does not allow me to admit that persons may be learning Christian truths from each other when I am not in their particular group. Second, I still feel badly when not everyone is involved in meaningful participation. The first concern with pride undoubtedly arises from an over-active ego, while the second concern about everyone's being involved probably arises from an over-active sense of responsibility.

To achieve greater participation in my confirmation instruction classes, I divided the classes into small groups. This was almost a necessity, since the thirty students in the class attended eight different schools. They had a real need to know each other before there could be any interaction among them in our groups. And just as this was true of students, it was also true of adults. Few in our congregation are neighbors, shop at the same stores, attend the same sporting or social events, or work in the same area of town. Yet when they began to meet in small groups for breakfast meetings, midweek morning and evening meetings, and overnight retreats, they began to know each other, open up to each other, and become concerned about each other. One recent case is illustrative here. A small group of women had been meeting for several hours each week for Bible study and prayer and just plain sharing. Suddenly, a six-month-old daughter of one of the group died. The manner in which the other women and their husbands ministered to her during her grief amazed the young mother. They cried with her, listened to her, and thus supported her in a marvelous fashion. Prior to the formation of this small group, most of the participants did not even know each other's names. Had I been leading the group in the lecture-type approach, this instance of faith active in love may not have happened.

These, then, are important goals for pastors: to seek and to help their leaders to seek; and to bring people into meaningful relationships with each other so they may participate creatively and redemptively with their fellow human beings and begin to interpret their life experience in Christian terms.

At the beginning of my ministry I felt satisfaction after leading a class which had been quiet and had paid attention. Now, I discover little satisfaction following such a learning situation. Rather, I gain personal delight when I see persons in groups participating and interacting with each other, or just opening up to each other. I see this happening more and more as I take the risk of "freeing up" learning situations so that there is interaction not only between me and others, but also between other persons in the situation.

One such "happening" occurred in a group of people gathered as a social concerns committee. Up until this past year, only adults were allowed to serve on a committee of the congregation. This year I encouraged three high school youth to participate in our social concerns committee meeting. The youth willingly became involved in the topic of discussion. Following the meeting, a woman walked over to one of the young people and said, "I learned a lot from you tonight. Thank you for coming."

Another example will serve to illustrate how I have come to prize participation over mere attendance. During the first five years of my ministry, I firmly felt it was the pastor's role to lead services of worship; this was his role and no one else's. Then, during my two years of graduate study abroad, I became more and more open to the leadership of laity in all areas of the church's life. Mainly through reading, I began to see the real need to involve laity in worship as well as in teaching and leading functions. I also observed lay participation in the services of worship in both the Church of Scotland and the Scottish Episcopal Church. During my first year back from studying abroad, I put lay men and women in total charge of Sunday services when I had to be out of town. I assisted them in preparation for reading Scripture, delivering the sermon, and conducting The Service. The people in attendance responded very favorably to the leadership of the laity. Even more gratifying was the remark of one layman who said to me later in the week, "You know, I've been a Lutheran all my life, and until I led The Service on Sunday, I didn't realize the depth and meaning contained in the words of our liturgy." This remark helped me realize anew that learning takes place through participation more than through mere attendance. Men, women, and youth now participate in the leadership of every Sunday service, even if that involves merely reading the Scripture.

From Remembering to Thinking

A study, I recall, revealed that most pastors teach according to the example of their beloved seminary professors—most of whom lectured and then gave tests to see how much the students remembered. At least I believe that was the model I was trying to follow in the beginning of my ministry. All too much of my time in educational ministry, I now realize, was spent in trying to teach persons to remember—remember facts and codes of behavior. Now I consciously strive more to teach persons to think for themselves than to remember a body of facts.

In order to attain this style of teaching, I needed, first of all, to treat people, especially youth, as person who *could* think. Second, I needed to view their minds as instruments to be used, rather than as storehouses to be filled. Finally, I needed to provide opportunities for such thinking to take place. Thus, with adults, we not only studied the theory of Christian ethics, we took three hours to wrestle with the issues of abortion, amnesty, and mixed marriage—all of which affected more than one person in the group personally. I sat with young people in confirmation instruction groups in homes and struggled with them in considering case studies pertaining to problems of youth. I asked the fellowship committee to define for themselves the purpose of their group in our congregational life. The next time they met, I played a fifteen-minute provocative tape recording for them which described one person's view of the role of fellowship in the church today. After hearing the tape, they modified their own thinking on the subject and arrived at their purpose. I could have given them my view of their purpose and they may have remembered it; but I feel that their view is more meaningful simply because it is theirs.

It takes a great deal more time and effort to teach persons to think than to remember facts. Yet I feel this is one of the pastor's tasks in educational ministry.

Some results of helping people think creatively in confirmation classes, adult study groups, and even in some committee meetings can be noted. First, I've observed that individuals are asking more and more questions about matters that affect them personally. Second, some adults as well as some youth are speaking to their peers with more depth of conviction in council meetings or in confirmation instruction classes. Third, I've seen persons grasp leadership opportunities after they have been stimulated through hard thinking.

From Absorbing to Acting

Pastors must not only help people think. They must also direct people toward action. This I personally find is a most difficult task.

So much of what we do in the area of educational ministry is geared toward helping persons remember facts and experiences, toward helping them think, èven toward providing experiences and feelings which they can absorb. One of the laymen in our congregation frequently comes up to me after a service of worship and says, "There it is again: a good sermon, but I'll bet nobody is going to do anything about it!" He also came up to me after viewing and discussing a short, stimulating film and said, "I doubt if anything will happen because we saw the movie and discussed it; it's too safe a setting to be in. No one will change his attitudes or actions."

That layman may be a bit too pessimistic, but he *does* challenge me with a real problem. How am I going to get people out of an audience and into the field of battle with changed attitudes and behavior? Most pastors, I feel, spend the greatest share of their time behind the lines of battle, and therefore must rely upon the rank and file to become involved in the steady day-by-day contest of life. Yet I also feel most pastors further realize that our Lord trained his disciples so they could give a good account of themselves after he left them. And most pastors realize *that* is their task as well. The crunch comes in trying to fulfill that task. I have struggled with this task and have only partially fulfilled it in some cases.

One example is the six-week adult-oriented course on marriage I recently led. In addition to reading books, listening to tapes, participating in small group discussions, and examining case studies in marital conflict, each person was to make a commitment. That commitment was for a one-week period only. I asked them to show five deliberate acts of love toward their spouse. When we met the next week, they wrote these five acts on a piece of paper together with the response of the spouse to each act. These descriptions were then shared with the group. It was clear that many of the people showed great creativity, ingenuity, and sensitivity in doing their deliberate acts of love. One wife, now twelve months later, still drives weekly to the downtown district from a suburb to have lunch with her husband—an action begun during our week of showing an act of love.

Beyond this one case I can refer to only a handful of examples where I was able to guide people in "doing the truth," as James Pike put it in the title of his book on Christian ethics. Such examples include various requests on my part for a commitment—to a week of prayer, to another six-week period of study, to an overnight retreat with other adults, to asking parents to share their views on a particular subject with their children.

A more concrete example of acting followed a two-hour presentation to adults on the plight of the poor in our county jail. Part of the response was in terms of money. The group voted (with many dissenting voices) to provide $75 worth of books and magazine subscriptions for the prisoners. Then when I asked for volunteers to act as friends for the poor awaiting trial, four persons responded. Another example of doing also followed one of our Sunday morning adult forums. A week after a guest speaker portrayed the problems of the elderly, one woman asked the group if they would help organize a monthly luncheon and party for the senior citizens of our congregation. A few persons responded. So she brought the idea to the Women of the Church at their monthly meeting and got a few more persons to respond. Currently, this group meets enthusiastically monthly (and have chosen "The Elderberries" as the name of their group). Yet another example of acting comes from a meeting of our social concerns committee. One of the young mothers told the group how frustrating and depressing it can be to stay at home every day with preschool children. So the group responded and helped her plan a monthly meeting of all mothers in our congregation who have preschool children. The mothers have free baby sitting for one afternoon each month, transportation to the church building, and an afternoon of crafts and fellowship together.

Another example of putting an insight into action comes from a group of teachers who spent the weekend in a teacher training workshop. During the hours in which they observed a second-grade class, only one person made a particular observation. One of the girls in the class was wearing new shoes and was constantly looking down at them and "polishing" them against her tights. After the class session she shared her observation with the other teachers in the workshop and said, "Oh how I wish the teacher would have noticed the girl's new shoes and told her how nice they were. But her new shoes, which were obviously important to her, went unnoticed by everyone, including her teacher." Several months later, the teacher who made the observation told me how she had made many similar observations in her own classes since that weekend workshop. She felt this helped her teaching immensely because she was now more aware that she was teaching persons rather than subjects.

A final example shows how one man transferred what he experienced in a discussion group to his job situation. In a Sunday morning adult discussion group on helping people of lower income groups, several men who are directly involved in employing persons argued heatedly against being "overly kind" to minority groups. They felt persons from minority groups were undependable and demanding. Toward the end of the discussion, I, together with several others, pointed how our Lord showed us the way of constantly giving of ourselves even when it isn't always appreciated. Three weeks later I was having lunch with one of the men who had objected so vociferously to helping continually those black people who didn't respond with gratitude. He related how he had just hired a young, unskilled black girl and had told her that his company would pay for typing and shorthand lessons that she could take during morning hours. "I've been thinking about that discussion the other Sunday morning," he told me, "and somehow I felt I just wanted to go the second mile in helping the young girl."

All of these illustrations make up only a small percentage of responses to educational ministry. Together with many other pastors, I feel the frustration of attaining the goal of assisting persons to become involved in action rather than to absorb some truths or experiences. But with others, I am still striving.

From Doing to Enabling

There is a related fact which grows out of the above discussion of doing and acting. That fact is this: pastors must strive to enable people to do the work of ministry rather than do it all themselves. I went a long distance down the road in the parish before I pursued this goal in educational ministry.

Part of the reason I waited seven years to pursue this goal stemmed from a mistaken idea that *my* way was the best way. (I assume there are other pastors with this hang-up.) Another reason for hesitating so long to allow the laity to develop their plans and programs was a lack of trust, faith, and confidence in the abilities and insights of others. But when I came to a large parish as its only pastor, I was forced by my busy schedule to allow the laity to carry out much of the work of ministry. So now I can say to fellow pastors, "Don't limit the vision of the people in your congregation by doing so much of what needs to be done. Rather, enable them to cooperate with you in your congregation's ministry."

Because I can now say this, I can also declare with joy that I receive great satisfaction from observing others as they receive compliments for their work of ministry. Three times within the past five months, persons have said to me, "You'd better watch out, you'll be out of a job!" One occasion was when a layman did an outstanding job in leading The Service while I was out of town. Another instance followed worship in which a layman did a fine job of reading the Scripture for the day. A final time this remark was made to me occurred when I entered the room at the close of a Bible study led by a layman. In all three cases I had helped train these men for their work, but they, not I, did it. Therefore they received the praise. At this point in my ministry I receive deep satisfaction that these occasions of ministry by laity are so well accepted and that these persons are being equipped for their tasks.

The committee established annually to bring resolutions and reports before the yearly congregational meetings now studies and probes before it begins to crystallize topics for resolutions. During the first six years of my ministry, other co-pastors and I always wrote the resolutions for this committee. Then the committee would edit and modify our resolutions. Most of our time as pastors was involved in selling the committee and then the congregation on *our* suggestions. But once again, the lack of time in my present congregation forced me to hand this job of writing resolutions over to a committee. The result is that more persons are involved in thinking through the role of the church in today's society and in carrying out the resolutions which they develop. They are eager to carry them out simply because the resolutions are *theirs*.

Another area in which I gain personal satisfaction at the present is watching the functioning of our open spaces, or interest center, Sunday church school program. In this area, as with the resolutions committee, after I got the ball going, I let others carry it.

To start the process, I passed along several articles on learning communities or the open space programs to our Sunday church school superintendent. After reading the articles she returned them to me, expressing her enthusiasm for the ideas. Then we called together other leaders of our Sunday church school and shared our enthusiasm and vision concerning this new concept. At the suggestion of a person from the national office on parish education, these interested people called in persons who were involved in this educational method in public schools. The Sunday church school leaders also visited these schools to see the open spaces concept in action. This contact with persons involved in leading youth in these situations and the contact with the students themselves sold the idea to our leaders.

During the summer months I conducted a family Sunday school session. In previous summers the congregation had cancelled Sunday school classes. Parents and their children now gathered into one large area. They sang songs and heard a Bible story or watched a biblical film. Then I asked the parents to discuss the main point of the story with their children. After the discussion each family, working together, had to depict the main thrust of the story with a banner, through a dramatization, with puppets, or in a newspaper article or poem of their own. They did this as they ate cookies and drank coffee or Kool-Aid at their tables. Toward the end of the session, the children came forward and showed the entire group (between 65 and 80 people) what their family had done. These sessions of family Sunday school gave the leaders of our Sunday school greater enthusiasm to develop one large learning area without using the plastic dividers to section the room into small areas. Because I had asked a person who taught in a public school with an open spaces type of program to observe the entire session, she was able to help me and the Sunday school leaders see some of the possibilities and problems of open spaces.

In the fall, I again met wtih the leaders of our program. Together we sought persons who would put our ideas and theirs into practice.

We met in a member's home and shared our enthusiasm for and vision of the open spaces concept. These two persons agreed to develop the program for us. At this point I continued to meet with the new leaders and regular Sunday church school leaders in planning possible themes to use for the program. From that time onward, I only occasionally met with the two new leaders. They then carried the idea through to development. They sought out the teachers or "enablers" for this type of Sunday morning program, and with them gathered the material and ideas for the open spaces type of learning situation. After months of planning and discussing and writing articles on the program for the parish newsletters, they implemented the program for Grades 1–4. Now they have five interest centers in one large room with a minimum of two enablers at each center. In addition, there are two persons who walk around the room as observers. The enablers and observers meet twice a month for evaluation and suggestions. The children think this new learning experience is great. As one of them put it, "Wow, this is fun!"

What It Takes

In reviewing the road I have taken to my present view regarding the pastor's role in educational ministry, I see that it has been necessary to develop certain ideas and beliefs in order to hold this view.

First, if pastors are going to listen as well as lecture, personalize their teaching as well as propound facts, encourage participation as well as attendance, strive to help persons think as well as remember, act as well as absorb feelings and ideas, enable persons to share the ministry as well as do the ministry themselves, then pastors must have a high level of trust in people. It means that pastors have to believe that God has created all people with talent and creativity. It means that pastors must then channel their energies more and more toward developing the talent and potential leadership of lay leaders and students. It means that pastors must take seriously the ability of youth and adults alike to ask ultimate questions concerning their faith without asking the questions for them. It means that pastors must view leaders and students as responsible, rather than irresponsible, persons. To be sure, people are recalcitrant, balky, sinful. Therefore, pastors must continually urge, prod, and forgive. And because this is required of them constantly, pastors too can grow weary and become frustrated. Nevertheless, I firmly hold that the more pastors become open to the leadership of congregational members, the more they can accept obstinance or foot-dragging.

Second, if pastors are going to enable others to develop their own ideas and programs, they must be willing to share the spotlight with others. Pastors may indeed stimulate, inspire, encourage, and even prod some persons in their appointed teaching or leadership roles. Yet, because the end result belongs to the people, the people themselves may receive most, if not all, of the praise. And for many of us pastors, this is not always easy to accept.

Third, if pastors are to grow as enablers in educational ministry, it means they must also be open to evaluation. In a team ministry, this evaluation can often come from fellow pastors. Those who serve a congregation alone often must allow the laity to evaluate their ideas as well as their work.

In the fourth place, if pastors feel that they too are learning with fellow members in their common educational ministry, then they must demonstrate that belief. Pastors must show as well as say to fellow believers in Christ that they also are pilgrims along the way, they also are sinners "standing in the need of prayer," they also are in the battle of life, not above it.

A fifth thing needs to be said. As important as listening, personalizing and enabling are for the ministry, pastors must maintain a creative tension between these vital aspects and proclamation. For there is always the danger of striving to do "meaningful things" and forgetting to confront persons with the claims of Jesus as Lord.

Finally, if pastors are going to be open to change regarding their role in educational ministry, they must believe that the Holy Spirit is going along the road of life and ministry with them. And the belief in the guidance of the Holy Spirit will do something for all pastors. It will free them from becoming depressed because they don't always see tangible results of the congregation's educational ministry. The Holy Spirit is always at work and may bring forth the fruit of Christian education at a later time. Most important of all, the belief that the Holy Spirit is present with his guidance in educational ministry means that pastors will realize they haven't arrived at the end of their journey. Rather, they can see that they have but traveled to their present destination. Pastors can be assured that their views will be changed and modified as they go along if they remain open to the Spirit's guidance. And thus pastors can know that they haven't arrived at the end of their journey on which they are seeking to understand their role in educational ministry. I know I haven't.

Thus in the unpredictability of parish life and their responsibility to fellow Christians and to the Lord, pastors may continue to seek a clearer understanding of their role in educational ministry. Yet pastors will ever realize that they are dedicated not to a role, but to a Person. Therefore pastors will trust the Holy Spirit to guide them as they, together with their congregations, seek to serve him as Lord of all life.

FOCUS ON ADULT EDUCATION

John Lundin

The Bible is one of the bases for developing my pastoral ministry. In the Bible I discovered patterns and practices that suggest that education was a primary concern of the synagogue and church and that education within the institution was basically an adult process. Of course the custom of the head of the family telling the story of Passover to the family, as well as indications that large amounts of the Torah were memorized, show that there was religious education occurring within the home.

In the New Testament, the patterns of Jesus' ministry suggest that most of his teaching time was spent with adults. The intensive training of the Twelve, the conflict with the scholars, and the teaching events as he encounters people in their everyday activities point to a priority of adult education in his teaching ministry.

Although children were among the crowds as he taught (cf. the feeding of the five thousand), the New Testament relates only one incident of how he dealt with children. Jesus rebuked those who tried to stop young children from coming to him. He welcomed them and blessed them.

The historical pattern of the Christian church shows a strong emphasis on adult education. Child education outside the home was given little attention until the Shepherd of Hermes in the second century wrote about providing instruction for fatherless children. The catechumenate of the early church was originally designed for adults to be equipped as carriers of the good news. The church's emphasis on teaching reached its height during the rapid spread of the early Christian church and then seems to have disappeared by the middle of the fifth century. The primary focus of what the church was and did during the period from Augustine to Luther centered around the Sacraments. Luther's emphasis reverted to the pre-fifth century model of the church as an equipper of adults;

children were to be taught within the home. His concern is typified in his *Small Catechism*, where the imperative for the head of the house to teach the *Small Catechism* to the children is given.

A further indication of the vitality that emits from an adult community of Christians that methodically gathers and studies the will of God can be seen in the early spread of the Methodist Church. The small group Bible study of the Wesley brothers patterned itself after the early church's focus on the teaching ministry.

Adult Education Essential

From this biblical and historical perspective, the central focus of my pastoral ministry is the teaching role. I am the chief teacher who equips the saints to do the work of the ministry. The biblical passage that gives insight into my concept of the primary role of the Christian community is Ephesians 4:11-13: "And his gifts were that some should be apostles, some prophets, some evangelists, some pastors and teachers, to equip the saints for the work of ministry, for building up the body of Christ, until we all attain to the unity of the faith and of the knowledge of the Son of God, to mature manhood, to the measure of the stature of the fullness of Christ."

With these assumptions, adult education becomes essential work in the church. It is a tool that God uses to call his community into existence. It is a means whereby he makes his word operational. When God says something and adults hear the word of God, reflect on the word and incorporate—make active—that word into their life and lifestyles, the church is on its way toward fulfilling its mission.

The church then has a primary responsibility to provide the arena where God may speak in such a way that all people can hear him and be led out, be freed, to act and think in ways not previously open to them.

Education allows adults to be better decision-makers as they attempt to interpret the will of God in the light of the experiences of life. Those making decisions then are able to interpret the information. It has been my experience that problems arise not so much from a lack of information as from an inability to interpret and theologize with the information.

If this is so, then the more capable the adult is of making decisions from a theological base, the healthier the whole church becomes, and the more we move together toward the "stature of the fulness of Christ" (Ephesians 4:13).

An adult education program presupposes that new days call for new responses both for the church and for individuals, and that change can take place. God is calling us into an "abundant life."

We can become more than we already are. I believe that changes taking place within a congregation to assure that it will become more than it already is must be done with adults who have experienced learning. If learning has taken place while they have participated in the adult education program, they have been freed to act and think in different ways. A Christian community can benefit greatly from adults who have been equipped to do better theology. Since the adults of a community are also the decision-makers of a community, the more capable the decision-makers, the healthier the decisions made for the community.

Adult education, as it acts as the arena where community is called into existence, provides not only the best environment for the creation of community but also a primary means whereby community has reason to celebrate.

The father's teaching the significance of the Passover within the family unit, the gathering of only twelve as Christ's initial cadre, and the effectiveness of Wesley's small group Bible studies indicate that when small groups consistently meet in the Lord's name, the spirit begins creating community. As individuals are encouraged to use the group as a laboratory of experimentation where they may risk what was previously taboo, such as anger, or test new ideas and actions that may cause rejection if known by the larger community, they discover what Christian community can become.

It has been my experience that the outgrowth of having participated in a Christian community at a small group level creates the desire to celebrate this community. A new dimension in worship then develops as one of the results of this previous activity of the spirit. Thus when worship services no longer bear the burden of being the primary arena where community is created, the direction and focus of preaching can shift. Rather than just calling Christians into community, worship then reflects the community already called into existence. Each member, as a vital participant in community, contributes to the vitality of the worship. The vitality and the stability of the community demand of the preacher a high quality of preaching, since expectations rise as theology is articulated. Yet this lends a stability to the total worship life that is difficult to maintain if the worship stands or falls on the capacity of the preacher to motivate the audience from the pulpit.

Motivation

Whatever our ideals for educational ministry might be, establishing that ministry is not an easy task. The primary problem that our congregation found as it developed an adult education program was motivation. We discovered that we had a wealth of resources. We found movie theaters with some excellent films, college professors and community leaders who were willing to give perspective to the Christian experience, and literature, books, and periodicals that contained a wealth of materials, all of which was of little value if there was nobody involved. The best curriculum in the world does no good if people are not involved. Not only must curriculum be provided, people must be motivated to come. As a means of motivating people, we relied upon the *P*rogram of *A*dult Christian *E*ducation (PACE, from Augsburg Publishing House) as a resource for planning our program.

With the constant pressure of demands placed upon every person's time, priorities for time and effort are developed by everyone. In our community, little time is left to do things that do not hold a high priority. This makes it necessary to help people decide that adult Christian education is important enough to take the time and effort. Defining expectations, working around busy schedules, offering help and resources for questions that the congregation asks, as well as asking for a commitment from each person each year, have been keys in assuring the regular attendance of classes. PACE has been our tool to accomplish these goals.

The PACE program enabled us to look at our situation in new ways. We are an open country church of approximately 400 adults, ministering primarily to farm people, but an increasing number of rural non-farm residents are joining our congregation. The rural non-farm people are residents of our community and work in the neighboring city. We are typical of rural congregations with a large age span among our membership, although the demographics are beginning to take new shapes as new people become part of our community. Our age graph is 18–30, 98; 30–45, 71; 45–65, 113; 65–80, 80; over 80, 32. Over 28 percent of the congregation is 65 or over. This configuration has an effect on the type of curriculum made available, since one of the main categories to be taken seriously in adult education is age. Other concerns must be the rural nature of our parish as well as the rapid change from being a primarily Norwegian community. These data show that each year we must make sure a course on visitation of the sick and shut-in is offered so that intelligent visitation of the elderly is assured. *Home Bible Studies* are placed in the home of every shut-in. Courses on death, dying, and grief are offered yearly. Courses on the problem of changes within the church, which have bothered middle age groups, are offered. Courses on the problems of dealing as a Christian with the dramatically changing rural scene, as well as with the problems of rural ecology and pollution, are directed toward the farmer. As target groups and concerns are identified, resources are found.

A Healing Ministry

However, the main problem confronting adult education programs is not the peculiarities of a particular congregation or age group. It is motivation. How can adults be motivated to get involved in education?

Priorities are measured and set up as much as possible in relation to how well the activity equips lay people to do the work of the ministry. If people see the benefits, their motivation is likely to be better.

My goal is to move away as much as possible from a crisis ministry into a community ministry where the community of faith, rather than the pastor, becomes the primary healing agent. As a person moves through a crisis (marital, spiritual, or another kind) with the pastor, at some point in the counseling he or she is, if possible, referred to a particular study course relating to the problem. At an appropriate time in personal counseling, an attempt is made to identify what adult course will best help the person to continue the growth that was stimulated by dealing with the crisis. I have found that the growth that takes place after a person has moved outside the initial one-to-one relationship with the pastor and into a relationship with the healing community is more significant for long-term results. A couple who has had to deal with the possibility of divorce can be most effective in helping others think through the alternatives of a floundering marriage. A course in Parent Effectiveness Training was an excellent resource already available in our community for equipping parents to find new ways to deal with parent-child relationships. With the training of an instructor within the parish and the growth of interest among parents, the course is now offered within our parish. The environment for learning is greatly enhanced when couples with similar interests gather to work through and solve their problems together.

The Pastor's Part

This kind of interconnected program fits my understanding of the pastor's role. As a pastor I must stimulate persons and organizations through a process which moves them toward commonly agreed upon goals and programs. For example, we studied the needs of the Sunday school and made it our goal to train enough persons as teachers to build a reserve of Sunday school teachers. After a period of time, we were able to develop twice as many trained teachers as necessary. This allowed for teachers to teach only half-years and to participate in adult education the other half of the year. More and more creative teaching methods (team teaching, and use of audiovisual resources, for example) are evident as teachers become more confident in their theology and their skills. As other needs are identified we mutually work out acceptable goals.

One of the first things I did was to seek out, through counsel of the board of education, those whom the community thought were the six most capable people to run our adult education program. If the program could not survive without me beyond the initial thrust to energize the program, adult education would have limited value for the community. Instead, through the direction of the PACE Program, we trained the six most capable people to run the program. After personally recruiting them, I met with them until they were willing to commit themselves to running the program. The PACE book carefully spells out the steps that they, as the board, would take to motivate and involve the congregation. They would interpret the needs and select the curriculum and enroll the people. I would function as a resource person when new things were tried.

With the emphasis on lay-developed programming the life of the congregation continues with a degree of consistency even as each pastor brings in particular skills.

My role is to act first as an energizer, as the one who gets new things going. Whether it be the adult education program or a new method of evangelism, the process is the same. I seek out and mobilize the leadership and train them; then I turn the program over to them. After this initial phase, I move into a resource position where policy and program is decided by and implemented by the board. My role in teaching courses is similar. I am responsible for teaching the courses the first time as I equip someone to teach the course. I then move into new courses and repeat the process. Other courses are taught by resource persons who have skills in special areas of interest. They contract to teach the course as needed.

Restructuring

I consider adult education as the program behind the program. Once the people in the parish have begun to be equipped to theologize and articulate their theology, I have found they begin to develop programs facilitating these expressions. This means the second phase of leadership is the restructuring of the existing congregational structures. As soon as the people begin to move toward some new awareness of their mission, our traditional structures become a binding force rather than a freezing force. Our adult education process would have become a self-defeating process if we could not have moved into the second phase of expressing the new awareness of mission.

This has resulted in completely redefining our structure with the aid of the concept of business systems, through which we attempt to define the viewpoint, objective, and goal of all the necessary areas in which a church must function. At this point, we are convinced many of the traditional problems, such as poor dissemination of information or unrealistic expectations of the minister, can be taken care of by the development of an appropriate management information system that describes tasks on the basis of commonly agreed upon objectives that have been worked out prior to the initiation of the program. As I grow in the ability to manage by objectives, everyone has a clearer idea of what is expected, and each person is able to work within his or her personal capabilities.

As a new project or event is proposed, we define its goals and I graph out what needs to be done. When the needs of the congregation are spelled out and the expectations defined, participants tend to be much more satisfied because they can measure what they have done and they experience success because they have accomplished what is expected of them. Each member of the congregation is asked to be involved in at least one adult course each year. They know what is expected and they are not made to feel guilty about not participating in the 25 or 30 other courses that are offered in any given year.

With expectations defined and jobs broken down into manageable segments I can be the initiator of each project and can then turn it over to people who are capable of running the show, freeing me to go on to other experimental projects.

Dealing with Change

Change does not occur without stresses and strains. I have discovered that no new form or structure, no matter how creative it may be, seems good to the persons who feel it will bypass them. Refusal to change many times comes not from unwillingness, but rather from the inability to change. Change happens when a person is given a better alternative, is shown the risk involved is worth it, and then is shown how to change in manageable pieces. If given an uncertain future with the promise that things will be better, or if given the choice of living with the certainty of what one knows, even if it is inadequate, most often people will choose certainty. This I discovered most vividly with my attempts to change the congregational constitution. Numerous attempts to change it failed because I gave no good reason to change it. As inadequate as it seemed, it was still better than some unknown. As we have been able to begin to define our mission as a congregation, emerging objectives have begun to dictate and define what the new constitution should be.

The awareness that the church is not a club where members are thrown out if they don't pay dues, the decision to open Holy Communion to all baptized Christians, and the removal of pastor as chairman of the congregation have been moves to facilitate the congregation's mission. We have been able to move from the constitution's dictating and defining the community to the community's dictating and defining the constitution.

Change, then, is the result of a community's defining a new need to be fulfilled. Change ultimately does not take place because we are against something already existing, but because we are for something helping us to live life more fully.

One quickly discovers that intensity of opposition is one way of discovering the success of a program. No one opposes anything which does not threaten personal ideals or lifestyle. We have been most effective in dealing with opposition by trying to listen to the objections and incorporating them into the program. One of the most successful courses we have had is entitled "The Church and Our Changing World." In the course, we talk about the things most disturbing to our people during a particular year. A thorough discussion of a change before the change is proposed minimizes the opposition because objections have not only been answered but have helped shape the proposed change. Two years of educational programs concerning the new structure for confirmation and first Communion preceded any proposals for changing our practice. When the change was brought to a congregational vote, the reason for the change had already been talked about and the deacons had been given a chance to develop a policy that fit our particular situation. With the congregation's views expressed, the questions answered, and opposition aired, the changes were approved.

I've discovered that even those opposed to the adult education program will attend classes dealing with their concerns. I believe it is unrealistic, even undesirable, to think opposition will at some time disappear. Opposition is constantly needed and used to shape the program. We attempt to offer a program ministering to those who normally will not get involved, rather than just to those who will participate, whatever the program. Much of the opposition seems to come from expectations being unfulfilled, and begins to be modified once proper management systems are developed as part of the process where the community discovers and defines its mission.

Evaluation

An essential phase of our program is evaluation. The first year of our curriculum development was the most difficult since we had no reliable measurement for what people were asking and what people wanted. After the first year, we had a composite of evaluations. These are written by each participant at the end of each course. The most useful way of evaluating what is happening in a program is by constantly asking those who are benefiting from the program for their views. This is about as accurate a measure as we have been able to develop, since it is defined by how well we are helping people to answer the questions that they are asking about their Christian life. If their questions are not being answered, then one of two things happens: either they stop participating, or they voice strong opinions on the evaluation sheet. Accurate records are kept of each person's year-to-year participation. If drastic changes take place in someone's participation, an effort is made to find out why.

Engaging in this process has made changes in my understanding, too. Adult education has been the greatest stimulant to my own continuing education. The more people become knowledgeable, the harder the questions are, and the more difficult it is to preach and teach. The more critical the listener and the more articulate the student becomes, the more one has to study to stay ahead.

Each year I have found it necessary to obtain refresher courses in preaching and teaching. I recently found it necessary to train in church administration concepts in order to help articulate new administrative structures. Each new course I teach results in my reading at least one book related to the subject. In the past few months the interest in death, dying, and grief has stimulated me to read numerous books relating to the subject and to attend three special conferences, including one conducted by Elisabeth Kübler-Ross. This has helped keep me theologically fresh.

The frustration some pastors feel of spinning wheels with very little visible progress has not been my experience. I see people asking theological questions about their farming methods and their marriages. I have discovered there are those who care more about profit than preservation of wild life tilling the land. There are those who are seeking to provide the kind of family environment that may challenge the lifestyle a particular profession forces upon the breadwinner. For some husbands, spending more time at home with their wives and children is becoming more important than making top money.

Of course, all people are not thinking theologically, nor are all problems solved. But the frustration of seeing these kinds of needs and having no way to deal with them has not been part of the experience. We have been able to have patience rooted in the knowledge that time is on our side and that the Spirit will work if we provide the environment.

CONSTANT CHANGE AND CONSTANT GOSPEL

John R. Cochran

Through the effusion of tears the words came tumbling out: "You white ——————!" Donald had just felt the "lickin' stick," didn't like it a bit, and gave free vent to his feelings. At some earlier point those words would have stung me. No more. Their utterance only signified how close to the heart of this neighborhood the ministry of education is hitting—close enough to earn that epithet.

The Scene Is Black

Fear constricts in the business of communication. And fear is probably the one word which would characterize the beginning of my ministry at Emanuel in Southwark—not fear of assault or robbery, but simple fear that communication could not, would not, happen. Sneaking through my mind came reminders of my whiteness and consciousness of blackness, so new to me. There were those awful times when I couldn't understand a colloquialism or got stuck on an accent. There were foods I'd never heard of and dances I'd never seen. Sometimes we fenced with each other with words, probing, jabbing, just to see what was there. Testing each other out was quite a game. There were people who deliberately stayed just beyond the pale of communication, coming close enough to be seen but never close enough to engage in conversation. Why? Was it because of color or culture or collar or cow manure on my shoes? Could we communicate? What shape would education take here?

I had everything so cleverly and conveniently arranged from experience in my first parish. Education was a matter of using the LCA curriculum according to the directions. Confirmation had to be a three-year program—more years, more education, better Christians. It worked so smoothly there, a little dull perhaps, but without major hitches. Then Archie's brother died in an automobile accident in

Philadelphia and my clever arrangements died with him. I had baptized Archie early in this ministry in Southwark and he had in the process become my best teacher, sometimes consciously, sometimes quite unawares. When his brother was killed I ministered to his family and found myself in such a wholly new experience that I nearly didn't recover from it. The grief process was so overt as to be overwhelming. The funeral blew my mind: nurses in attendance, open cries of grief during the service (as I read a lesson, a brother cried out: "I want my brother! I want my brother!"), and a graveside service in which we lowered the casket and watched as it was covered. The sense of panic I experienced can scarcely be described. The conventional way of ministering to that family, the conventional way (for me) of putting a funeral together, the conventional way of communicating and education just wouldn't work here. The scene was black, the culture was black, the communictaion was black, and I was white.

Much of the fear was for nothing. People do like to communicate, like to be listened to, and sometimes like to learn. And simple presence, persistence, and openness would work wonders in understanding and communicating. Lots of people would do more than was really required of them to show me, teach me, help me, lead me. And they did—until the fear subsided and the suspicion ebbed and the communication flowed. Some of the fear was well-founded, for the new situation demanded of me a creativity and imagination of which I was unsure.

The Word Is Hope

Grappling with the situation educationally was a primary concern. It was obvious that serious problems lay deep in this community—deeply rooted and bearing bitter fruit. How do you relate the gospel to a gang killing followed by a gang killing followed by an overdose *ad infinitum?* The gospel was born in the midst of violence. Our forebears knew the meaning of treachery and brutality and race hatred. The problem was a great deal less with the gospel than with me. The gospel announces liberty and healing and hope in Jesus in the midst of circumstances far worse than ours. Inexperienced parroting of that proclamation diminishes the gospel and shortchanges those on the receiving end. Clearly, my first task was to involve myself as widely and deeply in the life of this new community as possible, to find the means to listen and learn, to care and be tested, to discern the elusive lines where the gospel ended and my culture continued.

The situation was both worse and better than I had anticipated. Circumstances among families and in schools and on the streets were deadly. Families were fragments and functioned in ways quite strange to me (not all of them, of course), the schools wracked by violence and underachievement and the streets controlled by the worst elements, the mouthiest and least intelligent. Tardiness and irregularity were the rule rather than the exception. Good intentions were rarely matched by performance. Others who had preceded me and overlapped me vowed that normal classes and educational structures could never work. Children were incredibly social and abysmally undisciplined. Group functioning nearly always included more centrifugal elements than the normal group can handle.

But there were ways in which the situation was better. The previously mentioned openness was a large factor. No one pretended that the situation was the "best of all possible worlds." Generally, the people freely recognized the existence of major personal social problems. They, seemingly, wanted to work at retarding or eliminating them. If the situation lacked internal discipline in attacking problems, it surely did not lack the dramatic portrayal of our condition. And in many ways, having all our problems hanging out in full view affords didactic opportunities rarely found. The trick is to demonstrate, if only in a limited way, that we can deal with a problem, that by education and training and cooperative effort we can *win* one. The task is to give birth to hope in a situation so many view as hopeless. Hope was just waiting to be born. Hope lurked around in the shadows afraid to be articulated, to come out when there seemed so little ground for it. And our ministry had to be shaped by those problems and needs and the gospel which was born of the same stuff.

The Ministry Is Growing

We began, a seminarian and I, outside the building, beyond the existing program: visiting, talking, inviting, building. To be sure, the existing program carried problems in structure and language. Those who responded by participation in educational programs, such as Sunday school, confirmation classes, and *ad hoc* groups of every description, were not always responsive to the materials we used. But they came. Building a teaching staff was difficult because so many of the teachers were as tardy and irregular as the students. But we kept at it, so firmly convinced of the relevance of the gospel and its power that we could not be dissuaded by anything. We determined that two things were essential educationally for us:

1. That we be as experimental and eclectic as the situation required in teaching, in hours and days of instruction and discussion, and in the materials we employed;

2. That we needed to develop a core of well trained, dedicated lay ministers to touch every dimension of our work, who would be learners and teachers at the same time ("learning by doing," in the ancient phrase).

It required little effort for us to be experimental and eclectic, although the focus of that improved as our grasp of basic, cultural components improved. We learned how to use a piece of LCA curriculum here, East Harlem Protestant Parish curriculum there, Morse Press, Morehouse Barlow, Augsburg—pictures in place of print, story-telling in place of reading for those whose reading levels hit about kindergarten level, graphic illustrations of every description—in classes, in sermons, in street-side conversations, in school rooms, anywhere we could get in.

For building that core of dependables, we resuscitated the diaconate of the early church with our own adaptations. This revival, we learned after the fact, closely parallels the centuries-old diaconate of the Ethiopian Church. The use of deacons liturgically was already established at Emanuel. We had to expand the role and fill the ranks, both of which we did gradually. We introduced a six-month training course for deacons, using the Bible, *The Ministry of Deacons* (Geneva: World Council of Churches, 1965) and Lukas Vischer's, *Ye Are Baptized* (Geneva: World Council of Churches, 1961) as text books, together with exercises in liturgy and ministry. Gradually the age at which one could enter the course was lowered to include high school youth who were to work in teams of two with a senior deacon. The duties were vastly expanded to include hospital visitation; home Communions; new resident visitation; Sunday school, Baptism class, and day camp teaching; and even some semi-riot-condition control in the neighborhood. We normally have from fifteen to twenty actively functioning deacons at any given time, with others in military service or in universities. The use of deacons is calculated not to replace volunteers, but to stimulate voluntarism. All deacons are volunteers and each is responsible for generating a number of volunteer co-workers—hence the number of volunteers involved in leadership has soared and the numbers involved in the total program have gone wild. The deacons have gathered classes for baptismal instruction of more than twenty-five children at a time and have kept a liaison between church and home of surprising quality and extent.

The deacons' sense of belonging to church and neighborhood continues to amaze me. Through the most difficult experiences my most trusted companions have been deacons. When other paid staff has been sent home for fear of physical harm, the deacons stay with the problem until some kind of solution has been reached. In July, 1970, the loss of electrical power in a building of 200 apartments brought us, on a Saturday night, to near-riot conditions. (The riot was much more in the minds of the police than in the actions of people, but the situation was potentially very dangerous.) Three deacons labored with me from 10:30 P.M. until 4:30 A.M. to insure the absence of violence and the comfort of those without electricity. We averted a disaster through the efforts of those dedicated lay workers. That marriage of strong neighborhood consciousness and dedication to the Lord and his church have made the deacons some of the best teachers I have ever seen in action. Their strong guidance has helped many a budding gang fighter in Southwark to change direction. That we have experienced no deaths in that lethal warfare since 1971 can be attributed in part to the dramatic work of this corps of deacons and staff at Emanuel in shutting off the supply of younger gang members.

Just as the dramatic portrayal of problems assists our ministry, so the possibility of dramatic portrayal exists with our wins—with powerful effect in a community so addicted to the verbal and the dramatic. For us to be able to point to one youth who has made it to college from seemingly hopeless circumstances is worth a million written words of encouragement. And those who have changed directions, those who are making it, are more than willing to be used as the dramatic sign to turn the heads of their brothers and sisters. They ask for the opportunity—and we gladly give it.

The ministry is growing and it is educational at every point. From the *ad hoc* living room classrooms for adults (in homes of families) to a kitchen Eucharist on the eighteenth floor to a discussion around the ping pong table to a Baptism class to a college-bound meeting to religion classes in our parochial school to Sunday school classes to an informal corner gathering, *we are teaching and learning*. Our inner core is on fire with the gospel and its promise of hope and future, and the fire is spreading. Sometimes we burn out here or there and have to double back to rekindle, but our work goes on. It has not lost its sense of excitement and newness in these years. Somehow each time a flame is kindled, each time the gospel strikes fire in someone new, it is amazing and beautiful and so much more than we could really have accomplished with our own efforts.

Shaping Future Through Education

Our ministry is now to the point that we cannot concern ourselves exclusively (if we ever could) with religious education. As the meaning of our work expands in the lives of people and the lives and needs of people crowd in on the church, it becomes obvious that we cannot ignore problems of education and employment and family stability. In employment we join our efforts to those of the state, and in family stability we work hand-in-hand with professional counselors. In the area of education our maneuvering room has been narrowed to the point at which we have to teach reading and mathematics and science ourselves. Through our parish school we intend to raise a new dramatic sign of hope in this community. It is no longer enough for us to sidestep disabling lack of ability with printed communication, with clever teaching by pictures and speech —now young people must be taught to read! Not many beyond this situation will take the time for clever communication. Either you communicate on a par with your peers or you have no college placement, no job. . . .

More and more we see the need for development of critical faculties on the part of adults and young people—to prevent rip-off, but even more to seize opportunities and to comprehend the subtle implications of this or that. What that means is that our religious education is in, with, and under "whole life" concerns, a front-end undertaking to be sure, but not the whole. It is, in short, a sacramental undertaking, clothed in the flesh and blood terms of human elements and human needs and human lives, always hearing within the living presence of the living God. A great joy of our work is that both are obvious: our commitment to the Lord is shown in our daily worship and our teaching/our commitment to the human needs, to the people, is shown by our daily work—the old *ora et labora* of Benedict.

So Donald can hurl his epithet without turning us off. We hit too close to where he lives, too demanding, too much future for one small head. But that's where we're going to keep on working and hitting—where you live, in the heart, and in the seat of the pants. We'll do it because Donald will one day say, "Thanks so much," as so many before him have done.

2

THE BIBLE AND THEOLOGY IN TEACHING-LEARNING

A tutor should not be continually thundering instruction into the ears of his pupil, as if he were pouring it through a funnel, but induce him to think, to distinguish, and to find out things for himself; sometimes opening the way, at other times leaving it for him to open; and so accommodate his precepts to the capacity of his pupil.

—Michel de Montaigne

The greater the intellectual progress
of the ages,
the more fully will it be possible
to employ the Bible
not only as the foundation of education,
but as the instrument of education.

—J. W. von Goethe

If we work upon marble, it will perish; if on brass, time will efface it; if we rear temples, they will crumble into dust; but if we work upon immortal minds, and imbue them with principles, with the just fear of God, and love of our fellow-men, we engrave on those tablets something that will brighten to all eternity.

—Daniel Webster

If we go back to the world's greatest teacher we see that this is the way in which Jesus taught. The Gospel record shows that he sometimes taught from the Old Testament scriptures, but the major emphasis is his teaching from life. What we often fail to see is that the stories we now try to communicate as Bible authority began as life-centered experience to illuminate or cast doubts upon traditional ideas and attitudes.

—Ronald Goldman

ON THEOLOGIZING

For Lutherans the Bible has always had a central place in educational efforts, as well as in worship. Nevertheless the Bible has been interpreted in a variety of ways—some good, some bad. There appears to be a longing for new dimensions of the use of the Bible in the church. The formation of Bible study groups, the ALC-LCA churchwide survey of how congregational members feel the Bible should be used today, and the fact of biblical illiteracy among many younger church members all suggest the urgency of taking new looks at the function of the Bible in congregations.

Richard S. Hanson attempts to put biblical study in perspective. Pastors have been introduced to biblical criticism during their seminary years, but often the exigencies of parish duties have resulted in inadequate Bible teaching. Hanson suggests a perspective for studying biblical theology which takes seriously the variety of theologies and languages in the Bible and the context in which the theological interpretations have been made. He describes the pitfalls of helter-skelter use of texts for the sake of relevancy, on the one hand, and extra-biblical interpretive schemes, on the other. For the sake of appropriate contemporary theologizing, he urges a thorough study of the many distinct traditions in the Bible.

Through a number of perceptive examples he describes the multiform interpretations of the Bible and suggests how all of us might be helped to see more clearly our task of interpretation as Christians today. He makes a plea for helping people become aware of the variety of languages, e.g. poetic, Johannine, and Pauline.

Hanson uses his experience in college teaching to give examples of assignments which might prove fruitful for those who are searching for new meanings. He cautions against premature applications because the tendency to misinterpret is so great when ideas are taken out of context. He lays great stress on learning for the sake of learning and helping small groups of eager people take seriously the power of the biblical witness on its own terms.

Not content to urge pastors to dig deeply in biblical study, Hanson offers suggestions on making multiple use of these efforts. With a new lectionary series upon us it is particularly appropriate that pastors be involved in new efforts to understand the biblical materials used as an integral part of public worship. He is confident that showing people how to discover and understand the theologies of the Bible will enable them to produce insight and probe the difficult questions. Confident of those insights, Hanson sees the possibilities of renewal and reform emerging.

For Richard Luecke, educational ministry has the crucial task of helping individuals and congregations think theologically and act in the name of the Lord. Richard Luecke titles his article "Local Theology," suggesting the necessity of approaching educational ministry with this task clearly in focus.

In the context of contemporary society Luecke discusses the rationale for doing local theology—who does it, why do it, and what to do. He proposes a style of reflection within congregations which explores problematic areas or "topics" in order to seek responses which connect with the past, speak to the present, and are open to the future.

The "how" of doing theology, Luecke suggests, is through using arts or disciplines, such as: symbolics, hermeneutics, homiletics, and systematics. However, he sees the disciplines as opportunities to interrelate the functions of congregational activities and the sources of the faith, and to lead to insights for our time.

The "occasions" for these opportunities for theological exploration are located in acts of celebration, interpretation, procedures and polity, and organization. Outcomes of these disciplined probes during the occasions of worship, instruction, polity, and organization are then examined in relation to their effects on communication and to their development in the society.

Luecke applies his perspectives to the problems of symbols and community creation in the church and in society, interpretation and issue discrimination, procedure, polity, and common action. He also deals with the difficulties and possibilities of intra-congregational conflicts, organization for interrelation with the society, and the role of pastors.

He provides a useful analytic tool to look at parish life in theological-educational dimensions. Luecke's proposal can provide an excellent evaluative perspective, a model for what pastors and congregations could perform in their own locus.

BIBLICAL THEOLOGY

Richard Simon Hanson

Parish pastors are beset by questions and demands. Parishioners with various needs press them with difficult existential problems while their own inner selves insistently demand response to questions of role and profession. While answering the summons to stand at the side of those who suffer, busy pastors wonder when they will find time to minister to some of their own intellectual or spiritual needs. While they hasten to prepare for next Sunday's sermon, they agonize over the fact that there is seldom time to study for the pure reward of learning or pursuing an interest. And all this is in the midst of a host of trite and mundane demands that always seem to require more time than they deserve.

If we will allow it to happen, however, there are times when two or more of these questions converge and the answers to one become the answers to one or more of the others. Or, to put it in another way, there may be things we can do to meet two or three of these conflicting demands at once.

Knowing you are pressed by many demands and suspecting that you look back with some longing at a time in life when you could enjoy the luxuries of reading and study and the pursuit of answers to tantalizing questions, I am hoping to offer a way in which you can treat yourselves to a bit of scholarly pleasure and, at the same time, serve yourselves with spiritual food and deal with what appears to me to be a neglected area of concern in most of our parishes.

I suspect that for most pastors, study of the Bible is a frantic searching of pericope texts and commentaries for something to say in a sermon, or preparation for a study group that is made up of persons considerably less informed than the pastor. Biblical theology just is not being studied by parish pastors. If it was ever done at all, it was probably last done in a seminary classroom. But I also know of a limited number of lay people who feel cheated by the mill that grinds out the grist that most people want or need for spiritual or intellectual nourishment. These are people who are tired of being talked down to and earnestly desire something more challenging to the mind than they have had until now. I feel that their need can be met together with the need of the study-starved pastor. So I offer what may be a way of hope to some: a modest program for pastors and laity to use individually or together.

At the same time I am concerned about a good deal of fuzziness and ambiguity concerning the nature and usefulness of the Bible and, equally, the function and definition of theology. We are not at all agreed on what the Bible is good for. Some of us see it as the one and only source for what we call the Word of God. Others use it only reluctantly as a source from which one must quote in the preaching of a sermon in order to be heard and believed. For some, the Bible is a daily source of consolation as they live with it devotionally. For most, only parts of it are useful or relevant: the parts that make good preaching texts, the parts that least offend our modern sense of what is rational, or the parts that best undergird Lutheran theology. We are not even agreed on just how it can be or is the Word of God. Indeed, a good many would honesly rather say that it merely *contains* the Word of God. However, they would rather not be asked to defend that statement because they are not at all sure how they could demonstrate just how and where we find the Word of God that is contained there.

We are similarly confused about theology. Most pastors seem to regard it as the concern of specialists only. Maybe you, like they, are quick to confess that you (least of all suspects!) are not a theologian. You were a theological student once, but that was once upon a time. You seem to be convinced that parish duties prevent you from being that now.

The Business of Theology

Theology is the business of interpreting and articulating the message of faith that has been passed on to us by our fathers. It is a process of thinking and speaking what we think, and we do it whenever we have to give an explanation of what we believe.

It is done at both simple and sophisticated levels. An uneducated person struggling to explain why he believes what he believes is doing theology as surely as the theological professor who writes articles for learned journals. A missionary explaining Christianity to a prospective convert, a parent teaching a child what faith in God is all about, or a person explaining his own tradition to himself: all these are persons doing theology. Hopefully, parish pastors do theology every time they deliver a sermon. Indeed, one fails to do it only when one merely parrots clichés and slogans of the tradition without questioning what they mean.

When this theologizing is done in our own time and when it is an attempt to interpret and articulate the faith that has been handed down by the preceding generation, it is best called *contemporary theology*, for it is an attempt to articulate the faith of the past in contemporary language. And it is important to do this, for language and culture are steadily evolving phenomena that demand change for the very sake of preserving what has been passed on to us.

This means that contemporary theology is, by nature, a conservative endeavor. No matter how radical or daring its language, it is an attempt to make sense of a message that has been received from the past. Rarely does a contemporary theologian come up with new revelation, and when one does, it is almost always consistent with the revelation of the past. Contemporary theologians pursue a conservative double task: the task of preserving the tradition that they have received and of relating it in language that has clear meaning in the present.

Biblical theology is unlike contemporary theology in one major respect: it is theology of times and culture more ancient than our own and preceding us in the tradition. It is, in fact, the theology of the Bible, and the task of the biblical theologian is to understand the theology found there rather than to create his own. The only creativity permitted is the creativity of articulating what is discovered by careful study—unless we are so daring as to actually *do* theology the way it is done in the Bible! Biblical theology is the theology that is found in the Bible. It is the thinking and talking and writing of persons who lived long ago and pursued the business of interpreting and articulating the message of faith that was given to them. It is the contemporary theology of times long past. Like us, our theologian-forebears had to explain what they believed to others and to the generation that came after them. Like us, they had to do theology in order to pass on the faith from the past to the future.

The Nature of Biblical Theology

The Bible is full of theology—or, more correctly, theologies, for there are as many theologies in the Bible as there are persons who did the writing and the speaking. Each prophet, evangelist, or storyteller was a theologian. The Bible is not just revelation; it is revelation couched in the language that is theology. It is revelation being interpreted and articulated. That is as true of revelation that was fresh and new as it was for revelation that had already been passed on by years of tradition. Moses explaining to his people that he had seen a burning bush and heard a message from the God of his fathers had to do theology by having to explain it, and those who passed on the tradition of Moses' story did theology every time they explained that tradition to a succeeding generation. Theology is what we do when we communicate either the content of revelation afresh or the tradition that we believe in. It is what we do every time we give God a name, seek to describe a theophany, or attempt to articulate a conviction.

But are there really many theologies in the Bible? Yes, insofar as there are many names for God, many accounts of theophany, and many more repetitions of those accounts. Each body of material in the Bible has its own peculiar language or way of speaking, its own favorite names for God, its own favored events of revelation, and its own favorite terms for describing or explaining those events.

It takes little perception to notice this. Even untrained readers catch on to such differences between the writings of John and the writings of Paul or the Book of Micah and the Book of Hosea. John's language and manner of presentation just is not much like the language and style of Paul, and the material that each of the two favors is unique. Micah's way of defining the problems of his day is significantly different from the way of Hosea. And if it is easy for the untrained eye to catch some of these differences, it is possible for the discerning eye to perceive many more.

This idea of discerning different theologies within the Bible might be easiest to understand and accept if we think of the obviously different theologies of the contemporary church. No matter how our message may be the same, we Lutherans do not tell it the same as our Presbyterian, Anglican, or Roman Catholic brethren. We have a vocabulary peculiar to ourselves with distinctions of law and gospel, a doctrine of two kingdoms, and careful concern for what we mean by the sacraments. We treasure certain features of the tradition or message that are of less significance to the others and they, in turn, each emphasize their peculiar distinctions. Yet we insist, most of the time, that we are the "one, holy, catholic, apostolic church," the Communion of Saints. We feel that our differing theologies are differing thrusts of emphasis or differences of language.

The situation of the Bible is like this. Though it is all of one historical tradition and grounded in a few common events, there were various groups who preserved and passed on the tradition, each in its distinctive way, and various prophets who called attention to particular aspects of what was happening. The particular theology of each group or individual speaker/writer is the particular language and focus that is used in telling the story or proclaiming the message at a particular time in history.

Examples of Biblical Theology

The Book of Judges is a relatively simple demonstration of how theology functions in the process of passing on the tradition. The book is, for the most part, a collection of hero stories plus a few other patriarchal legends. As for subject matter, it is here that we meet such personalities as Deborah, Gideon, and Samson, or hear such a sordid tale as the story of the Levite's concubine. The stories are of varying length and varying style. Their origin is from here and there in the Confederacy, spanning some 200 years. In the telling, however, they are bound by a common theology, a common interpretation of what was going on.

The stories were clearly passed on through several generations before they were gathered together into what came to be called the Book of Judges. However, the persons who gathered the stories were not content merely to repeat what they had heard; they put them into a framework that is a clear and simple theology. They told the stories in such a way as to make them illustrations of a certain way of understanding the world and God and the times. That scheme is set forth in the second chapter of the book:

> And the people of Israel did what was evil in the sight of the Lord and served the Baals; and they forsook the Lord, the God of their fathers, who had brought them out of the land of Egypt; they went after other gods, from among the gods of the peoples who were round about them, and bowed down to them; and they provoked the Lord to anger. They forsook the Lord, and served the Baals and the Ashtaroth. So the anger of the Lord was kindled against Israel, and he gave them over to plunderers, who plundered them; and he sold them into the power of their enemies round about, so that they could no longer withstand their enemies. Whenever they marched out, the hand of the Lord was against them for evil, as the Lord had warned, and as the Lord had sworn to them; and they were in sore straits.
>
> Then the Lord raised up judges, who saved them out of the power of those who plundered them. And yet they did not listen to their judges; for they played the harlot after other gods and bowed down to them; they soon turned aside from the way in which their fathers had walked, who had obeyed the commandments of the Lord, and they did not do so. Whenever the Lord raised up judges for them, the Lord was with the judge, and he saved them from the hand of their enemies all the days of the judge; for the Lord was moved to pity by their groaning because of those who afflicted and oppressed them. But whenever the judge died, they turned back and behaved worse than their fathers, going after other gods, serving them and bowing down to them; they did not drop any of their practices or their stubborn ways.
>
> (Judges 2:11-19)

This part of Judges 2 set forth the theology of those who put the stories together and recorded them for later generations. The words are not revelation; they are interpretation. Revelation is to be found in the happenings that inspired the stories, and that is precisely what this theology implies. The hard times that came upon the tribes of Israel were revelation through which God was saying that all was not well. Conversely, the good times that came when they were saved by a judge were ways of God's revealing his mercy. According to this theology, the revelation was in the happenings—the very history that the people lived. The stories, as accounts of those happenings, were the first theological form in which that revelation was articulated. Those stories, in turn, were seen together as forming a kind of pattern which is described in the words that are repeated at several points throughout the Book of Judges: 3:7-9, 3:12, 3:15, 4:1-3, 6:1, 6:7-8, 10:6-7, 10:10-16, and 13:1. Looking it all over, the authors saw revelation just that way and declared it in simple, straightforward, dogmatic statements. As they saw it, all those stories put together declared eloquently that God was the Lord of history giving special training to the tribes of Israel.

Quite another perception of how God exercises his sovereign authority is found in the Book of Ecclesiastes. The theology of the Book of Ecclesiastes is not much like the theology of the Book of Judges. The writer of Ecclesiastes, after considering the events and ways of the world, has this to say:

> I have seen the business that God has given the sons of men to be busy with. He has made everything beautiful in its time; also he has put eternity into man's mind, yet so that he cannot find out what God has done from the beginning to the end. I know that there is nothing better for them than to be happy and enjoy themselves as long as they live; also that is God's gift to man that every one should eat and drink and take pleasure in all his toil. I know that whatever God does endures for ever; nothing can be added to it, nor anything taken from it; God has made it so, in order that men should fear before him. That which is, already has been; that which is to be, already has been; and God seeks what has been driven away.
>
> Moreover I saw under the sun that in the place of justice, even there was wickedness, and in the place of righteousness, even there was wickedness. I said in my heart, God will judge the righteous and the wicked, for he has appointed a time for every matter, and for every work. I said in my heart with regard to the sons of men that God is testing them to show them that they are but beasts. For the fate of the sons of men and the fate of beasts is the same; as one dies, so dies the other. They all have the same breath, and man has no advantage over the beasts; for all is vanity.
>
> (Ecclesiastes 3:10-19)

Though we cannot accuse these ancient theological groups of being directly opposed to each other at every point, we can obviously say that they saw the whole matter of life and history quite differently. We may have no doubt that they believed in one and the same God, yet they did not see the same thing when they looked at history in their respective times. One group saw a clear pattern that might be called divine justice at work. The other saw, quite precisely, the absence of any such pattern. One articulates the notion that God was disciplining and training his servants, the tribes of Israel. The other articulates the mystery and obscurity of the ways of God.

Differing theologies can be seen in the New Testament as well. The Epistle to the Hebrews is theology in its purest sense. There are no eyewitness accounts of revelation, no Jesus-stories, no visions, no oracles. From beginning to end, Hebrews is *interpretation* of the revelation that was Jesus. It is, in fact, a discussion of various ways in which God had revealed himself to the Hebrew people and how the revelation of God via the Messiah has superseded all others and introduced a new era. According to the anonymous author of the epistle, the Christ is even the great high priest. The author made this statement for a distinct purpose. It was not because Jesus ever said that about himself, nor because it was ever said that explicitly in any prophetic oracle, but because that was a powerful and valid way to explain Jesus' death and resurrection to a people who understood full well what the priesthood and sacrifice were all about. And to counter any argument that Jesus could not be a priest because he was of the family of Judah rather than the family of Levi, the author argued brilliantly for a priesthood after the order of Melchizedek on the basis of the great messianic hymn in Psalm 110.

When we turn to the Gospel of Mark, however, we find no such talk of sacrifice nor any suggestion that Jesus is a priest. His death is not even depicted as an atonement of any kind. Mark proclaims his message of Jesus in a theology that centers about the idea of the power of God. His Jesus is a wonder-worker who heals the sick, casts out demons, and aggressively challenges the scribes and Pharisees because he embodies the power of God. Jesus is the Messiah, pronounced to be the Son of God as he steps from the baptismal waters of Jordan. As the Messiah—the Christ, the King—Jesus possesses God's power and authority.

The story is a story of action, as God's power erupts in the world of the first century Jews of Palestine. Indeed, it is a story of conflict in which the powers of demonic and human evil oppose the power of Jesus and are drawn out by him. But out of the conflict comes victory for God and his Son. The Christ is killed, but as he dies, the curtain of the Temple is split, and three days later he has risen: two clear signs that the power of God is triumphant in Jesus the Christ. The theology of Mark focuses on the power of God rather than the meaning of Jesus' death. To learn the theology of sacrifice we must turn to portions of the writings of Paul or John or, most especially, to the anonymous Epistle to the Hebrews. We will simply not find that theology in Mark's Gospel.

Theology in the Tradition

Down through the ages the theological task was done by those persons who cared enough about the faith of their fathers or the ongoing revelation of God to speak of it to their contemporaries and write it in their own way for the sake of passing it on to the next generation. It was not often startlingly new and fresh, however. Because several generations may share a common world of experience, there have been times in the transmission of the tradition when theology has experienced so little change that it seems to have been static or even stagnating. But the world does change, and those who rose to the theological task in times of change forged out the strikingly creative languages of Moses, Samuel, Amos, Jeremiah, Jesus, Paul, John, Irenaeus, Athanasius, Augustine, Abelard, Bernard, Francis, Luther, Calvin, or Thomas. . . . The list could be impressively long.

These persons whom we call theologians are an important part of the tradition itself. They are the creators of language. Without them the tradition would die for lack of meaning. They are the members of the community of faith who have succeeded in communicating the message of faith to the other members of the community in ways that speak with sense and power. The theologians are essential as revelation itself, for the theologians are the preachers and teachers of the message.

The Bible is an impressive collection of what the earliest theologians of our tradition succeeded in speaking to the generations that came after them. It is the record of the faith of our fathers as it was transmitted from its beginnings to the latest book of the New Testament—an ever expanding record, to be sure, as new revelation was added to old, but still a tradition that was being passed on in new and newer forms of speech.

To study biblical theology is to study the theologies of the first historical periods of our tradition of faith. The task is to study rather than to do. One can study contemporary theology as well, but most of us who are involved in preaching the message of faith are involved in doing rather than studying contemporary theology. Contemporary theology is theology being done.

In fact, the only theology that can be *done* in our day is contemporary theology. Whether we use ancient or recent sources as our starting point, our explanations are contemporary, and that is what makes it all contemporary theology. It is the creative language of faith being spoken in our time. Biblical theology, on the other hand, is something that has already been *done*. It is the theologizing that was done by the biblical writers when they articulated the words that are now preserved for all generations. Their task cannot be done again, for their time is past. They were the contemporary theologians of bygone ages. What we can do is study what they did. We can draw from their labors and drink from their wells. We can explore them, admire them, and learn much from them, but we cannot do their task again because it is too late. They, in their times, have done it. We have no option to *do* biblical theology; we can only *learn*. To be a biblical theologian is to be a student or a scholar.

There is evidence that we confuse the content of faith with theology—the results of which are ridiculous displays of intolerance and fear toward those of differing theological traditions or points of view. We also fail to realize that the theological task is precisely the task we are called to every time we need to articulate our faith.

To put it simply, theology is language. No matter how inextricably interwoven the two may be, theology and the content of faith that theology articulates are not the same thing. Theology is not what we believe in; theology is the way we talk and think about what we believe in. All may believe in one and the same thing, but our theologies may differ because we typically find many different ways to apprehend and articulate that one thing we perceive in common. Theologies are and should be as different as we are.

What I have been calling awkwardly the content of faith is another matter, for by this phrase I mean to refer to that which we believe in: God as revealed to us in the many revelations that make up the story of our tradition.

Much of this distinction was explained very well by G. Ernest Wright in an unpretentious little volume entitled *God Who Acts* (Naperville, Ill.: Allenson, 1952). Wright, perhaps more than anyone else, has helped us see that the revelation of God came or comes in *events* that are historically recitable and this, in turn, helps us distinguish between the events and the recitation of those events. The events are the revelation that is to be belived in; the recital of the events is done by language which is properly called theology.

The Nature of the Task

So far we recognize two factors essential to understanding biblical theology: (1) that it is theology of long ago, written in languages of the past and growing out of an environment that has passed away; (2) that it is many theologies rather than one.

In consideration of these two observations we now ask two corollary questions: how does one learn these theologies, and how does one teach them? And the first proposition that suggests itself is this: to understand the theologies of the Bible one must learn something of the life and times in which they came into being.

The task is not so hard as it is time-consuming and delightful. There are hundreds of fine scholars who have dedicated their lives to the study of ancient Hebrew culture and the world into which Christianity was born, and they have produced some marvelous books for the rest of us. Fr. Roland deVaux's *Ancient Israel* (New York: McGraw-Hill, 1965) is an example of the best. It discusses in detail and in historical perspective almost all of the facets of the culture that produced the Old Testament. Because Fr. deVaux spent his life in and around Jerusalem, the book is rich with an intimate understanding of the area. For more purely historical approaches, we have such fine works as *A History of Israel* by John Bright (Philadelphia: Westminster, 1972), and *The History of Israel* by Martin Noth (New York: Harper & Row, 1960). For additional recommendations of useful books related to the study of the Old and New Testaments, see the Helpful Books and Resources section (p. 282).

A trip to Israel does not help as much as people expect it to. It stimulates the imagination, to be sure, and it refines our sense of romance, but if it is not backed up by a generous amount of study of ancient times, it gives us precious little information about the distant past. Contemporary Israel, after all, is a modern country and much of what passes as being of biblical times is pure "touristica." Beware of the person who knows only because he has "been there!"

Part of understanding the times in which the Bible was written is the necessity of understanding its languages. Most simply, this means learning Hebrew, Aramaic, and Greek. No one should set forth to be a teacher of biblical theology without some knowledge of those languages. There is simply no substitute for it. But *language* means more than the original tongues versus an English translation. It means differentiating between poetry and prose, or between the language of law and the language of story.

Every year I teach Bible to some 300 college students who haven't had a bit of Hebrew or Greek but do some language study to increase their understanding. When we study the prophets, for example, I talk about the language of poetry and the language of vision so that the students can understand when they are in the midst of metaphors or symbols, and when the words are intended to create pictures in the mind rather than have meaning *per se*. Or I spend a good amount of time explaining the language of story so that they will read with imagination and perception that penetrates deeper than the surface facts of the material.

One of my favorite assignments is the reading of the case laws that one finds in Exodus 20–24 or in much of the Book of Deuteronomy. "In these laws you will find the daily happenings of the lives of those people," I tell the students. "As you read each law, try to reconstruct the actual case and how the people brought it to the judges and how the judges dealt with it." The aim is to show them that there is real life—albeit of another age and culture—behind the words of the text, and a few of my students have caught on to the extent that they declare that the case laws are the most interesting part of the Bible! I wonder if a follow-up study of those persons might reveal them to be budding law students.

Poetry as Theological Language

The language of poetry proves to be very difficult for many people, perhaps because it is so unlike the language of our daily discourse. The language of daily discourse is a language of shallow perception and simple, two-plus-two kinds of observations. It does not see deeper than the surface of things, nor does it create picture frames around what is seen. The language of the poet, on the other hand, it the language of insight. The poet is one who sees deeply. The poet is one who sees life as pictures—moving pictures, too.

Part of the problem for our generation is the fact that we do not even understand the poetry of our own times. We have lost the art of understanding poetry. We have come to think that poetry is a purely esthetic thing to be enjoyed by a few purely esthetic people. Poetry just is not a popular language today.

Unfortunately for us, however, poetry was a popular kind of language in ancient Israel and Judah. As far as we can tell, poetry was the language of the street-preaching prophets, the language of temple worship and the language in which many of the most well-known stories were transmitted from one generation to another, not merely for the sake of speaking esthetically, but for the sake of speaking with power.

Poetry is powerful language. Poetry is language used to arrest our attention and cause us to focus our thoughts on a single thing for a longer time than we would normally be inclined. Poetry is language that says, "Stop! Look at this! Consider this that I hold before your eyes! Think about it! Do not let it pass!" And the point of focus may be a thing of delight or a thing of sadness, a moment of beauty, a moment of horror, or just an ordinary moment that shouldn't be missed because it is worth a second look.

Perhaps we can illustrate from the pages of the Bible itself the kinds of moments that poetry arrests us to consider.

A moment of horror—the fall of Nineveh as portrayed by the prophet Nahum:

> Woe to the bloody city,
> all full of lies and booty—
>   no end to the plunder!
> The crack of whip, and rumble of wheel,
>   galloping horse and bounding chariot!
> Horsemen charging,
>   flashing sword and glittering spear,
> hosts of slain,
>   heaps of corpses,
> dead bodies without end—
>   they stumble over the bodies!
> And all for the countless harlotries of the harlot,
>   graceful and of deadly charms,
> who betrays nations with her harlotries,
>   and peoples with her charms.
>
> (Nahum 3:1-4)

A moment of delight—the voice of the bride in the Song of Songs:

> The voice of my beloved!
>   Behold, he comes,
> leaping upon the mountains,
>   bounding over the hills.
> My beloved is like a gazelle,
>   or a young stag.
> Behold, there he stands
>   behind our wall,
> gazing in at the windows,
>   looking through the lattice.
> My beloved speaks and says to me:
> "Arise, my love, my fair one,
>   and come away;
> for lo, the winter is past,
>   the rain is over and gone.
> The flowers appear on the earth,
>   the time of singing has come,
> and the voice of the turtledove
>   is heard in our land.
> The fig tree puts forth its figs,
>   and the vines are in blossom;
>   they give forth fragrance.
> Arise, my love, my fair one,
>   and come away.
>
> (The Song of Solomon, 2:8-13)

A moment of insight—prayer of a wise person:

Two things I ask of thee;
deny them not to me before I die:
Remove far from me falsehood and lying;
give me neither poverty nor riches;
feed me with the food that is needful for me,
lest I be full and deny thee,
and say, "Who is the Lord?"
or lest I be poor, and steal,
and profane the name of my God.
(Proverbs 30:7-9)

A moment of accusation—God speaks through a prophet:

Hear, O heavens, and give ear, O earth;
for the Lord has spoken:
"Sons have I reared and brought up,
but they have rebelled against me.
The ox knows its owner,
and the ass its master's crib;
but Israel does not know,
my people does not understand."
(Isaiah 1:2-3)

A moment of judgment—Isaiah describes the Lord's power:

For, behold, the Lord, the Lord of hosts,
is taking away from Jerusalem and from Judah
stay and staff,
the whole stay of bread,
and the whole stay of water;
the mighty man and the soldier,
the judge and the prophet,
the diviner and the elder,
the captain of fifty
and the man of rank,
the counselor and the skillful magician
and the expert in charms.
And I will make boys their princes,
and babes shall rule over them.
And the people will oppress one another,
every man his fellow
and every man his neighbor;
the youth will be insolent to the elder,
and the base fellow to the honorable.
(Isaiah 3:1-5)

A moment of vision—Zechariah sees beyond harsh realities:

Rejoice greatly, O daughter of Zion!
  Shout aloud, O daughter of Jerusalem!
Lo, your king comes to you;
  triumphant and victorious is he,
humble and riding on an ass,
  on a colt the foal of an ass.

(Zechariah 9:9)

A moment of devotion—a psalmist sings with spiritual intensity:

How lovely is thy dwelling place,
  O Lord of hosts!
My soul longs, yea, faints
  for the courts of the Lord;
my heart and flesh sing for joy to the
  living God.
Even the sparrow finds a home,
  and the swallow a nest for herself,
  where she may lay her young,
at thy altars, O Lord of hosts,
  my King and my God.
Blessed are those who dwell in thy house,
  ever singing thy praise!

(Psalm 84:1-4)

A moment of faith—the awareness of a believer of the power of God:

Come, behold the works of the Lord,
  how he has wrought desolations in the earth.
He makes wars cease to the end of the earth;
  he breaks the bow, and shatters the spear,
  he burns the chariots with fire!
"Be still, and know that I am God.
  I am exalted among the nations,
  I am exalted in the earth!"
The Lord of hosts is with us;
  the God of Jacob is our refuge.

(Psalm 46:8-11)

A moment of sadness—the death of great leaders lamented by a historian:

Saul and Jonathan, beloved and lovely!
  In life and in death they were not divided;
they were swifter than eagles,
  they were stronger than lions.

Ye daughters of Israel, weep over Saul,
who clothed you daintily in scarlet,
who put ornaments of gold upon your apparel.
How are the mighty fallen
in the midst of the battle!
(2 Samuel 1:23-25a)

What more eloquent speech is there than the speech of poetry? What more powerful way to say anything? Because the poet is one who seeks to arrest us, we must allow ourselves to be arrested. We must stop and give attention. We must slow the pace of the mind so that the poem can do its work of painting its pictures and creating its moods. This is what we have not been trained to do, for we are a generation concerned with data and facts and speed-reading and efficiency. Poetry stands in defiance of our way of life, demanding that we interrupt our mad pace to pause and behold what we are missing in all of our haste.

The Bible is loaded with poetry and is poetic in spirit even where the words do not have poetic rhythms and colors. The Bible requires slow reading rather than speed. There is no rapid way to read it and grasp its messages. That makes it out of style, and that is why we have to pause and teach people how to read poetry at the beginning stage of learning biblical theology.

The best of the biblical writers were poets. Their messages are missed if we do not develop a sense for the sounds and shapes of poetry. Poetry was the prophetic way of doing theology—the prophetic way of articulating the revelation that was heard and seen—and once we understand this, we will not settle for the narrow dimensions of those who see prophecy as merely precise predictions of future events. However, this is the greatest difficulty of introducing modern readers to the prophets of the Bible. Having explained the times of the prophets and the ways of those times, we may find that there are people who cannot fathom what those prophets said simply because they cannot understand what poetry is. As a result, the teacher may have to spend most of his time patiently illustrating the most basic and simple features of poetic communication.

Various Languages of Theology

There is no such thing as one certain kind of theological language. In the Bible, theology is done in several different languages: the language of poetry, the language of story, the languages of ritual, law, drama, and proverbial wisdom, the language of vision. and the straightforward and direct language of letters that was used so often by Paul. Because those we in the West have come to call theologians tend to bind themselves to a language of abstract concepts and logic, which is the language of philosophy, we have come to think that there is a special language of theology. But we are wrong in thinking that, and it may well be that we have failed to recognize some of our best theologians because we have failed to realize that theology can be done and is done in many ways.

Consider how effectively the language of story has served as a way to talk about God. To remind ourselves of the obvious, anyone who has thought about it knows that God is not a person in the sense that we normally use that word. God is not tied to a body, that "he" must see with eyes or hear with ears. All anthropomorphic talk about God is false and inaccurate. As a matter of fact, all talk about God falls short because talk must compare this to that and God is beyond all comparisons. If speech must be true to its subject, no speech about God is even possible and we must remain speechless. But that is a restriction we cannot abide, for thoughts of the mystery we call God demand expression.

How liberating it is to be able to cast God as a character in a story. If we can make him the one who walks in the Garden of Eden, we can talk about creation itself and how we grow up in "his" presence. "He" can visit Abraham and speak words of command and direction. "He" can hear our cries of despair and our hymns of praise. "He" can judge us or save us. "He" can be as a father to children. "He" can be king, shepherd, or lord of hosts. All of this is necessary for an articulation of the awareness in us that refuses to be identified as anything less than awareness of God.

To apply this point to our present task we say this: when you set forth to read any part of the Bible you must ask, "What is the special language of this part of the Bible? Under what guise does the writer write? Does he speak as a poet or merely as a reporter? Is he telling a story, discussing an idea, or preaching a sermon? Is the language painting pictures or is it leading me into abstract realms? Is the writer speaking of ordinary life, as in codes of law, or relaying visions? Are the words telling it as plainly as it is or do they speak in metaphor and parable?" To relate this point to an earlier point, we must say: there are not only many theologies in the Bible; there are also many languages.

Each theology has its own language and must be approached and understood on those terms. If one wishes to understand the theology of the writings of John in the New Testament, he must take time to learn John's special vocabulary and way of speaking. If one would study the Book of Deuteronomy, he must be willing to learn the language of law and the language of ritual. If one wants to get the message of Genesis, he must surrender himself to the language of story.

And one must be careful to not mix two languages as though they were one. At the beginning stage at least, John's writings should be studied by themselves. Those who dash back and forth between the Synoptic Gospels and the Gospel according to John, or between Paul's Epistles and the First Epistle of John, will soon lose track of the peculiar and distinctive features of John's language and will cease to hear the message of John in its clarity. The theologies of the Bible cannot be learned unless they are learned one at a time by taking the amount of time required to give each its proper due.

Bible Study in the Parish

The most common kinds of lay or parish Bible study groups mix the theologies of the Bible in a most indiscriminate way and garble them all as a result. Even in our preaching and in our sermon preparations we are not accustomed to distinguishing between the language of Paul and the language of John. We lump the four Gospels together as a common pool of preaching texts rather than observe their very important differences. We read the stories of Genesis in the same way that we read the records of 1 and 2 Kings, ending up with outlandish notions of ancient history as a consequence.

Consider the Bible study group that meets for personal enlightenment. Noble as its purposes are, such a study group is not apt to understand any part of the Bible on its own terms. "What the First Epistle of Peter can mean to me" is apt to be its stated goal, and the words *to me* are underlined. It is a self-centered approach to the Scriptures and, at its best, it produces an existential experience. The focus is on the person or persons doing the study rather than on the material that is being studied.

Or consider the kinds of Bible study we so often do for catechetical instruction. We are not really after what the Bible says and certainly are not aware of its diversity of parts. Our aim is to demonstrate the rightness of our denominational beliefs. We use Scripture to show that Lutheran doctrines are backed by Scriptural truth or, at our worst, to prove that ours is the only true way to understand the Bible. We are not after biblical theology.

A similar evaluation must be given to the now-famous Bethel Bible Series. Underlying it is a Lutheran doctrinal position. The whole study is a well-framed, conservative, contemporary theology. The important feature about it is its overall view. It is a comprehensive construction that cites many passages of Scripture to validate its parts, but it is not designed for getting at the distinctive theologies of the Bible. It is a rather sound contemporary view of the Bible that does increase our familiarity with it in a very general and indiscriminate way while pushing a certain doctrinal position as part of the package. My good friend, its author, advises us to "think Hebrew," but he does not really teach us to do that and he does not undertake the task which we are exploring here.

If we really want to learn the theologies of the Bible, we must take an approach unlike those described above. We must take one part at a time, take the time that is necessary to enter its world of thought and learn its language, and free ourselves to let it say what it will even though it surprises us with insights we have never encountered before.

How can this be done? (And we recognize that the question is being asked by parish pastors who are already busier than they ought to be with hundreds of odd tasks that may never get done to a point of satisfaction!)

Sample Assignments in Biblical Theology

Since I teach religion at a liberal arts college, every year I face the task of teaching Bible to persons who are lay members of the church and most likely will be for the rest of their lives. As college students, they are in a situation where assignments and learning are the normal fare of the day and academic credit is part of the reward. This makes my task unlike the educational task of the parish pastor. But insofar as these students are at the level of understanding where most interested lay people can be found, the tasks are similar. I am not teaching professionals or, for the most part, people who are going on to be educated for the parish ministry. Therefore it might be helpful to share some sample assignments that have worked in the classroom over the past few years in terms of discovering the theologies of the Bible.

Sample Assignment 1: The Gospel According to Mark

Mark was a servant of the church in the second generation of its existence. He was a servant with the particular task of putting the Jesus story into manuscript form in order that it might be recorded for future generations and used for the instruction of persons who were interested in learning what Christianity was all about. If the only known tradition about how Mark did it is correct, he got the various stories about Jesus from others. His was the task of putting them together and writing them down.

The people who gave these stories to Mark were, like Mark himself, believers. They were not unbiased reporters. They had convictions and a point of view about this Jesus whose story they wanted to tell. So the materials came into Mark's hands as theology, i.e., as explanations of who Jesus was, not merely as reports of the known facts. Mark, as one of the believers, shared those convictions and that point of view, but added to them—or stamped upon them—the uniqueness of his own point of view and convictions.

The result is a particular presentation of the Jesus story, a particular way of understanding Jesus and explaining who he was, a particular theology. When we read the Gospel according to Mark, we meet Jesus as seen through the eyes of Mark and those other early Christians who told him the stories they knew. In many ways, the view is distinctively different from the view you will get if you read one of the other Gospels in the New Testament.

To make sure that we are seeing just what is in Mark and neither something more nor something else, let us follow some simple guidelines.

1. Do not fill in Mark's story with what is not there. If Mark has told us nothing about the birth of Jesus, we must leave that out of the picture. It simply is not part of Mark's view of Jesus.

2. Let Mark's writing make its own points of emphasis. Certain things seemed important to him and he had his own way of drawing them to our attention.

a) Like many writers, Mark wrote an introduction in which he very clearly proclaimed the main points of what he had to say. To be honest, we must accept those points at face value and allow them to be as important as Mark wanted them to be.

b) As in all conversation and writing, Mark betrayed what is most important to him by frequent repetition. When, again and again, we read his stories of Jesus performing miracles, his point is clear and strong: Jesus, according to Mark, was a miracle worker.

c) Like many storytellers, Mark wrote with some sense of plot. There are tensions and confrontations in the story, and the tensions move to a point of crisis which is resolved. Look for that plot—for the point of crisis and the resolution—and it will tell you something that is message and interpretation. It will say something about Jesus and what he came to do.

3. When you are done, try to articulate what you have learned in Mark's Gospel. Include everything you can recall, add nothing more, and try to be as true to Mark as possible. If you see it all as a picture, then picture it. If you see it as a play or a movie, recreate it for yourself (or others) that way. If you can say it in words, then try writing it down.

4. There may be words or episodes in Mark that you do not understand. If so, try to discover what they mean by talking to someone else who has studied the Gospel of Mark or knows it better than you, or by going to a Bible dictionary or some book which tells you what you need to know about the times in which Mark wrote. Or use a good commentary. But do this last of all, after you have had your own chance to discover what Mark has to say. It will be much more rewarding that way, for you will learn more and gain more respect for your own learning ability than if you go first to a handbook or commentary by someone who supposedly knows all about it.

Now go to one of the other Gospels and try the same thing. You will discover some important and refreshing differences.

Sample Assignment 2: The Message of a Prophet

There lived, in the eighth century before the Common Era, four great Hebrew prophets by the names of Amos, Hosea, Micah, and Isaiah. Though they shared uncanny agreement in what they saw and what they had to say, each had a unique way of seeing and saying it. Choose one of the prophets whose writings are brief—Amos, Hosea, or Micah—and learn his message well enough either to describe it or to articulate it in your own way.

The prophets were people, unusual people, to be sure, but as real as any persons who ever lived. Like all people, they lived in a certain time and in a certain place. And there were things happening in that time and place which had never happened quite that way before and would never happen quite that way again. It was *their* time and place in history, and everything they had to say fit that time and that place.

1. If we would understand what those prophets said, we must understand something of the time and the place in which they lived. What was it like in Israel and Judah and the ancient Near East during the eighth century B.C.? It was a unique time in history: a time when one super-power, Assyria, set out to overpower and plunder all other nations for purely despotic reasons. It was a time of crisis that led little countries like Israel and Judah to do extreme things to save themselves from the disaster which came upon them. Some detailed examination of those times must be done before one can proceed to an actual reading of the books of the prophets who lived and worked during the crises.

2. Now that we know something of the circumstances in which those prophets proclaimed their message, let us scan any one of the three books which we have named. Doing that, we discover that

they are not prose, but poetry. Most translations make that obvious by setting the contents in stanzas.

Poetry is a special kind of language. A poet uses language in beautiful and powerful ways to make an impact with his message. A poet is not satisfied to say a thing once and leave it at that. A poet repeats what he has to say in as many ways as he deems wise to drive his points into the consciousness of his listener so impressively that his message will be remembered. To give the poet a chance to do his job well, we must be receptive to each repetition of the ideas. We must let him hammer it to us as many times as he pleases.

Hebrew poets, like many of our poets, used words to paint pictures in the mind. So once again, we must be receptive. As we read the words or listen to someone else reading them, we must let the pictures happen. We must let them form in our minds. Then we must remember these impressions *as picture*, even to the point of forgetting the words themselves.

3. When we read through one of these prophetic books, we find that our train of thought often is broken by abrupt transitions or changes in thought that do not make sense. The reason is simple: the messages were not originally written as books. The prophets were preachers, not writers. As with Jesus, their words were normally recorded by disciples who noted or memorized what they had to say. Disciples saw to it that the messages were written down and later on were gathered into scroll-books to preserve them for future generations. When the various oracles or sermons were finally gathered together, they could be grouped in a dozen different ways, topically to haphazardly. So the best way to read the works of the prophets is to take them as a series of short messages once spoken and preserved only in the abbreviated form in which we have them. Do not worry much about the order in which they come, but take them as they come and let each message make its own impression. If we relax and do that, we shall come away with a feeling of a total message as well, and that will be something of a comprehension of the theology of that particular prophet.

Such assignments as these get at the task of biblical theology. Students who do all three of the prophets assigned are able to envision those prophets as individuals with distinctive messages for their people, yet they are just as able to see that all three said much the same thing. Students who do all three of the Synoptic Gospels this way usually come up with some understanding of the distinctive message and language of each. This kind of short-term assignment is reasonable enough to be used in a parish course of a few weeks' duration. We are not talking about the verse-by-verse plodding that is so often done in an existentially-oriented study group.

There is such a thing as moving so slowly as to miss that essential message and the power of its thrust. We are talking about comprehensive reading in an effort to grasp the major points of emphasis and absorb the total impact of a distinctive message. The aim of this kind of study is to let an ancient prophet or evangelist speak his whole message in a bold and distinctive way.

Applying What We Learn

But there is one pitfall into which we may stumble no matter how we proceed to our task. That is our own anxiety to apply what the Bible says as quickly as we see the hint of a correlation between a prophetic word and a situation of our own time. The reason for this is obvious: we are so accustomed to using biblical texts for preparing and preaching sermons—and our lay people so accustomed to hearing it done that way—that we cannot restrain ourselves from doing it. Like monkeys trained to respond to certain signals, we automatically begin to prepare sermons in our minds as soon as an insight hits us. As soon as we understand a little bit of it, we find ourselves anxious to preach it.

For the sake of learning biblical theology, it is necessary to resist that urge as long as possible. Not that it is wrong to use what one learns of biblical theology in the preaching of sermons—it just is better to wait until one has learned more, and all of it has settled together into a stable perspective. We may rest assured that it will, in due time, affect our preaching and our thinking in a dozen different ways. If we really learn the message of Hosea or 1 Peter, nothing will hold it back from influencing what we think and say—or even what we do!

I have seen a good many college students get all turned on when they read the Book of Amos and discover that he attacked the same social ills that plague us today. "Isn't this marvelous!" they say. "Amos is speaking directly to us." And they are right, of course, in the sense that there is something universally and ever true about the justice and judgment that Amos proclaimed. But the trap is sprung when the students then jump to the conclusion that everything in the Book of Amos must be aimed directly at us, for they then go on to miss much of what Amos had to say to his own people in his own day, or they badly distort it to fit our contemporary world. How easy it is to conclude that America or all the Christians of today are the modern equivalent of the ancient Israel and Judah whom the prophets addressed. Yet how few similarities there really are. In how many ways is this giant, modern industrial nation of America like the tiny, primitive, agrarian society of ancient Israel? The differences are far more overwhelming than the likenesses. If we want to draw parallels, mighty America should be compared to the mighty powers of old, such as Egypt, Babylon, or Assyria. But if we read the prophetic oracles against those great nations of old, they do not put us in nearly so hopeful a situation as the oracles about Judah and Israel. It is so nice to be part of the chosen nation, and not nearly so nice to be one of the mighty!

But the truth of the matter is that we should make no categorical comparisons at all. The modern world is not a duplicate of the ancient world and this prevents us from applying directly an ancient word to a contemporary situation. The nations of biblical times have, for the most part, passed away, and the great national powers of today had not yet been born when the Bible was being written. Nor are the personalities of today resurrected forms of ancient pharaohs, Herods, or Caesars. Life has moved on and the world is new in a thousand ways. Human nature remains much the same. The laws by which God governs the universe have not changed. The essence of the ancient prophet messages remains valid, but the specifics have changed enough that the messages need to be spoken in daring new forms.

If we would apply the messages of the Bible, let us not go searching for quotable quotes to aim at the first target that suggests itself, for there is a truer way. Let us, instead, imbibe the messages of Scripture—drink them in until they form a part of our consciousness and have an effect upon our convictions and our points of view. Then let us behold our world with wisdom and with open eyes and ears. We will see the truths of Scripture demonstrated and validated over and over again. We will see justice and judgment and even salvation. We may even hear the voices of prophets who speak in our day!

The Value of Learning

Learning for the sake of learning seems at times to be such a useless task. We are prone to think that we are wasting our time if we are not studying for the sake of immediate application. It seems worthwhile to study for the sake of next Sunday's sermon but a luxurious waste of time to gather with a few interested people to study something only for the sake of learning it. We have trained ourselves to be pragmatists.

Yet it is learning for the sake of learning that produces wisdom as well as depth and breadth of understanding. The pragmatists get their assignments done and the pragmatic pastors may be a flash in the pulpit, but their wisdom is shallow and narrow in scope. And we Americans are far too often the flashy but shallow pragmatists. We are active and busy. We do so much and plan so much and build so many things, but we starve ourselves of study and exhibit the results of that starvation.

Practical Possibilities

There is a need, I think, for devoted study groups in most of our parishes. Huge numbers of participants are not necessary. Large attendance figures look impressive in annual reports, but may not accomplish the task which I have in mind. The task that I see is the task of gathering the few people who really need and want something that is educationally challenging, and administering to that need. I see the pastor functioning as the leader or teacher of that group but also as one of its members, because he may be the first to know that he has that need.

I recently had an opportunity to travel throughout the United States in an adult education program that is funded by the National Endowment for the Humanities and administered by the Woodrow Wilson Foundation under the program title of "The National Humanities Series." Our task was to go into towns and small cities with the equipment of artists and lecturers to meet the needs of those citizens who thirst for education and exposure to various forms of art. We went to a town for a week at a time, presented our programs in various places and to various groups, and actually sought out the people who felt some need for what we had to offer.

The people whom we sought out and came to know might be called the people who really want to learn more than they now know. In a church situation, they would be the people one could most easily recruit for an education program that would demand something of their time and interest.

As a result of my own observations, I would estimate that up to three percent of the population of any given community is apt to fall into this category of willing learners. Indeed, I would rate a community as very healthy if as many as three percent of its total population were of this type; even one percent is good. A community is noticeably weak when this minority is smaller than that.

This observation may help us to arrive at an estimation of how many people there might be in a normal parish who would enlist themselves in a course designed to teach them a bit of biblical theology. In a parish of 1000 members, we might reasonably expect twenty such people—providing we do not keep them so busy with trivia that they cannot take the time that is essential for a course of real study and learning. So let us suppose that we have a parish of 1000 in which there are twenty adults able and interested enough that their pastor can form a small class of biblical students. How can the pastor so manage his or her time and abilities to do it?

The secret may lie in learning to make the time serve two purposes. As a college teacher, I face the problem of having to meet more than one kind of need, and so I seek ways in which more than one need can be met at one time. There is, on the one hand, the demand that I teach the students who paid their tuition for the privilege of learning something from me, and, on the other hand, there is my own personal need for challenge and further learning for staying alive intellectually and remaining equipped adequately to do my job well. It would be easy to slip into a pattern of repeatedly dishing out old and familiar stuff to the students in the interest of keeping things at their level and myself in a secure position. It would be just as easy to become so busy with student demands that I would have no time to do the reading and research I need to do.

One way out of this bind is to do a course in which I do fresh study or research in the process of preparing material for the course. Getting ready for class thus demands that I work with unfamiliar material and new problems. The teaching duties no longer conflict with my need for personal study. They help it.

There are few parish pastors who will not admit that they do not take enough time for personal study and the furthering of their own education. Perhaps they can do something about that by serving the needs of that interesting minority of people who are ready for intellectual challenge and whose needs are so easily neglected along with the same personal needs of their pastor. More pastors might do well to neglect something else from time to time to meet this need.

The pastor could begin the course by sharing what he knows from his own personal training but then dare to plow into something he dearly wants to study for the sake of his own intellectual growth. He will risk a bit of security but gain much in learning, for when the teacher has to wrestle with what he is teaching, he always learns more than the students. All sorts of challenging courses could be offered: a study of some biblical book or group of writings, a study of necessary backgrounds, or maybe even a beginner's course in Hebrew or New Testament Greek. We peddle our goods at the level of the lowest common denominator often enough. Why not try to sell something more valuable and expensive for a change?

Reasons for an Elementary Approach

Or, on the contrary, is this approach too elementary? It may be somewhat insulting to suggest that a seminary graduate should be asked to operate at such a basic level as has been outlined here. Should a person who has feasted on such sophisticated stuff as the writings of Von Rad, Cullman, Eichrodt, Dodd, or Bultmann be asked to go back to elementary techniques of how to read the Bible? Is this not regression?

The best of our lay people are not ready for the level of work done by the great names in biblical theology. They must first be oriented to the Bible as something they can read, and they must first learn to read it in such a way as to understand it as literature that speaks for itself. If this is done first, then we may well be able to lead them to the intricate realms of textual criticism, form criticism, tradition history, the tracing of sources, and the rest. I fear that we would lose as much as we would gain if we began at such a sophisticated level, however. The student must first gain control of a good amount of the content and apparent message of biblical material.

I also am inclined to believe that many of us who have gone through seminary were led into a sophisticated level of biblical study before we were ready for it. Lacking knowledge of the material and lacking the language skills that were necessary to an understanding of the problems being dealt with, we failed to appreciate fully what the masters were saying and, as often as not, we regarded their work as irrelevant to our cause and something to be left in the notebooks that gather dust in the darker recesses of our libraries. Many of us could well afford to begin once more at such a basic level as that which I have outlined—for the sake of doing something we didn't do well enough the first time around, to gain a new appreciation for some of the heavier stuff we endured in our student days.

When I began teaching fresh out in the academic world with a Harvard Ph.D., I threw all sorts of sophisticated material at my college students, mostly to impress them with how much I knew and how familiar I was with the great scholars of my field. The students received the material with patience and gullible admiration. Many of them learned about things they could only pretend to understand and doggedly displayed their knowledge in essays and examinations. Now, a short ten years later, I have come to understand that my own display of wisdom must take second place to a worthier goal: the learning that the student can actually do on his own with good direction and guidance. So, more and more, I engage myself in the task of *showing* students *how* to discover and understand the theologies of the Bible with their own wits and talents—and I am rewarded by gratifying results. Many of them come to the very insights that great scholars have written about and, time and again, they stumble into the very questions that demand a critical analysis of material and a discussion of profound problems. When this happens, we do not avoid the problem; we use it as the awaited opportunity for going deeper and inviting even more difficult questions.

Readiness is an extremely important factor. We must begin at where the level of curiosity is met and proceed from there.

There would be something immensely healthy about a group of intelligent Christians who knew how to read the necessary books that have to do with cultural-historical background, went into the Scriptures on their own, read with understanding, and were able to think and talk about each biblical book on its own terms.

A Reason for Doing It at All

We say, often enough, that the Bible is our source of inspiration. We practice our belief by preaching from pericope texts that come from the Bible, by using portions of the Bible liturgically, and by encouraging Bible study groups. This falls short of being a good thing, however, if we fail to measure the huge leap of years we take when we jump back into those sources directly from our present point in time, and fail to comprehend that the Bible is the message as it was told long ago and far away.

The sources of Scripture have been relayed to us through a thousand channels over a period of two thousand years. Our understanding of Scripture has been conditioned by that long period of transmission. To a great degree, our understanding of those sources has been determined by the history we have come through. The problems of the Middle Ages, the turmoil of the Reformation, the discoveries of the Age of Enlightenment: all these have gone into our understanding of familiar portions of Scripture and shaped our theologies down to this time. None of the theologies of the churches today is the same as any of the theologies of the Bible. It could not be so and it should not be so. Time has gone on and life's processes have done their work. Only if time had stood still could theologies have remained unchanged, and that would have been disastrous. Yet the biblical sources remain the root of it all. There is where we find our beginnings.

It is something of a pilgrimage to go back to the Bible and that is what it should be. We cannot go back just to get a word that fits our day. Indeed, as often as not we shall find words that cannot fit our day. What we can do and should do is go back to see how it was back there in times that were nearer our beginnings as a people of faith. Doing this, we will find refreshment, insight, encouragement, and a depth of understanding that will make us strong. Our perspective will be stretched and we will become people of the ages who do not bend to every wind that blows or snap off from the bough in sudden changes of the breeze, because we have an awareness of the roots beneath us, and we know how the bough can be traced to the trunk that is grounded in those roots.

LOCAL THEOLOGY

Richard Luecke

We have received sharp reminders in our day of the senses i which all theology is situational. All theologizing, including that o basic Scriptures and subsequently adopted Confessions, addresse questions present within the culture from which, and partly agains which, it speaks. It takes up terms and notions from that cultur along the way to supplying its own meanings and designations methods and structures. If we wish to focus the tasks of theologica education in a local congregation, we must begin by pointing to tha located company of people as the agents and to the particula events and issues of their setting as helping to set the agenda.

THE PLACES OF LOCAL THEOLOGY

Agents and Topics

Already we have turned up two meanings for the word *local* ir our title, one bearing on the *who* and the other on the *what* of loca theologizing. The *who* is an individual or group identified by some location in time and space, or within a configuration of functions and institutions which is characterized by interrelated physical, technical, social, and cultural factors. The theological activity of a local pastor or congregation is never fully discharged in the transmission of doctrines formulated in previous times or other places. Even classes in biblical literature and courses in Christian doctrine, which lean heavily toward recovery of previously formed and more widely shared meanings, employ personal and social involvements as indispensable aids to understanding. Sermons which give over eighteen or twenty minutes to unfolding the historical meanings of their texts, no less than those swiped up from pulpit magazines, are likely to fall short of the particular purpose of this function. Neither he statements of theologians assembled in distant seminaries or retreat centers, nor their articles in theological journals, helpful as these may be in pointing directions and clarifying disciplines, can be expected to deal sufficiently with the particular people and specific data peculiarly commingled on any given congregational scene.

This truism extends to policies and programs conceived in another place. These are seldom adequately received or implemented by local clergy and congregations responding simply as line to staff. They are appropriately adopted, in part, through conscious expansion of the "congregation" to include people assembled in other times and places and, in any case, through adaptation to local needs. A local congregation must deal with its own environment on the basis of its own lights. Since environment and lights, judgments of fact and aspirations, are mutually determinative, it becomes essential that the constituency of a congregation consciously share some discussable and actionable time and place. Achieving agreement on its location helps constitute the *who* of local theology.

It also helps determine the *what* of congregational theologizing. *Local* may be taken to refer, if we allow a classical pun (*loci* in Latin, *topoi* in Greek), to places or topics or areas of problematic inquiry and exploration. Local theology is topical, first of all, in taking up issues which are timely and pressing for the people involved. Technological and social changes are producing much shock of surprise and pain today, not least because they do not seem interpretable or processable in customary ways—whether because older interpretations are inadequate, or because it is no longer possible to gain agreement on them, or both. Some original attentiveness and fundamental reconsideration seems needed in the face of private uncertainties and waged disputes. It was this unease which produced Action Training in the churches during the past decade, with its twin notes of "engagement" and "reflection."[1] It seemed that people would find their faith quickened—find themselves liberated from advertisement, propaganda, money, publicity, superficiality, and banality—only when they exposed themselves to the questions within which they actually live, whether these questions produced an initial wonder or doubt or anguish.

Classically, a *topos* or *locus* referred not to a ready-made definition or judgment but to a problematic "space" which could be cleared for inquiry and exploration (*hunting* was a favorite word in Aristotle's *Topics*). Within those commonplaces one could find or invent various arguments, ways of proceeding with a question, and possible organizations of things. Historical theologies were sometimes set up in terms of *loci* or regions for investigation prior to proposing fixed definitions or set doctrines. This facilitated consideration of the fathers and of alternative formulations and objections on the way to making a fresh proposal. That is still a good approach, in a pluralistic and ecumenical day, to questions of 'God', 'Christ', 'freedom', 'love', 'beauty', 'community', 'family', 'education', 'health', 'death'. It helps people to understand what others have said and are saying, to find previously unnoted spheres of agreement, and even to explore and invent common actions. Here we propose a "topical" approach to questions raised by the events of the day in a particular community, and by the issues raised among people who are diversely affected by them and make conflicting responses. It is a frequent question among educators today whether creativity, as something more than bizarre or extraordinary behavior, can be taught. The church, for its part, has always referred to the Spirit as a source of discovery, innovation and creativity. Might not its educational activities include a use of "topics" in which invention and judgment actually take place?[2]

Most of the questions now vexing the society have manifestations within local communities. There are newly apparent reasons why these questions should be addressed at that scale. Expressed disenchantment with social action programs mounted during the sixties has been accompanied (and perhaps fortified) by withdrawal of federal authorities and national church judicatories from projects aimed at that distance toward felt crises of the city. Causes assigned for the failure of those programs differ significantly,[3] though almost all authorities also point to diminishing funds or a needlessly circuitous routing of funds for such purposes. The official word is that urban crises must now be approached through regional and local programs, though it is by no means clear that regional civic authorities are more responsive to initiatives in communities of the poor. Some "radical" leaders agree with this shift of focus for reasons of their own. Large scale social movements, like that of labor and, in some degree, that of the Blacks, have tended to become bureaucratic in their own way, no longer imparting a sense of identity to their members nor facilitating initiatives on the part of constituent groups.

A familiar dispute in the churches over whether funds and efforts should be expended in behalf of "individual souls" or "social action" was for some years rendered gratuitous by showing how action groups vitalized souls. That response appears to require modification today.

Such mingled considerations provide charter and necessity for local reflection, which is time-conditioned to the point of distinguishing the seventies from the sixties, and place-conditioned to the point of actually dealing with basic issues (shelter, economic development, education, health, communications) also at the scale of local communities. The issues are deep and vexed enough to require fundamental inquiry and exploration in terms of places or topics wherein alternative judgments and arguments, procedures and structures, may be found.

Disciplines and Occasions

To the questions of the *who* and the *what* of local theology we must now add those of *how* (since it is "theology" we wish to do, which does have disciplines in common with that done previously and elsewhere) and *when* (since we wish to name the spheres and occasions of congregational activity in which it is to take place). In seeking the disciplines of theologizing within a congregation, let us once again invoke a local metaphor, for we wish to spread the needed arts or skills in such a way as to see how, taken together, they cover the field and help to define one another. When the church speaks of educating the 'whole person', or speaks of the responses of the 'whole person', it sometimes spreads terms like *heart and mind, body and soul,* or seeks to cover the whole range of human faculties with pairs or sets of terms like *feeling and thought,* or *habituation and aspiration.* We may think similarly of the faculties of a congregation for feeling and thinking together, for following procedures and organizing things; and we may proceed to name the arts or disciplines by which it does so theologically. Words for these theological disciplines are all at hand, but it is important that we understand them by virtue of their interrelationships. There are specialists in each of these disciplines; but each in its own way points to the others.

A first theological discipline or art deals with congregational symbols as such—with those words, objects, gestures, and ideas which serve to identify the congregation and form a common bond for all its members. These are, primarily, Scriptures and Confessions, sacraments, the cross and sign of the cross, words like *gospel* and ideas like salvation. But other symbols, some quite local, come to serve in secondary ways. The art involved is one of making sure these actually serve their practical bonding function which is prior to, and in some ways stronger and more pervasive than, any discussion or action which follows—*and* of making sure they actually convey a disposition and basis for subsequent communication. We may call this an art of canonics or *symbolics.* It addresses primarily the faculties of feeling or will. It is the basis of invention; for symbols unite people who have offered, and will offer, diverging meanings and designations. Such differences are not divisive in the moment when symbols are being voluntarily affirmed. It is possible to have many tongues but one voice; and that common voice may serve to loosen many tongues. Even the best and most abiding statements are yielded up to the common voice, for they can become falsified through hardened and inattentive applications. A theological use of symbols guards these moments of passion or passivity in which participants are expectant and apperceptive. As someone said, "There is more light yet to break forth from that holy word."

A second theological discipline, which follows from the first, is that of interpretation based on shared symbols that now become sources. It is an art because it brings into juxtaposition or interplay a recovery of previous symbol-based interpretations and a discovery of (perhaps otherwise unnoted) current realities. We read ancient texts, as John of Salisbury said, in order to improve our perceptions in the present. Without a memory of previous interpretations, which is closely linked with a sense of identity, there is little precedent or guidance with which to approach (or even to form) present questions. There is little disposition for standing against the stream or for directing items purposefully in it; people are likely to be carried on a more conservative or a more liberal stream or even in a revolutionary current. A group is not actively conservative without some remembered convictions concerning what sort of things need conserving. It does not become actively radical by forgetting its roots. Merely to stay focused on the past (however rigorous one's determination of the text and its historical meaning may then become) or merely to become immersed in the present and its dreams of the future, were states of mind which Kierkegaard characterized as 'despair'. This art of maintaining continuities between past and present interpretations is called *hermeneutics*. It is not exercised by simply repeating, nor even by simply applying, past judgments in new situations; it is a matter of trying, through a use of discoverably similar procedures brought to new materials, to do as well in the present or nearly so. A certifying result of this practice is found when new perceptions arise at both ends, in new understandings of what was going on in the ancient writings or actions and of what is going on in the present scene. This provides a basis for saying, as Karl Barth did, that, "One voice calling 'forward' and the other calling 'return' do not constitute a contradiction."

An early discovery in the course of this interpretive activity is that a variety of interpretations arose side by side in most previous periods and that a similar diversity arises today. Controversies arise which cannot be resolved simply by referring back to the unitive symbols themselves; for diverging interpretations may have found their meanings and designations by taking hold of the same symbols at somewhat different poles of the unexplicated region they encompass and moving across the area from there. Such controversies have sometimes proved wholesome, even when they were theoretically undecidable, by virtue of enrichments introduced on both sides as a result of interaction. Those who live and work with a tradition learn that, while truth is one, it is subject to several sorts of statement; and that, while truth is changeless, it can be subverted by wooden applications.

Agreement in interpretations of the present scene is vexed both by differing definitions of basic terms and by differing prudential assessments of consequences. This brings us to a third discipline by which a congregation comes to adopt a common statement, or at least a common action, even though arguments have differed. This discipline may be called, if we expand a common usage, *homiletics* (which means "saying the same thing"). Even when a clergy person stands quite alone in the pulpit, he or she means to be speaking the proper mind of the congregation. This helps to discipline his utterances, both vocabulary and sequence of parts, in that place; it also accounts for the practice in some congregations of interjecting "Amens" when he is actually succeeding. On many complex issues, however, the congregation must try to come to common voice or action through discussion. This requires an appropriate procedure of discussion, which (no less than the clergy person's homilies) points backward to interpretations and symbols and which also provides for adequate participation. Such procedures toward agreement are necessitated by events of the day which call for freshly formed congregational responses; the object of this art is valid innovation.

Our final theological discipline is one of relating new judgments and actions, when they are taken, to understandings, policies, and institutions previously formed, and of making whatever adjustments are required. Only through such an art of organization do words finally come to objectivity and does thought actually join action. This theological art of the congregation may be called, if we allow the word to refer to constructions not only of thought and exposition but also of physical properties and established roles, *systematics*. It moves necessarily from the use of symbols as shared objects or spheres for exploration, the use of shared texts for discovery, the use of acceptable procedures in argument and discussion for innovation, to the establishment and reformation of institutional structures for creativity.

These four related arts, taken as such, are not new or confined to the church; they are employed by all who engage in theoretical, practical, or productive activity.[4] We wish to see them, however, as functioning very specifically within Christian knowledge, community, communication, and institution. Since the purpose of Christian education is not merely to impart information or directives to passive recipients, but to render people active as Christian knowers, doers, and communicators, we wish to see them as the very skills or disciplines to be cultivated. All congregational activities are, or may be, educative in this basic sense; and without special care, any congregational function may become counter-educative. It should not be difficult for us at this point to spread a fan of congregational activities which, like these disciplines, are distinguishable but not rigidly separable, and which may then be inspected for their educational import. The range of congregational functions might be encompassed by the following set of terms: *celebration*, or worship, *interpretation*, or instruction, *procedures* and policy of discussion and decision, and *organization* which implements and unifies all activities in an organic way.

By scanning such a sequence of functional spheres, one is led to ask whether celebration has become co-opted for purposes of imposing judgments or promoting programs to the neglect of its primary capacities for creating a communal bond and disposition among people whose determinate judgments and actions may differ somewhat. Or, conversely, has it become simply fervent without throwing lines outward toward communication and common action? One is led to ask whether instruction is being imparted without a sense of the exploration needed to deal attentively with diverging statements and changing circumstances. It appears plausible that early instruction should focus on the practical use of symbols and on communal loyalties which underlie ethical rules concerning obedience, violence, sexuality, property, reputation, and vocation. One is led to examine whether congregational opinions and decisions are being formed without reference to Christian identity, tradition, and imperative, or without regard for appropriate interaction and assent. Are organizational matters being resolved (despite a perfunctory prayer at the outset of business meetings) in such a way that the church's convictions stay hidden under a bushel and its institutions are not worth setting on a hill?

Since topics explored in the congregation are raised in part by events in the surrounding community, we may expect the behavior of its members to become quickened and styled in that wider sphere. It is possiblè to name the public functions to which church members will come with a practiced eye, i.e., to deal appreciatively and critically with community creating symbols and traditions, with emerging issues and arguments, and with revision of institutional procedures and utilities in the public arena. Moreover, since the congregation is itself an institution interacting with others in the public order, it becomes a matter of congregational imperative to examine its own institutional provisions—especially those bearing on properties, charitable services, and professional roles—in terms of their effect on communication and development in the society.

The disciplines, congregational functions, and community engagements can be charted.

DISCIPLINES AND THEIR RELATIONSHIPS

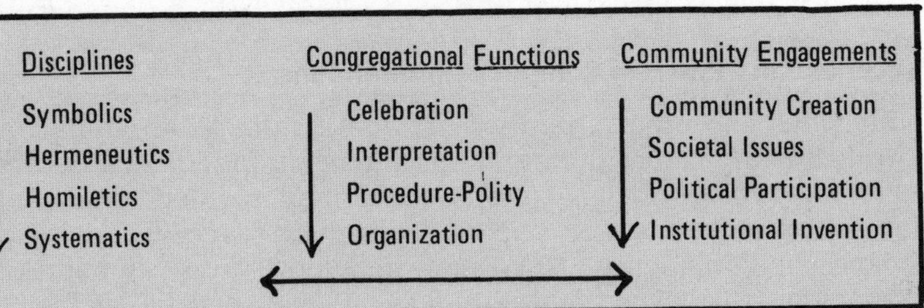

It is the disciplines in the first column which are being cultivated, and which point, in each instance, to the shifts which must take place on the way to (or as a result of) interaction with the wider community. We now need to examine carefully the terms in the middle column which are related to congregational functions. It is interesting to speculate whether the "religionless Christianity" of Dietrich Bonhoeffer, much cited in recent decades, finds explication in the activities of the third column, providing those of the first two columns remain functional but hidden.

A specific course in Christian education could in fact be developed by reflection on any one of the disciplines we have named, as may be seen in almost any seminary curriculum. Or it might focus attention on some particular congregational function: on worship or doctrine, on congregational life or church institutions. Our purpose is to show that the goal of Christian education is Christian activity, and that such activity is itself educational. But Christian activity always implies bringing a number of elements together, as is indicated by the arrows in our chart. In his *Journal* for 1847, Soren Kierkegaard described Christian learning and activity in terms of "reflections."

> Reflections must not so much mollify, reassure, persuade, as awaken and provoke men and sharpen thought. *Their purpose is to rightly set all the elements in motion.* . . . Reflection ought to be a gadfly; therefore their tone ought to be quite different from that of edifying discourse, which rests in mood. But reflections ought in the good sense to

> be impatient, high-spirited in mood. Irony is necessary here and the even more significant ingredient of the comic. One may well laugh once in a while, if only to make the thought clearer and more striking. . . . Reflections must fetch men up out of the cellar, call to them, turn their comfortable way of thinking topsy-turvy with the dialectic of truth.[5]

On a good day, in any congregation, Christian education is like that.

A DISCIPLINE OF SYMBOL AND COMMUNITY CREATION

Precedent and Praxis in Religious Communions

Religious and other group symbols have suffered an ambiguous and fluctuating career during the past generation. For two decades following World War II, cultural spokesmen pointed with confidence and enthusiasm to scientific explanation and technological advances in conjunction with a new "religionlessness" and an "end of ideology." Today we find ourselves on what seems a backswing, engulfed in new religious manifestations not only in churches but on streets, theater stages, and communal farms. We shall not undertake here to judge how representative were the former religionless interpreters nor how hardy is the new religiousness, except to observe that a swing from politics-without-religion to religion-without-politics (especially in a time of vast executive takeovers and of warfare waged on the backs and from the purses of the poor) invites careful critical reflection.

One consequence of that earlier distaste or aversion is a simple unawareness of functioning group symbols, which are no less able to cast their spell for being unnoted and uncultivated. When asked to identify symbols, we say "the cross" or "the flag" and then there is silence. Cultural observers have written about a decay of symbols; such a phrase may actually help to shroud them in antiquity and mystery. A suggestion is offered that symbols pertain to primitive peoples and must disappear when societies grow more advanced. A symbolic logic has distinguished cognitive from non-cognitive expressions in ways which diverted attention from manifestly emotive symbols. An understandable fear of ideology (gained by many from memories of nationalistic, mass, and "pan" movements), which can, without clarification of practical issues, turn inter-group disputes into something like religious warfare, has led to a notion that group-defining symbols can and should be left behind.

All this has helped deflect attention from a quite non-mysterious, practical dynamic in the life of every community which today calls for self-conscious clarification and attention. The churches, for their own part, have suffered attention through neglect of this matter. Yet they at least have always been required, on pain of losing their very identity and identifying function, to recognize and guard their symbols in such a way as to keep them functional and to keep them from doing more harm than good.

A basic precedent for this practice has always been at hand in the biblical prophets and their dealings both with the ceremonies of the temple and with those of the cultural religion. A simplistic notion, partly supported by a previous generation of scholars, that the Old Testament prophets were congenitally or vocationally opposed to religious practices, and that there was a direct standoff between prophets and priests, seems refuted or at least complicated by evidence to be found in historical and poetic texts. Cultic prophets are described as being associated with shrines and holy places, as performing sacral acts, and as quite possibly being included with the temple personnel. Priestly and prophetic notes are closely juxtaposed in liturgical songs like that of Psalm 95.[6] A reflective practice, both appreciative and critical, developed alongside religious ceremonies. It was when the voice of regular prophets had been tamed (cited by Amos as an ominous sign) that angry, unofficial prophets declaimed outside the shrine or stayed home and wrote their prophecy. Even they, so far from opposing ideological symbol and story, actually based their utterances on a traditional formula concerning the Exodus and a shared notion of covenant which constituted Israel a people. What the prophets opposed was the absorption of religious objects and practices from the surrounding culture without criticism or reconstruction, or the employment of religious symbols as though they had no importance in the determination of action in that culture. They opposed a combination of "iniquity *and* solemn assembly."

Thus it became a theological practice to go after simple introduction of the Baalim, phallic pillars, and prostitutes of both sexes within the temple precincts, and any simple immersion in the fertility rites of Canaanite agriculture, in such a way as to comprise the Bride of Jahweh. On the other hand, prophetic reflection and utterance was needed to counter any resulting notion that this "separation" meant most favored nation treatment in terms of assured prosperity or exoneration from demands imposed by social circumstances. Amos began by citing *many* nations under Jahweh's watchful eye and avenging hand and then drew a straight line from Israel's "chosenness" to the likelihood of her being punished for her iniquities. It was in a time of comparative prosperity and religious revival that Amos told worshipers at Bethel to take home their peace offerings and their songs. He called the gentlewomen of Samaria (kind of eighth century B.C. suburbia) Bashan cows for demanding everything their husbands could buy while there was abject poverty in the land. He also scored the men who stretched out on ivory couches in blissful neglect of growing divisions in the society. This behavior violated the very covenant which was celebrated in Zion. Symbols which were meant to open the eyes of worshipers to new realities were actually serving to close them—to bring on the doom.

We wish to note, first, the practical power of symbols as such to create a common bond and motivation within religious communions (as it also happens within other groups). Arguments move from generalizations afforded by doctrines or theories to making their point with respect to concrete particulars. Symbols *are* vivid and concrete particulars which communicate more directly, forcefully, and universally among those who hold them than does any deduction. The Greek word *symbolon* referred to tallies like two halves of a broken bone which, when produced, assured the bearers that they had found the right party to their contract.[7] In a similar way, specially designated objects, gestures, or verbal formulas as such may serve to incorporate and motivate members of a group. Subsequent arguments which make reference to such symbols add nothing to their practical strength. The fact that the meaning of a symbol is unspecified in its contractual or celebrational use does not diminish its practical effectiveness, which may actually depend on a certain degree of ambiguity. Both as a convert and as a bishop, Augustine learned from Ambrose to welcome initial unclarity and mystery in the Scriptures on the way to understanding or expounding them.

We wish to note, second, that by virtue of this primary practical function, symbols provide a ready basis for subsequent communication and action in which they take on specific meanings and designations. Without shared symbols, people are likely to lose their own communal modes of speech to some imposed technical language, their own communal story to some more general history, and their own activities to some assumed universal technology. The first thing any active community requires is a language of its own; otherwise proposals tend to become a function of outsiders or a domain of experts.

A first reflective discipline of the church, one neglected at peril, is accordingly that of identifying Christian symbols and clarifying their function, but of doing so in such a way as not to displace their intrinsic bonding power and effect. This discipline extends not only to the primary biblical and confessional standards, and the primary liturgical practices of gospel and sacraments, but also to secondary images, expressions, and actions which come to serve in supplementary ways. Thus symbolics requires some exercise with the special materials and consciousness of particular communions, including that of the local parish. Cultural accretions, like that of a white Jesus, may require local surgery or even suggest bold reclamations like those taking place at the Shrine of the Black Madonna or in Chicano marches with the Virgin of Guadalupe.

Not a few experiments have been mounted which seek to combine old themes with new postures, sights, and sounds from contemporary culture, as in the jazz mass or the freedom *seder*. A question to be asked of all such experiments is whether a new unity of expression is actually achieved or whether old and new forms simply have been juxtaposed in ways which are insufficiently appreciative of either. Occasionally ceremonies have been carried outward to make a more pointed demonstration at the gate of a national cemetery or federal prison, to declare a "liberated zone" amid city tenements, or to exorcise a court house. Participants testify to finding new power in old symbols when they are taken out of quarantine. Questions arise, however, whether such ceremonies are rooted as well as pointed, and whether, in any case, possible ambiguities are borne in mind. Religious symbols are never to be taken utterly captive to prudential judgments. There remains a basic sense in which celebration is for its own sake, as Romano Guardini put it, "A waste of time for God." Only God can create value; men can only enjoy it. One adores for no ulterior reason at all.

Symbols which produce community and common apperception always do so at the peril of producing community introversion and navel-gazing. In a time of unsettling technological and social change, many congregations understandably choose to retain familiar ceremonies. It becomes the educational task, at such times and in such groups, to point outward toward new content which may find development and illumination in the waiting elements and familiar movements of the service. The confession of sin may then include complacency with respect to issues stirring in the community. Thanksgiving may reach out to encompass new vitalities rising among the previously powerless. Lesson, creed, and sermon constitute a movement from historical affirmations to present ones, causing participants to respond as courageously and perspicaciously to new circumstances as did their forebears.

The Lord's Supper brings surpassing heights and depths to every human celebration by requiring a memory of Jesus' death and an eschatological hope. By uniting people of every kindred and class, it imposes a social demand no less painful for those who have been discriminated against in the past, as for those who have been the discriminators. But it thereby holds out a hope for the future of the city, which can become all the richer for present diversities. But if worship connives with present social exclusions, as Paul said, it shares in the city's sickness and death.

Though the practical function of symbol may be distinguished, it requires reflection and leads on—necessarily—to interpretation. The art of congregational symbolics is maintained by the functional commonplace of word and sacrament—from which may be drawn forth things both old and new. Symbols without words are empty; words without symbols are blind.

Transposing the Discipline to Wider Communities

We have noted an apparent shift from the end of ideology and the secularity of the sixties to a new religiousness in the seventies, whether because people really couldn't live without religion after all or because it wasn't any fun. Theologians, no less than others, have gone along for the ride, some of them publishing affirmative books at both ends of the swing.[8] The civil religion, decried as an inveterate national idolatry in the fifties, has been resurrected as a necessary and constructive feature of national unity in recent years. There is much new attention given, especially by theologians, to the symbols of smaller social groups as previous notions of a melting pot yield to revived claims about "unmeltable ethnics." Since alarms have been sounded and visions have been shared, we may suspect there is here a matter for situational interpretation and *praxis*. The task of theological reflection is not to hail every new cultural enthusiasm as pure gain, or (citing one well-known theologian) as progress from law to gospel, but rather to find and distinguish law and gospel within every new situation.

Social activists have come by their own route to taking a new interest in social symbols. This enthusiasm was spurred by the demonstrations of the sixties and by an awareness that many public communications tend to be epideictic, a matter of display, rather than apodictic, a matter of specific statement in a mass-media-oriented day like our own. Social movers hope that symbolic communications can be raised to offset present technological rigidities in knowledge. "People who proclaim the end of ideology," said one Chicago organizer, "sound like old men proclaiming the end of sex." They also see in the refurbishing of community symbols a neglected resource for recreating urban communities.

We have already observed that the biblical prophets did not confine their attention to the religious practices of the temple, but also focused outwardly on the culture ideology and folk religion which characterized agricultural activities and city building in the Canaanite society. A point to be noted is that they did not summarily reject all elements of the fertility rites and annual festivals in the land.

Sacrifices, sacred songs, festivals, the ephod, and the sexual imagery became adapted and used even in Israelite worship and theology. While seeking to preserve the wonder of nature both in germination and procreation, however, they did cry out against any connivance with public idolatry. In much the same way they de-idolized and yet provisionally affirmed the temple. The result of this negotiation between faith and cultural symbols is described in Genesis. The deep is no longer monstrous; the heavenly bodies are no longer divinities but "lamps set in the heavens"; man is to cultivate the earth without attacking the tree of life; man and woman are to share the gift of sexuality as glad creatures who did not invent it.[9] A similar prophetic practice seems needed today among people who require symbols for community and productivity in a mass society which has co-opted both fertility rites and annual festivals to an earth-destroying and socially-divisive economic growth.[10]

The familiar pictures of congenital opposition between the prophet and the king—kingly attempts to keep the prophets, prophetic excoriations of the king—have become modified through more penetrating interpretations of historical texts. The ambivalence of Samuel in the establishment of the kingship is seen by some scholars not merely as an expression of distinguishable traditions or a divided mind in Israel, but as the prophet's attempt to develop the consciousness and watchfulness needed in an increasingly complicated and organized society. Prophetic warnings to people on their way to establishing a kingship may be read in the light of the expository admonitions to people who had adopted the covenant (cf. Joshua 24). It appears likely that, in addition to covenant-renewing ceremonies, Israel also observed kingship-renewing festivals in which the king was newly identified with the struggles of his people and pledged to activity in behalf of the poor. Images from such a humiliation rite are employed in the royal psalms and still stir in the passion accounts of the Gospels.[11] Thus the kingship becomes corrupted when it endorses public neglect of the poor, to say nothing of using the poor as scapegoats in securing public favor. Conversely, the appropriate functions of kingship become circumscribed by a corrupt public.[12] There is always a danger that political authority will co-opt cultural symbols in entrenching or expanding its powers; and there is always a danger that indifferent citizens will allow it to do so. "Power corrupts," says Lord Acton, looking at government; "Powerlessness corrupts," says Rollo May, looking at the citizenry. The manifest perils, even tragic fatefulness, which attends any expanding institutionalization of public power is offset not only by development of counterpower but also by assiduous and disciplined dealing with societal symbols and ceremonies.

Here let us point to a discipline of symbols in public arenas analogous to that required in the church. A first task lies in the very identification of social symbols, including both society-wide and sectoral symbols. Their legitimation lies in the very right and necessity of human association. Arts of tending them supply a quite particular meaning of the notion of the priesthood of all persons in the society. New attention to national symbols seems crucial in a time of vast bureaucratic and economic expansion accompanied by a drying up of political discourse. The danger of using national symbols—including those of the civil religion with its reference to providential chosenness and destiny, to bless and harden patronizing and imperialist policies toward other nations—is sufficiently apparent. Less clear is the left-hand power of social ideals like freedom and equality, if they become confined to familiar civic or market practices, to harden racial attitudes and discriminations. If all persons are free and equal, but you need bondsmen to scrub your cotton or to produce slack in the labor market, you are likely to think of a black as less than human.[13] Thus we must point old ideals toward extended applications. The notion of rights, freed from confinement to particular civil and political rights, might become opened toward the economic and social rights on which political power depends, and even toward cultural rights of communication without which economic benefits may only serve to pacify an invisible minority.[14] Primary symbols, present at the creation and functional for the duration of a nation, may also become expanded by the addition of secondary symbols which unfold and enliven its tradition. Such symbols may arise from many sources: from political events, as we add to the Declaration of Independence and the Constitution the Second Inaugural of Abraham Lincoln, Roosevelt's Four Freedoms, the United Nation's Universal Declaration of Human Rights, or add to the list of previous public liberators the name of Martin Luther King, Jr., or to the old image of the frontier the notion of New Frontiers and New Direction; from art, literature, and drama as critical and exemplary images arise; perhaps even from sport as we add to the present enthusiasm for football the notion of the Non-Zero-Sum-Game in which nobody really wins unless everybody does.

But recovery and elaboration of symbols are needed, at the same time and for the same reasons, within special sectors of the society. Functional sectors (law, social service, education, entertainment) have become self-protective professions rather than publicly-oriented guilds; without inspiration and vision they may become increasingly rigid and cynical. Without communal symbol, story, and carnival, residential neighborhoods remain mere bedroom accommodations without amenities or mutual functions. Racially or economically ghettoed neighborhoods remain slums of isolated individuals or of externally imposed services. It seems unlikely that any tenants' union, block club, or community organization can overcome apathy or violence, which seem two sides of the same coin (apathy may be seen as frozen violence, violence as exploding apathy), without shared stories, images, and slogans providing a basis for mutual appeal and activity. It is when they tell their stories and find them merging toward a common formula, and find themselves responding in rage or ribaldry to the same images, that any group begins to move toward catharsis, solidarity, discovery of leaders, and the development of socially creative institutions.[15]

Such community creation raises the specter of inter-group conflict, which might become all the more intense by virtue of symbolic fervor on all sides. Public consternation in this matter often fails to discern the need for community identity, the function of symbols in producing a sense of identity, or the reflective practice by which their use becomes constructive. One of the vagaries of group symbols is that they often get their start by helping to wall off outsiders or enemies. National symbols come out of mothballs during times of war and are sometimes kept alive as propaganda for a cold war. Bumper stickers are mostly *against* somebody. What is required, accordingly, is a conscious practice which points community symbols toward tasks of internal development during times of peace as well as war, and toward eventual cooperation with differing groups as well as identification of enemies. In inter-group controversy it becomes important to avoid a clash of symbols by finding and defining the practical matters at issue. The discipline required in a plural society is one which takes all group symbols very, very seriously and none of them too seriously. It requires an ability to belong to several communities at once—both special communities defined by private symbols and embracive communities united by overarching ones. It takes skills to utilize the symbols effectively.

Following are two examples of a use of community symbols for internal development and external cooperation. In exercising a role at once kingly and prophetic in the black community, which pays general homage to the slogan "Black Power," the Rev. Jesse Jackson has moved to the formation of an organization called PUSH, a militant-sounding acronym which enfolds a constructive impulse: People United to Save Humanity. In his Saturday morning Chicago rally, he is likely to take a familiar, honored story, like that of Joseph and his brothers, and add it to the shared lore of this community. A young man, sold into slavery and carried to a distant, oppressive land, worked hard in the fields and then in the household of a slave master who became very rich. Because his manly vitalities proved fascinating to the slaveholder's wife and threatening to her husband, he was confined in prison. There he has been held in chains to this very day, awaiting the moment when he, and he alone, will be able to interpret the nightmare now disturbing the oppressor's sleep. The Joseph story has been lifted, for this use, from its biblical context, somewhat like reference to the New Israel in American presidential utterances. Yet it carries an analogous plausibility and constructive effect.

During a rally of war resisters in which speech after speech had flung charges of imperialism and oppression at powerful American institutions and high placed officials, the Rev. Richard Neuhaus of Brooklyn announced that the assembly would then sing *America the Beautiful*. The audience gasped. He explained that the words of this anthem did not describe America as it is or had ever been, but as it was meant to be or may think of itself as yet becoming in the future of the Creator. The description was (borrowing a word from theology) eschatological. The organ played; some voices joined in; and evening news found us all listening to a song we did not expect to hear at that time or from that place.

Such reflective dealing with symbols, both local and overarching, at once shared and unspecified, merges necessarily with a discipline of interpretation.

A DISCIPLINE OF INTERPRETATION AND ISSUE: DISCRIMINATION

Christian Interpretation As a Verb

Christian communions regularly turn from celebration to explication and are, in fact, committed to keeping these two functions in interaction. In interpretation, symbols begin to take on fixed meanings and designations; verbal symbols (gospel, salvation, soul, grace, love, freedom) come to stand as subjects or predicates of statements. What people assert in a specific way helps determine what they will come to see and not see, and what they may be willing to undertake, in practical situations.

Interpretation is brought in a primary way to the text of the Scriptures or, rather, *its* interpretations are unfolded in current expositions. It is also based on confessional and other valued writings, as well as on significant non-literary actions and objects. Even communication of traditions depends in some degree on reference to present quandaries and engagements of the members. But beyond this, since theological commitments are assumed in their very confession to have import for all of life, present as well as past, outside the church as well as in it, theological interpretation is also brought to practical issues and problems as such. Thus interpretive activities actually help to constitute the situation in which members find themselves.

This continuity of interpretation may be observed in the biblical prophets who began invariably by citing the Exodus and the covenant and then pronounced on the idolatries and the imperatives of the promise in matters at hand. "Now, then, hear the word of the Lord." The word of the Lord *came* to Samuel, Nathan, Micaiah, Isaiah, Amos, Jeremiah, and Ezekiel, who made successive pronouncement. Jeremiah, in fact, got into trouble for saying something materially different concerning the future of the Temple than Isaiah had said in less advanced circumstances before him. Jesus began by affirming the law and the prophets—not one jot would pass away until all had been fulfilled—and then spoke a word which claimed similar authorization. "You have heard that it was said to the men of old . . . But I say to you"; "Amen, Amen, I say to you." Something of this authority for direct statement and action was communicated to the disciples. "And he appointed twelve, to be with him, and to be sent out to preach and have authority. . . ." (Mark 3:14-15); "Behold, I have given you authority . . . over all the power of the enemy" (Luke 10:19). The fourth Gospel uses the word *Spirit* to authorize a practice of interpretation in the future: the departing Jesus could not tell his followers all the things they would have to say and do in times to come; when the Spirit came he would lead them into all truth; he would teach them what they were to say; he would take what was Christ's and give it to them, so that the things he did they would do, too, and greater than these (John 16). This serves to juxtapose transmissions of interpretation with interpretive activities. It suggests there are new interpretations to be made and to be welcomed when they appear. The ancient proclamation of the Kingdom of God implies as much; as Bonhoeffer pointed out, "God is always God for us exactly today."

Interpretation raises the possibility, in a way celebration did not, of differences in statement or judgment and of resulting partisan oppositions. Such oppositions could arise in the New Testament and even among apostles (Galatians 2). They arise, in fact, already at the point of interpreting the Scriptures, as the history of interpretation abundantly and significantly shows. A shift in modes of interpretation sometimes brings a Reformation to the church or a Renaissance to the society; of both there have been many more than one. After a long period of dialectical interpretation, during which Scripture-based doctrines were compared and then synthesized, and in which allegorical interpretations of the Scriptures came to abound (a method which could cite no less an interpreter than Augustine), Erasmus called for a return to a grammatical study of the text itself (for which he cited Jerome who had distinguished between a *veritas Graeca* and a *veritas Hebraica*). Luther agreed on this return to the biblical text as sufficient and clear in itself; but he called not for the arts of the grammarian (or any academic doctor) so much as the simple submission of the believer to divine matters in which he must despair of ordinary human powers. (In this respect he preferred Augustine to Jerome.) He made a virtue of uncertainty, appealing to the spirit for insight, knowing full well that his rejection of reason rendered his own position impregnable and undiscussable—at least until much verbiage had been flushed out and humankind had found once again the changed heart of faith. The battle between the dialectician and the grammarian (and these are not the only hermeneutic methods which may be distinguished) has burst into flames many times in history and burns again today. For that very reason, it seems unlikely that such controversies can be laid to rest once and for all by referring to the latest fashion in interpretation, or even by saying, "Back to the Bible"—to which all interpreters make appeal.

The task seems, rather, one of maintaining coexistence and confrontation of differing modes of interpretation in such a way as to allow each, if it cannot convince the other, at least to understand it, to criticize it, and to push it. Does the dialectical interpreter acknowledge in his own terms the living God who is not to be taken captive to human intentions, and also the deceitful heart (and therewith the undependable mind) of humankind? Is the grammarian able to find the full meaning of an ancient text for present belief, beyond repetition of abiding moral platitudes? How does the anxiety-stricken true believer expound, by some description of human intentionality, the necessity he finds for individual interpretation? Must he not emerge from his demonstrative pose long enough to compare the particular meanings ventured by his opponents? It seems desirable to discriminate the several sets of determinate meanings which arise from differing modes of interpretation, perhaps even to produce such a dictionary as an educational project. It seems that communication in the Spirit may continue so long as it is sustained by the common celebration which asserts a Pentecost over Babel, and so long as it moves toward addressing specific new questions and problems in which a movement of the Spirit is discerned. The apostolic controversy described in Galatians 2 and Acts 15 addressed a practical problem bearing on common action for which there was no precise precedent, and it was resolved in a practical way through reference to the Spirit. When Luther sought to justify a perpetuation of schism between the reformation parties which met at Marburg, he did so not by pointing merely to unresolved differences of formulation, but by raising the charge of "a different spirit."

Christian social interpretation is the art of bringing basic symbols to the exploration of social questions. We may cite as an example the thorny discussions during the past decade of relationships between white and black communities and specifically of black economic development. The issue was raised for a time in terms of guilt and reparations, though these conceptions proved too vague or heavy to sustain discussion for very long. It may be asked, however, whether biblical images might not have served to perpetuate reflection and develop explication of this matter within many congregations. 'Israel' in the biblical understanding has a corporate and historical identity, such that children do bear the sins of their fathers to third and fourth generations and also take up responsibilities for a future which is not merely a matter of private volition. The 'Body of Christ' is comprised of many members, past, present, and future (ultimately embracing all people in the vision of faith), and has a corporate history. Those who take up life with Christ take up socially inherited burdens they did not themselves create, and do for the sake of a future they do not arbitrarily project. Though 'guilt' is a familiar term in theology, so is 'forgiveness', which serves to turn attention from the past to the future. While the notion of reparations may have limited validity at present in the right and need of black people for compensatory opportunities, such a legally-minded notion becomes enlarged through biblical concepts of restitution or reconstruction. Socio-ethical notions of corporate identity, societal integrity, and historical responsibility, to use Gibson Winter's phrases, are much required at this time and are no doubt amenable to broad theoretical explication.[16] But they are very uncustomary conceptions and are likely to be approached somewhat differently by people whose social theorizing differs by virtue of being more the grammatical or more dialectical, whose arguments are more experimental or more rational, more utilitarian or more moral. Religious images could conceivably function to get people on the track and to sustain inquiry in crucial but complicated social questions which might otherwise be abandoned.

The most basic theological dispositions of faith, hope, and love serve both to preserve internal communication and to direct attention outward. Does not faith imply a disposition *toward* self-determination in primary communities, since people are to make their own responses—a disposition *against* saying, "The people aren't ready"? The *only* way to develop responsibility is to exercise it. Does not love seek such opportunities for all, including those strangely different from ourselves, even enemies? Does not hope envision a social future all the richer by virtue of many centers of initiative—not one altogether programmed by the special competencies of some of us, or even by the many?

Finding Where Social Issues Lie

Social symbols may become hardened through usage into designations of specific institutionalized customs. We have had occasion to note how a universally acclaimed freedom may come to refer primarily to market practices, and how free enterprise may become confined to modes of economic competition which seemed equitable in the past. Similarly, we have observed how universal rights may remain confined in conception or debate to certain political actions like voting, or to certain civil liberties like publication, even when economic, social, and technological realities have removed much of the substance of such freedoms. It is when such symbols become cleared of specified meanings that they become spheres for broader social issues, for finding new arguments, and for inventing new structures.

Virtually all Americans affirm the founding ideal of liberty, yet during the past decades we have witnessed a remarkable opening of the topic of freedom to diversified interpretations in American society. Sentences fly which suggest that freedom is found by doing one's own thing or doing as one pleases, by breaking free from one-dimensional thought and achieving new universal consciousness, by acting in accordance with human virtues or by ignoring ordinary procedures to take direct action in behalf of one's self or one's group. Freedom becomes variously defined in such utterances as self-motivation, self-perfection, self-development, or self-creation. Social proposals offer correspondingly different designations of the obstacles, the motions, and the agents of freedom. Freedom is customarily viewed in the business sector as liberty to expand technologically and economically in response to the market, which may itself be expanded by mass advertising techniques and foreign ventures. The counter-culture sees human wants as constricted and mobilized at present, and seeks to expand consciousness and therewith freedom for development in communal and cultural ways. Civic-minded citizens chart freedom in terms of human rights and democratic procedures which make possible some control of institutional development when it intrudes on the thoroughfare of individual liberties and social interaction. Certain minority groups describe freedom in terms of direct action and liberation from oppression by any means necessary. Similar oppositions flourish in interpretations of *power, communication, education, health,* and result in differing scenarios with respect to questions bearing on the development of technology and public policy.

Amid this rich diversity of social interpretation, a discipline seems needed which is not unlike the one we have sketched with respect to diverging interpretations in the church. This is a discipline which enables one, in addition to forming his own judgments, also to discriminate the meanings employed in those of others. It enables disputants to understand one another even if they do not agree, and perhaps to discover that their differing statements, while not homogenous, are not directly opposed. It enables them to develop their own arguments to take account, in their own way, of considerations raised by others. Such a development of arguments provides a foundation within the various modes of argument for proceeding toward common policies or practical actions which can be justified, in separate ways. But for this it becomes necessary not merely to discriminate meanings, but also to find the practical issues on which they agree and disagree.

When Augustine undertook in his *Confessions* to set forth the questions which are basic to all practical inquiry, he distinguished three investigations to be taken up in sequence. He borrowed these questions from Cicero's *De Inventione* which, he said, had derived them from God since they were logical. This previous rhetorician had set forth three constitutions of causes: Whether a thing is (*An est?*, the conjectural question); What it is (*Quid est?*, the definatory question); and what sort it is? (*Qual est?*, the qualifying question). To these Cicero also added a fourth question bearing on where exactly the matter can be most auspiciously taken up, since circumstances might become such as require alternating the form of leading or transfer to another court or sphere of action (*Cur est?*, the translative question).[17]

Thus, with respect to the present widespread malaise over rapid technological, economic, and social changes, we would ask, first, whether there really is a problem to worry about—and consider, perhaps, the widening divisions in domestic and world society, the think-tank projections which chart a terminal expenditure of natural resources and a conjunction of crises, bringing mass starvation in some countries, near the end of the century. We would ask, second, how to define the problem: whether as a temporary technological and productive lag, or as increasing dependency and powerlessness on the part of mass consumers. If there is agreement on the latter as a basic designation of the problem, then we would ask, third, whether present forms of technology, bureaucracy, and professionalized service systems are not serving to make rigid certain social functions on the whole, rendering people passive rather than active with respect to presently unmanageable problems. If agreed, we would ask, finally, at what points initiatives need to be taken, and what innovations need to be made, in order to make some alternative forms of development possible.

Do we look forward to restoration of large scale federal programs which might expand the service sector, perhaps through election of a liberal candidate? Such programs, in addition to their present unlikelihood, might serve to advance the crisis of dependency. Watergate may have served to expose dishonesty and bungling in high places; but it did nothing in itself to supplement or supplant self-augmenting and interlocking bureaucracies. Do we mount a mass movement? Such movement seems now subsided. If its purpose is simply to affect national programs, how much would it accomplish beyond a change of personnel? Do we form a commune or return to the land? Harmless proposals, but not such as have thus far produced viable and stable forms for an urbanized society in general. Through such inquiry, we might come to see that no genuine alternative to present modes of development is possible without a reconstitution of primary civil communities, which must entail something more than the community organization familiar in recent decades. Communities must be created which are able not only to struggle for client participation in the implementation of national service programs, but also to invent and use new vehicles for direct citizen activity in health care, education, housing, peace-keeping, rehabilitation—all of which must be taken as verbs and not as packaged products. In some cases, present top-down delivery systems would need to be dissolved into networks of components to which citizens have direct access. But many communally invented structures for activity might not even be those that initially require "throwing federal money at the problems." They might not be the sort which anyone has ever thought of calling illegal. In their behalf, some old but newly laundered symbols (independence, self-help, free enterprise) could be cited.

It is not our purpose here to offer interpretations or to conduct inquiries, but rather to show how disciplines like those cultivated within the congregational community, and accordingly in Christian education, are also applicable to discerning the signs of the times or the movement of the spirit in the wider society and to finding a way through present verbal standoffs in the public arena. It seems conceivable that the technologist (in any case, one interested in retooling society), the guru, the politician, the social mover, would agree—for divergent reasons—on a practical course of making new initiatives and activities possible in the society through community creation and structural innovation. The discipline of interpretation leads on necessarily to a discipline of procedures, not only in thought and inquiry but also in polity, which is productive of institutional decisions and actions.

A DISCIPLINE OF PROCEDURE AND COMMON ACTION

Polity and Proclamation in the Congregation

Religious communions do not merely sing and talk; they also make decisions and take actions to implement their celebrative and interpretive functions, usually augmenting them to include many extended functions. In coming to practical decisions, deliberations cannot remain mere matters of suasion, though there are some communions which wait until a full consensus is reached or pronounced. Unlike grace which is boundless, time and energy, funds and properties, are bounded; if they are expended in one way, they cannot be expended in another. The movement toward such decisions requires an art, for it must combine religious commitments with practical decisions by means of an appropriate procedure and polity, in the course of which participants must consider not only their own material interests but also inevitable and often indirect effects in the surrounding community. Since discussions leading to decision and expenditure are clearly more than academic, they often draw some blood—and in doing so provide occasion for additional Christian learnings.

The very mode of decision-making within a religious communion, if unreviewed, may serve to countermand the intentions flowing from its faith. Such a disjunction may arise by neglecting to provide, on the one hand, for appropriate participation in various sorts of decisions or, on the other, for appropriate reflection on the occasion of making them. There is much to be said for delegating authority in ways which maximize actual employment of talents and energies. Many active people prefer, so long as it functions well, a benevolent directorship, sometimes fondly called a participatory autocracy, which arranges for them to do their own work freely without time-consuming discussion of what those arrangements and that work should be. Yet in a time of personal displacement through over-developed administration, and loss of gratifying spheres of relatively independent initiative, there is a new demand and need for participation in governing decisions. To be sure, such participation does not in itself produce a reconstitution of functions; but it may help to do so if it compels an assembly to take note of special interests and initiatives.

A long history of discriminatory and limited roles for women in the church has now been reviewed in the light of a revised social consciousness and the desire of competent women to share administrative and pastoral offices. In certain of their pronouncements, women have pointed to desirable revisions which they in particular could bring to those offices. The youth have come awake to their exclusion from deliberations and decisions which, in their view, require the voice of those who face a longer future. Nor will simple assembly suffice if minority views and initiatives are thereby submerged; hence the emergence of racial and youth caucuses. Increased participation in the procedures leading to decision seems a provision not only for equity but for edification and effectiveness.

But new demands for participation need to be conjoined with some old demands for reflection in the course of decision-making. In the First Letter to the Corinthians, Paul took up one by one a sequence of practical decisions and organizational quandaries confronting that cantankerous but never dull congregation. There is little in the letter or the manner of Paul which will help us with tasks of democratizing discussion and suffrage in a modern congregation. However, he does not disapprove of the fact that women are preaching and prophesying, and he insists that wealth gives no distinction in the church. What we get, with respect to every issue, is a demand that Christological reflection must precede decision, accompanied by an illustration of how that reflection is to be made. Whether the question is one of scholarship or leadership, of sex and marriage, of social custom or congregational function, it is subordinated from the start to a consideration of the astonishing gospel and the peculiar nature of the congregation—of how it has been created, and how its procedures are to be shaped, by adherence to Christ. Every problem becomes, first, the occasion of a fresh proclamation.[18] First he reflects on the story of Christ and the story of the congregation, then gives the practical advice. The latter may appear somewhat high-handed, stringent, or idiosyncratic to the modern reader. But the prior theological reflection has served in each instance to open a space around the discussion and its resolution, lest the readers in Corinth, or elsewhere, should be left with nothing but particular rulings. It was not sufficient for the Corinthians simply to do the right thing without reflection on Christ and context which helped them to think and say the right thing. The apostle himself could go to hell for simply insisting on his ordinary rights.

In modern congregations, as in Corinth, theological reflection is to provide a backdrop for practical decisions. Provisions for such reflection becomes a matter of polity. Perhaps a congregation will defer to its pastor for guidance; perhaps it will accept guidance from a study group which has brought theological exploration to the matter in hand. We will consider the usefulness of such issue-directed reflection groups in a moment; but let us pause to note that a similar method of reflection is often observable within issue-oriented community groups even though the sources employed may be very different. When any such group faces organizational problems, there is always a first disposition to lay down a familiar rule and be done with it. But then someone recalls the group's own inception and story, identity and purpose. At the regular meeting of a Squatters' Association, for example, the following organizational matters might come up for decision (in fact, did come up at such a meeting in South London in the memory of this writer): certain members were not paying their monthly dues; a woman, frantic over her sick child, could not wait any longer for her turn to be visited by the glazing crew; costs needed to be recovered for use of the cooperatively owned pick-up truck; newspapers and newscasts had produced consternation by presenting very unfavorable views of squatter actions. The first proposals to come from the assembly recalled rulings handed down by every established authority from grade school to the General London Council; if members didn't pay their dues, they should be thrown out; the importunate lady would simply have to wait her turn like everybody else; the truck should go for so many cents a mile; a new public image should be pursued by a public relations committee, since the organization had lately achieved a quasi-legitimate status from reluctant public officials.

Before action was taken, however, someone offered second thoughts by recalling the squatters' own story. Unlike others in the society, they knew in their vitals what it was to be poor—not as statistics, but as persons caught with their families in a web of immediate needs which could not be met. If people could not pay their dues, perhaps they should be visited by a committee with whom they could air their special problems; and, of course, you didn't have to be paid up to serve on the Arrears Committee. Though public bureaucracies could remain immune to the cries of an anxious and indigent mother, the squatters could not; she would be visited the next day by an informal crew conscripted at that meeting. It was hoped that she would not have occasion to scold the assembly again. The fact that one squatter's new digs were farther removed from the city than those of another was not any fault of his own; the truck would be paid for by the trip, not by the mile. Since squatters did not begin in a publicly respectable way, it was not a *primary* concern to gain such an image now; they would continue to do what they thought right, and would be happy whenever they found that what is right is also legally and socially proper. So the process of decision-making finds its way.

Conflict and Congregation

Controversy virtually is inevitable in the churches when it comes to addressing prudential matters. Moreover, public conflicts tend to reproduce themselves within the churches, which can scarcely avoid reference to public issues in their tasks of forming interpretations and making practical decisions. Two circumstances conspire to make controversies unusually trenchant in the church. The first is that the church's faith does entail, in ways we have observed, a certain impulse, imperative, and purpose toward all social life. So far from being merely indifferent or neutral in social matters, the church requires that habitual and corporate judgments be repeatedly subjected to radical question. Its gospels present one who sides with the poor and the excluded in publicly offensive ways, proclaims forgiveness from the past and a new calling for the future, and lays non-negotiable demands on every follower. He proclaims a divine intent of release for the captives and liberty for the oppressed; though in the text he refrains from espousing specific political actions, he nevertheless suffers public trial and execution for sedition. He is vindicated in the Resurrection by God himself.

The other consideration is that, by the very nature of its commitment, the church cannot be identified simply with a particular public, party, or program. While the divine will does pertain to particular judgments, it is not always infallibly discerned by the faithful who seek it; moreover, even if it were discerned, it would not invariably correspond with presently available public policies. The church is an *ecclesia*: a company called out of diverse sectors and parties of the society. The demands of faith, when they become clear, may indeed divide people, as the gospel says, but not necessarily along the lines of political divisions in the society. Participants in this company are required, on the basis of the faith they have in common, and in spite of their differences in prudential matters, to sing and dance, to listen and speak together. Their assembly becomes a preserve for affirmation of a truth and leadership which are distinct from the particular programs of any party; it would have a song to sing and an affirmation to make even amid the failure of all parties. It is a peculiar gathering in the society, peculiarly demanding and peculiarly inclusive. It is an unassimilable foreign body in the sense that it is not assimilable by any public establishment. It may, by virtue of this very fact, exercise an indirect political influence which is not unimportant, but it does so through its own kind of activity which has its own kind of rules. "If you don't wish to play chess, then play some other game," said Ivan Illich, "but don't try to change the rules of chess."

This pair of considerations often produces an operational dilemma which itself requires interpretation. When a Conference on Church and Society met in Geneva in 1966 to develop Christian interpretation bearing on social matters, it offered some specific statements in condemnation of national policies, especially of American military intervention in Vietnam. Moral theologian Paul Ramsey took exception to the procedures and pronouncements of that conference in a harsh tract entitled *Who Speaks for the Church?* He objected that its specific judgments on foreign policies advanced beyond the special competence of church people, and gravely judged responsible public officials; that it over-estimated the power of conciliar statements to influence officials who know how to distinguish between such statements and votes; and, above all, that it forfeited the church's distinctive institutional power to prompt deeper consideration of the issues involved. He argued that a direction-pointing, ethic-stressing guideline was the appropriate form of statement for such an assembly.[19] Yet it is important for our purpose to appreciate the very ambiguity which produced this controversy. For it seems possible to agree in general with the institutional wisdom of Ramsey's proposals and still to appreciate the fact that this assembly undertook, in this instance, to acquit itself like human beings and speak, at least for itself, the full import of its lights.

Similar dilemmas emerge not only in the work of multi-church commissions but also in that of local congregations; and local procedures become, accordingly, a matter of inventive practice as well as of established program. Since preaching and routine instruction do not ordinarily enjoy sufficient time, concentration, and interaction to press beyond the surface of complicated social topics, it has become a familiar practice to form task forces, which make use of the special competencies and insights of many members in sustained inquiry and research. Sometimes neighboring congregations contribute members to such work groups, and even free a pastor for such a specialty through establishment of a cooperative ministry. Task forces are ordinarily composed of members having a particular interest or engagement in the question at issue, though they remain officially open to all lest they result in an unannounced schism. Such a work group brings symbol-sustained, theologically-reflective, methodic, and factual investigation to its topic; it conducts campaigns of information, discussion, and education among fellow-members. It may on occasion seek from the congregation a public statement or funds or facilities in support of some public action.

For the most part, however, such groups within the church remain "talk forces." Many social topics dealing with such areas as shelter, health, education, and communication require fundamental exploration reaching beyond public statements and familiar social actions.[20] Ordinarily, social action and experiment find their most appropriate and most effective base in the wider community. For instance, low-cost housing in the industrialized suburb of Elk Grove Village, Illinois, when faced with congregational opposition, moved their action outward to form Neighbors at Work with other motivated citizens. Friends of FIGHT, an inter-church group organized to lend support to a new black community organization in Rochester, New York, went public as Metro-Act to take on issues besetting that city in housing, education, welfare, and media. In shifting the base of their action in this way, members may also shift some of their contributions. Providing they do not therewith shift their presence, they may also help to sustain a distinctive suasive process in the church.

Shifting the action where possible need not be viewed merely as a means of avoiding division in the church; it may also be a means of keeping faith. It is a function of any congregation to watch for its souls. How can it sustain hope for the stranger it hardly ever sees while abandoning hope for the brother it sees? Or listen to one but not the other? *Something* is to be gained, even for societal movement, if a process is maintained which requires neophyte souls to become reflective, and stubborn souls to stay discursive. It is a small step for humanity but a great step for Charlie Wadanoby! If and when a decisive division comes to pass within a congregation, the reason must be assignable to dissatisfaction with the very demands imposed by the church's faith; at least the separating soul should be led to ask himself whether this is not the case.

Yet not all controversy over expenditure of church funds or use of church properties for socially significant purposes can be avoided —or should be. As we shall have occasion to observe, physical properties are in the public sphere, and it is appropriate that they should have wider communal uses. Following is a scenario in which an institutional contribution to a social cause produces conflict which is full of educational import for the congregation. It is a plausible understanding and often an outright policy that certain congregational funds and other resources should be available to the needy on an emergency basis without waiting for a meeting of the assembly or the board. Not to respond promptly is often tantamount to not responding at all. While churches are not without institutional constraints of their own, they are free from many restrictions placed on other institutions; hence they are often able to make immediate response to special needs when other institutions cannot. Many a chapel or church house has afforded a meeting space for groups denied a room elsewhere, or has provided a floor or kitchen for use while they worked through their questions. Mimeograph machines belonging to the church have helped the youth of a community to find a voice or have helped to balance the record for groups who were without a public relations office of their own. Churches have provided sanctuary for draft resisters even when their membership did not espouse resistance. In doing so, the church has lent its auspices to the right of conscience and the right to be heard; instead of being spirited away in silence, the young man is taken in publicly, in the presence of other citizens and perhaps also of microphones and the press.

A pastor or trustee or board acting in behalf of the congregation on such occasions should indeed be held accountable for such decisions in a later meeting; and if the needy in question are identified with a controversial social issue, that meeting is likely to be a lively one. Exactly because materials are involved, the debate affords a rich opportunity for clarifying the intentions of faith and the peculiar dynamics of the church. Sometimes this can be richer than any Bible class or discussion group by itself. It becomes possible on such occasions to air realities often overlooked: the respects in which church properties and funds are in fact involved in the economic and social order and serve, for the most part, to sustain present structures; the sense in which the church must treasure, on the basis of its own understanding of faith, a free and independent response to changing circumstances; and the manner in which it is therefore disposed to defend the right of people to raise issues, even if its members differ in their own conceptions of how those issues should be resolved. Since there seems comparatively little need, in the interest of opening or sustaining communication, for supplying space to the captains of agribusiness, such use of the church hall is more likely to fall to the grape workers.

In the controversy which ensues, it is inappropriate to manage discussion in a simply bureaucratic, compromising, or interpersonal way. In a congregation, as in a marriage, two courses are ruled out from the start: either to avoid a fight or to fight dirty. Psychologists have described destructive consequences which may result from suppression of conflict or from allowing it to express itself through scapegoat mechanisms. They have offered evidence of how group conflict, if welcomed as a sign of vitality and conscientiousness on both sides, can help individuals and groups grow. Lewis Coser points to the following benefits which may accrue from facing up to group controversies and working them through: the institution may achieve stability where there was underlying instability before; group norms may become revitalized by being called upon in the fray; new norms may be created in responding to new situations; new procedures for research and decision may be invented; group communications may become improved; as various issues are ventilated, it becomes possible to avoid polarization along one particular line of cleavage; the balance of power is repeatedly adjusted; and a deeper mutual knowledge comes to pass.[21]

To this we may add the fruits of theological reflection when brought to bear on this very experience of controversy among fellow members of a church. Among the special learnings: a rediscovery of the values affirmed by faith; a return to the roots of those values in the gospel and the history of its interpretation; a bumping of heads against the stubborn reality of the cross and the need for actual reliance on the Holy Spirit; and possibly even a new appreciation of the congregation as a paradigmatic community bearing a promise for the future of the city. It becomes an educational experience for people to endure their differences with one another in the church, and to make those differences functional rather than dysfunctional. This education can help equip members for conflicts being waged in the larger society: how, on the basis of overarching symbols and values in the metropolis, can social hatred be diminished, common ground be found for practical agreements, and social differences serve for mutual enrichment?

A DISCIPLINE OF ORGANIZATION AND ROLE

Appropriate Properties

Each of the disciplines we have named required a sense of organization. We found it necessary both to distinguish and to relate community-creating symbols in a horizontal way. They are to be found in words, concepts, gestures, and objects. Yet every symbol is an object, is expressive, requires recognition, and must be specially used. Primary and secondary symbols need to be distinguished in order to keep them interrelated, and we found analogies between them doing so in the church and doing so in community, metropolis, nation, and world. We also found it necessary to see organic relations between a discipline of symbols and other disciplines on a vertical axis: we found in symbols not only a means of community-creation, but also a basis for forming interpretations, actions, and communications in that community.

Similarly, it is important to relate theological interpretations, as they are formed, to one another; this is the task of 'systematic theology', which helps to determine meanings by drawing them into relationship. Theological meanings are determined and enriched further when they are related to those of science, morals, and art, a task which may require some philosophic grounding in principles which relate words, thoughts, actions, and things in a most basic way. But we do not wish theological interpretation to remain merely on an intellectual plane; we see it rather as the activity of a community moving toward practical discussion and action.

The discipline of procedures seeks to achieve united action by a congregation, using whatever expert knowledge, theological wisdom, parliamentary skills, and leadership are available. In doing so, it must give attention to events, values, movements toward participation, and existing structures in the surrounding community. But action which is really on target requires something more than democratic participation in decision-making; it requires keeping shared aspirations and beliefs behind the discussion and envisioning material results that can be drawn into organic unity with them. To the extent that such organization is maintained, all functions of the congregation come to objectivity.

Institutional structures and properties are perhaps the most usual objects in view when we speak of organization. It seems worth noting that the word *property* has often referred in the past to more than immovable and movable goods; it has also referred to proprietorship of knowledge, virtue, and skills. The phrase "Life, liberty, and happiness" was at one time interchangeable with "Life, liberty, and property," and there was no pejorative overtone. Yet we may, in taking up the discipline of organization, refer quite specifically to acquisition and disposition of physical properties, a topic we have not aired until now, and one which is a perplexing question for the church. This is a matter in which all the disciplines we have named may come to a certain fulfillment or to grief.

We have found it inappropriate to speak of the church's mind as neutral in social matters, even when it refrains from advocating specific political candidacies or policies. Here we find it utterly impossible to speak of the church's established institutions, programs, and properties as indifferent to, or inconsequential for, economic and social structures in the public sphere. The very ownership of properties and investments gives the church a stake in the maintenance and expansion of the market. Many of its present mission activities, including some of its most experimental projects, appear to depend on economic prosperity. Church-sponsored charities and social services have enfolded definitions of poverty and opportunity that rode along with those governing public service agencies; and any decision to live off church-sponsored agencies will also have its public effects. Churches have played implementing roles as non-profit institutional sponsors in federal housing programs, especially for the aged;[22] and it is plausibly suggested that they might as well forthrightly lobby in the interest of helping to shape those public measures.

It is well known that properties have accrued to church bodies during recent decades by virtue of their preferential tax status which is not shared by donors. A National Council of Churches study commission estimates that churches in the United States hold well over $100 billion worth of real estate (most of it withheld from tax rolls), and more than $10 billion in securities (much of that in professionally managed portfolios and in guarded pension funds). Inevitably there comes the proposal, accompanied by quotations from the Gospels, that the church should divest itself of securities and properties, turning over its wealth—no strings attached—to communities where the need most exists. Difficulties which arise in trying to name those communities are, perhaps, not insuperable. However, one denomination which voted to release 15 percent of its uncommitted funds to socially significant enterprises found it had turned up a mare's nest of disagreement over which funds were uncommitted and which enterprises were socially significant.

A similar proposal has become implemented at a congregational level during recent years by a shakedown of radically committed members (who often also characterize themselves as politically radical) into underground or believers' churches—which also produces some shake-ups into politically rightist church assemblies. In certain respects this is an attractive measure: it enables newly formed groups to develop specific projects and make directed expenditures without prolonged debates in a more mixed assembly. Yet, aside from the demonstrative value of property-less congregations, this does not provide an immediate solution to questions pertaining to present church properties and investments—and perhaps not even a long-range solution. Underground congregations acknowledge a *de facto* dependence on established church institutions: they are disproportionately comprised of seminary-trained members; they surface to make a primary witness at church conventions; in many further respects they live in a symbiotic relationship with above-ground churches.

Some need may be cited for providing institutionally and materially for the functions of celebration and nurture, including the special training of leaders, in churches which value distinctive traditions. There even seems a social wisdom in preserving religious spaces and facilities within a society. These have provided zones in which groups and individuals remain comparatively free from interference by state officials, in which voices may be raised in the event that permits for assembly are denied or in the event of rain in the park. They have provided temporary sanctuaries to temper justice and facilitate communication in many societies. By reference to certain European precedents, the institutional desirability of a noneyless church is by no means obvious; for this diminishes the)pportunities for emergence of viable social initiatives and experinents within the independent sector. The rise of community organzations within American society during recent decades was sup)orted in large measure by funding from the churches, a likely ource of funds for further community development.

A first step in the matter of church securities is to make full edu:ative use of the portfolio. The discovery that funds contributed for 'alid purposes have contributed along the way toward discriminaory employment, weapons manufacture, and destruction of the)iosphere is eye-opening.[23] Such demonstration lessons about a nilitary-industrial-educational-ecclesiological complex have been ınfolded in many church assemblies and then carried to annual :orporation meetings. A second step is to shift such funds, where)ossible, as either investments or gifts, to enterprises facilitating :ommunity development. New agencies have been created (the nter-denominational Fund for Community Organization, the National Council on Industrial and Business Opportunities, and similar ıgencies formed in particular cities) to package such funds in auspi:ious ways, providing for developmental periods and needed training, and to offset the old double standard implied in helping ninority enterprises, but not very much, and then saying, "Well, ve tried."

Over-built, over-propertied, over-invested, and over-organized :hurches are a matter for review and reform (highly educative activties) during the next years. Offers of assistance will also come in the 'orm of publicly instituted proposals to define "religious purposes" nore closely in defining church properties, and perhaps even to vithdraw tax exemptions from congregations whose activities are udged political in some way. The latter sort of measure must ılmost certainly be resisted, both by reference to ambiguities, which ıre always present in religious study and action, and by reference to ı long history of wholesome, tensile interaction between church and ;tate. Meanwhile, denominations are themselves dismantling certain ıational boards and occasionally yielding real estate for innovative :ommunity development. There is perhaps some reversal of the :entralizing tide which during the past years rolled over an earlier :ongregational intent in many American churches, separating the ıdministration of the churches from their nurturing units. "Power is without faith and faith is without power" (Gibson Winter). For)etter or for worse, the responsibility for holistic church organization may be falling to units and members closer to home.

A discipline of organization seems necessary for a time when congregations can neither take their present structures for granted nor send away for packaged programs. Such a discipline will accept it a axiomatic that physical properties and resources not deliberatel offered for purposes of exploring new definitions and structure will remain, in fact, in the service of older ones. It is a disciplin which reaches outward to reorganization in the civil community anc inward to a reorganization of one's own property, liberty, and life

Demanding Roles

Every organization implies a structure of functions and roles; role bring initiative and guidance to functions. The most pervasive rol in the church is ordinarily that of the clergy person, and reflectior on the enactment of this role may serve to throw light on that o others. Even the clergy role may be focused in a variety of ways it may be seen as primarily that of a celebrant, priest, or guru; of a preacher or teacher; of a moderator, administrator, or maintaine of process; of an executive director or a comparatively independen actor. Yet any such basic selection of concept requires a reachin out in practice to embrace other functions in its own way. Exercis ing the clergy role, like any other, is an art which may not invidi ously be described as playing the role. In some circumstances th role needs to be played outward into the civil community; in rar instances it becomes necessary simply to play it out.

Any particular alteration of the clergy role has an obverse side In a time of institutional over-development, universal education and demands for increased participation in decision-making, w may expect a partly imposed, partly assumed reduction of paternal ism and omnicompetence on the part of the clergy. It become important for them to divest themselves of such functions and pre rogatives as tend to reduce responsibility and authority on the par of other members. The very function of ministry to foster intentior and initiative in other people self-destructs if the minister refuse to cast himself as an auxiliary. Historical titles like *father* and *mon signor*, while valuable in specifiable respects, raise attending image which require revision; the term *pastor*, left to itself, may serve tc cast people as sheep. Reshaping the clergy image can furnish a precedent for reforming other callings in the light of new socia impulses.

Yet with every such reform of image, it becomes a task of minis try to clarify the hard authority for which it stands, namely, th *exousia* signaled in the symbols of faith and exercised in the wisdor and courage of faith. Such interventions of authority may take plac on the very occasion of performing sacred acts. An appropriat understanding of Baptism may be set on its head if plumbers repai clergy persons' faucets free of charge, while clergy persons baptize plumbers' babies for a fee. What Baptism "costs" is nothing less than the life of the subject and a lifetime of unpaid ministrations to him by fellow members. Discipline attending the performance of pastoral acts, theologically explicated, may help prepare ears for authoritative interpretations and appeals on other occasions.

A certain image or status is also accorded the clergy in the public realm. This can scarcely be denied so long as tax benefits and draft exemptions (to say nothing of rail certificates, baseball passes, golf privileges, and professional discounts) are extended and accepted. To be sure, certain present prerogatives and immunities linger on the basis of very old precedents; tax and service immunities go back to provisions under Constantine which extended the privileges of pagan priests to Christian clergy. These may appear somewhat anachronous in view of official disestablishment, pluralism, and extension of higher education; and they may be losing hold in the public mind as well as in the churches. A few denominations officially discourage acceptance of tax-free housing; some clergy devote these savings provisionally to societal purposes; certain seminaries formally discouraged acceptance of the 4-D draft status. Such proposals bear reflection and prove educative. But even if older marks of clergy status diminish, the question arises concerning a newer public image and function. It seems unlikely, in spite of predictions concerning "the vanishing clergyman,"[24] that this role will completely disappear from the public stage—or that it should.

It became familiar during past decades to see clergy marching with the black, the poor, and the young in American society. For a time they walked at the head of the procession and spoke into the microphones. The reason was only partly a tradition of charismatic leadership in black communities. An exploited minority often required a moral cover simply to get itself up to the place where it could be heard, and (at least in first appearances) needed a voice which was accustomed to speaking and being heard. More recently, clergy presence has been less up-front and less patronizing. The clergy stand *beside* the resister, occasionally chained to him, or *beside* the organizer-spokesperson, while the latter speaks for himself or the group. The point is that this person be heard, that listening be patient and respectful, and that the use of force on fellow citizens be restrained. The clergy stand there as a reminder of the right of conscience and perhaps also of moral convictions basic to consideration of the issue in question.

There seems little point in denying that the clergy image employed in this way does in fact exercise a certain indirect political influence. Yet it seems that any healthy society must allow some intrusive, delaying moral suasion in the arena of political contention, especially if it is exercised in behalf of virtually disenfrancised people who stand to be ignored. The fact that this is achieved by a public clergy presence, to borrow a favorite distinction of Ivan Illich, deserves "sarcasm but not cynicism."

Once again we are hard upon a practice requiring discipline, rather than a proven weapon requiring simply to be put in place. A public exercise of the clergy role need not mean simply throwing the weight of this office or its special pronouncements into the lists of new movements and programs. It might very well include lending them to the right of people to be heard. It does not mean promoting a particular candidate so much as the right of candidacy, nor does it mean adding unction to a particular political project so much as bringing the weight of moral authority to the right of people to act socially in their own behalf.

In their professional capacity, the clergy are disposed to support others in their social advocacies and actions, rather than seek a position of spokesmanship or leadership for themselves. But as citizens, the clergy may actually help form such groups and even contend for leadership. In the latter case, the use of clergy prerogatives, whether within the group or on its behalf, may with some justification be brought into question. There are many overlapping circumstances, and during recent years the public activities of clergy frequently raised suspicions that publicly-granted prerogatives were being suborned to political ends. In the glow of mass meetings, faithful imperatives are likely to be heard as specific political exhortations, especially if the clergy persons involved are known to hold strong political views—as well they might.[25] Moreover, the press of events may actually push the clergy into positions of public leadership. In the heat of political contention, their public role subtly, or not so subtly, shifts. Priests become competitors for political leadership and power.

Institutional ambiguities are rife, and there is no sure way to avoid them which is either safe or honest. Deliberate avoidance of controversial events on the part of the minister would bring the ministry itself into question. Clergy immunities do not exonerate anyone from responsibilities as a human being; one is a human being before he or she is a clergy person. "For God when he makes the prophet doth not unmake the man" (John Locke). Functionaries who allow the role to cloak the person place a shroud both over themselves and over the role. If there is a certain political neutrality in the professional role of the clergy person, there is no personal neutrality on that account—on the contrary. His sweet skin may not forever hide out behind others, as Dan Berrigan put it. Timidity and temporizing are quickly detected, especially by the young who have grown suspicious of these very things in the clergy. A spokesperson for faith may least of all stay bland or avoid every dispute in the interest of purity or favor.

In many instances it is a comparatively simple matter for the clergy to disclaim institutional spokemanship in expressing a political judgment—to which their own faith has disposed them but which cannot be deduced infallibly from the sources alone. ("I think I have the Spirit," was the inspired way in which Paul qualified a prudential utterance.) Such a disclaimer may actually foster an understanding of the nature of faith and of the responsibility it nurtures in every believer. Nevertheless, the question may stick: can a person stand on one side of a bitter social dispute, especially if he assumes leadership there, and remain able to minister adequately on both sides? The answer must be given in part by the person himself, but also in part by the people the pastor is asked to serve. Commitment to a partisan cause can become absorbing and even blinding; in that case the partisan personally stands in need of ministry. As an institutional rule of thumb, when the prophet becomes a king, it is time to look around for another prophet.[26]

No discussion of the clergy role and its educational import would be complete without giving attention to the discipline involved in quitting this function or in being dismissed from it; for the clergy may serve as theological teachers in either of these extraordinary events. To relinquish a post in the ministry because of increasing political identification, where doubts have arisen in the incumbent or his constituency whether he can maintain the freedom needed to minister adequately, is no personal or institutional disaster. A person changes neither his faith nor his character by quitting; he only changes a public career. This is no irreparable loss for the church in a time when there are more clergy than posts, and when many administrative functions presently served by clergy might be as well served by other persons. If the number of clergy is to become diminished, let this take place through a loss of men and women to lively social causes. A former parson becomes a stronger partisan; his skills in guiding reflection will be carried to new social deliberations.

If, however, complaints are raised in the interest of procuring a less demanding minister, one who does not disturb unexamined social opinions at all, then the charges must be contested. Then it is the objecting brothers who are seeking to take the Kingdom captive. It is no act of ministry to let this succeed with a struggle. In every contention of this kind, the plaintiffs must be referred not merely to their political differences with the minister but to the symbols of their faith and to the possibility that they are evading its demands. Persons charged with ministry are to exercise their calling to the end, and at the end.

Even here we discern the need for an appropriate praxis, one which requires a careful use of speech and a design of action based on elements to be found within the scene. If clarifications are needed of what seems a doubtful use of clergy prerogatives, let them be made. If our clergy person has placed facilities at the disposal of the poor or of moving elements within the community, he knows how to account for such actions on the basis of convictions shared within the church. If he has preempted discussion of such matters, he knows what to confess, what to affirm, what to promise. He need *not* climb into the pulpit to claim the will of the Lord for actions which are in themselves debatable or to condemn his detractors for unbelief or rancor. (These would then have a justifiable complaint.) Despising the judgment of people in the very course of ministering to them would itself serve to compromise the ministry in question.

Measurements have been made during the past decade of a growing cleavage between younger clergy and their congregations and projections have pointed to a gathering storm.[27] Not measured were the subtle, yet eminently germane, considerations of how these men and women were playing the game. Some of the most memorable clergy of the past generation have succeeded in working closely with social movements while retaining credibility as pastors. They have done so by guarding and cultivating their ability to bring inspiration and reflection to the very terms of the struggle.

The strain of ambiguity in religious institutions and professional roles itself bears witness to the reality for which they stand. Perspectives and facts are never separate in the pursuit of truth. Structures and initiatives are never separate in the exercise of power. Word and deed can never be neatly divided between separate institutions or separate callings. Disciplines are required which distinguish conviction and action only to unite them, and which therefore help to reform institutions and vocations. It is only when religious institutions are treated as dying that they live, and it is only when religious professionals are treated as imposters that they are true.

NOTES

1. Gibson Winter struck and expounded these notes in *The New Creation As Metropolis* (New York: Macmillan, 1963), chapter 3.

2. "Creativity and the Commonplace" was the subject of a paper read by Richard McKeon at a meeting of The Society for Philosophy of Creativity held during the meetings of the Western Division of the American Philosophical Association, Chicago, April 26, 1973. This choice discussion of "topic" and "invention" is to be published in the journal *Rhetoric and Philosophy*.

3. Daniel Moynihan assigns the reason of failure to "maximum feasible misunderstanding" between sociologists and politicians in a book by that title (New York: Free Press, 1969). Sherry Arnstein assigns it to "maximum feasible manipulation" of target communities by city government; her paper appeared in *City* (November, 1970) or may be procured from the North City Area Wide Council in Philadelphia. Saul Alinsky said the obvious: to imagine any city administration standing by while public moneys went to help communities fight city hall was to imagine "what never was and never will be."

4. Among the many writings in which Richard McKeon seeks to recover for our own age a practice of the liberal arts as pervasive disciples (in addition to their conception as subject matter fields) is one which uses the very terms, familiar in theological studies, that we have named. See *Humanistic Education and Western Civilization: Essays for Robert M. Hutchins* (New York: Holt, Rinehart, and Winston, 1964), pp. 158-181.

5. Reproduced in the translator's introduction to Soren Kierkegaard, *Works of Love* (New York: Harper Torchbooks, 1962), p. 12, n. 2. Italics are mine.

6. This psalm is regularly sung as the entrance hymn at Matins, but some churches break it off at verse 7b where the prophetic voice intrudes—a liturgical practice which is perhaps symptomatic. On the close relation between prophet and cult, see A. R. Johnson, *The Cultic Prophet in Ancient Israel* (Cardiff: University of Wales, 1944) or Walter Harrelson, *From Fertility Cult to Worship* (Garden City: Doubleday, 1969).

7. More generally, *symbol* could mean a mark, sign, or token; it served in medicine, in the plural, to refer to symptoms; it referred in law to a contract or covenant. The seventeenth century philosophers referred repeatedly to the mark of a signet ring on wax or to footprints or vestiges, all immediately formed "matches." Socially, symbols have served to circumscribe rhetorical communities in ways distinguishable from their function in arguments—as anyone knows who has tried to refute Marxism by attacking its view of history or theory of knowledge. Such attacks may actually serve to congeal the group in question. For a discussion which distinguishes this practical function of symbols see Richard McKeon, "Symbols, Myths and Arguments" in *Symbols and Values: An Initial Study*, ed. Lyman Bryson (New York: Harper, 1959). The anthropologist Konrad Lorentz describes a triple function in all ritualization: bond-formation, control of aggression, and communication. See Victor Turner's introductory chapter to *Forms of Symbolic Action: Proceedings of the 1969 Annual Spring Meeting of the American Ethnological Society* (Seattle: University of Washington Press, 1969).

8. Gibson Winter's *New Creation As Metropolis* (1963) was succeeded by a less-functional, more counter-cultural *Being Free: Reflections on America's Cultural Revolution* (New York: Macmillan, 1969). Harvey Cox's *Secular City* (New York:

Macmillan, 1965) became, to say the least, qualified in *The Feast of Fools: A Theological Essay on Festivity and Fantasy* (New York: Harper & Row, 1969) and again in *The Seduction of the Spirit* (New York: Simon and Schuster, 1973).

Will Herberg described the civil religion as inevitable and idolatrous in *Protestant, Catholic and Jew* (Garden City: Doubleday, 1955). Sidney Mead has described it as necessary and constructive in a plural society. But the present resurrector of the Rousseauian concept is Robert Bellah, whose much published paper, "Civil Religion in America," appeared with responses in *The Religious Situation 1968*, ed. Donald Cutler (Boston: Beacon, 1968). On ethnic symbols and community creation, see (in addition to Daniel Callahan, Andrew Greeley, and others) Michael Novak, who shifted his hopes from the New Left, expressed in *A Theology for Radical Politics* (New York: Herder, 1969), to a hardhat populism in *The Rise of the Unmeltable Ethnics* (New York: Macmillan, 1972). For the liveliest of many critical responses, see Richard John Neuhaus in *Worldview*, October, 1972 and January, 1973.

9. See Gerhard von Rad, *Old Testament Theology* (New York: Harper & Row, 1962) 1:19-35.

10. We may refer here to many Christian criticisms of the "Playboy Philosophy," as of its counterpart in *Cosmopolitan*, with their straightforward dedication to the old-fashioned practice of pushing products. The Danish art critic, R. Broby Johansen, has produced charts to show that the rise and fall of hemlines in industrial societies coincides remarkably with that of their Gross National Product. A repeated advertisement in the Sunday business section shows an unclad woman with a message: "Let me outsell your salesman at the next trade show—convention—business meeting." As for national festivals, John Strietelmeier proposes that these should now be dedicated frankly to the Seven Deadly Sins: Thanksgiving Day—gluttony; Christmas—avarice; New Year's Eve—lust; Easter—envy; Memorial Day—sloth; Independence Day—pride; Veteran's Day—wrath. All seem characterized by shorter memories, longer weekends, and heightened consumption. The American Revolution Bicentennial in 1976 affords an occasion for present exercise of a national symbolic discipline.

11. See Sigmund Mowinckel's chapter on the royal psalms in *The Psalms in Israel's Worship*, tr. D. R. Ap-Thomas (Nashville: Abingdon, 1962), Helmer Ringgren's reference to those psalms in *The Messiah in the Old Testament* (Naperville, Ill.: Allenson, 1956).

12. The Old Testament has its sympathies for the king, whose art is that of the possible, in his confrontations with the prophet who told him he might very well go to *gehenna* with what was possible. Limitations placed on royal policies by an unwilling populace were not relieved by pronouncements of doom; on the contrary, the prophet's words helped produce the very fate they envisioned. Hence the many scenarios in which a harrassed king makes the prophet's task seem cheap (think of Jehoiakim making paper dolls of the prophet's scroll in Jeremiah 36). Yet if constraints were such as to require a ruler to offer policies invalid in the longer run, someone had to see it and say so. The peace of the city was to be sought not merely by enlarging the palace but by altering policies, and there came a time when it was too late for that.

13. This counter-function of ideals was documented by Gunnar Myrdal, *The American Dilemma* (New York: McGraw-Hill, 1964), chs. 1 and 4, apps. 1-2.

14. The Universal Declaration of Human Rights adopted by the United Nations General Assembly in 1948 was supplemented by two Covenants, one on Civil and Political Rights and one on Economic, Social, and Cultural Rights, in 1966.

15. Such a sequence in community creation and development is unfolded by Richard Hauser in *The New Society* (London: Centre for Group Studies, 1969; available from the Urban Training Center for Christian Mission, 21 E. Van Buren, Chicago, Ill. 60605), pp. 235-258. A formalized common story was basic in the information and perpetuation of Israel (Deuteronomy 26). Hannah Arendt has remarked that the Greeks founded their cities in order to have places in which to tell their stories, but she might have turned that analysis around. A shared story of oppression and liberation, together with a panoply of liberators and liberation colors, has been formative in the creation of black consciousness and community. Something similar is to be found in almost every lively tenants' association. In suburban communities some new ritual seems emerging within story-telling and story-merging groups, as well as in grope groups, local arts and festivals, and communal applications of play-theory which sheds a new light on work.

16. See Gibson Winter, *Elements for a Social Ethic* (New York: Macmillan, 1966), pp. 264-279.

17. Augustine, *Confessions* x.9.16—10.17 (cf. *De Diversis Quaestionibus* lxxiii.18). Cicero, *De Inventione* I.viii.10 and throughout.

18. A procedure illustrated from this letter in Robert W. Funk, *Language, Hermeneutic, and Word of God* (New York: Harper & Row, 1961).

19. Paul Ramsey, *Who Speaks for the Church?* (Nashville: Abingdon, 1967).

20. Contributions to such fundamental exploration and research ("counter-foil research," in the phrase of Ivan Illich) seem appropriate institutional actions at present. The network of separate services (land, finance, materials, tools, design) proposed by John Turner in "Housing As a Verb," *Freedom to Build* (Cambridge: MIT Press, 1972) seems most able to expand personal and communal choices, values, and economy, but it is not available in present packaged housing systems. Illich's similar proposals for education in *Deschooling Society* (New York: Harper & Row, 1971) are not approached by actions for reform or control of schools. This radically inventive approach to social structures and utilities is further sketched in his *Tools for Conviviality* (New York: Harper & Row, 1973).

21. Lewis Coser, *The Functions of Social Conflict* (Glencoe: Free Press, 1956), pp. 72-85, 151-157. For applications in the church, see Martin E. Marty, "The Nature and Consequences of Social Conflict in Religious Groups," in *Religion and Social Conflict*, ed. Robert Lee and Martin Marty (New York: Oxford, 1964); also Robert Lee with Russell Galloway and William Eichorn, *The Schizophrenic Church: Conflict over Community Organization* (Philadelphia: Westminster, 1969). Alongside many manuals on modes of conflict resolution and negotiation, see J. M. Brown, F. K. Berrien, D. L. Russell, *Applied Psychology* (New York: Macmillan, 1966), pp. 478ff.

22. For one truculent description of difficulties too-innocently encountered in such church-sponsored housing programs, see Virgil E. Murdock, "Wheeling and Dealing in the Vineyards of the Lord: Churches as Real Estate Entrepreneurs," *Faith and Form* 5: Fall, 1972.

23. See among many similar studies a publication by the North American Congress on Latin America, *The Benevolent Empire* (Box 57, Cathedral Station, New York, N.Y. 10025) or Charles Powers, *Social Responsibility and Investments* (Nashville: Abingdon, 1971).

24. Cf. Ivan Illich, "The Vanishing Clergyman," in *The Church, Change and Development* (Chicago: Urban Training Center, or New York: Herder, 1970).

25. One of the first attempted crackdowns by the Justice Department on resistance to the Vietnam War cited a mass meeting on October 16, 1967, in Arlington Street Church, Boston, where William Ellery Channing (who signed the "Call to Resist" in the War of 1812 and in whose office the Massachusetts Peace Union was formed) once served as pastor. In the ensuing trial, the defense drew a distinction between supporting men in moments of conscience and actually exhorting them to resistance. But drawing such a line on that occasion, in that building, seems a lawyer's task indeed. In the ultimate dropping of charges, social wisdom prevailed.

26. Thus Fr. Hidalgo was led by imperceptible stages and by a sudden plot of the authorities against the local organizer from a comparatively simple Operation Breadbasket to leading a ragtail (by no means non-violent) army against Mexico City—at the age of 57 years. When his head was stuck on a pole at the top of the *alhondigo* in Guanajuato, Hidalgo was no longer officially regarded as a priest, but he had become the first patriot of Mexico. Remnants of his army were led by Fr. Jose Morelos who, by order of the Bishop of Oaxaca, was publicly defrocked and made to suffer the ordeal of having the holy oils scraped from his palms. While onlookers wept openly, Morelos suffered this impropriety without a whimper.

27. Jeffrey Hadden, *The Gathering Storm in the Churches* (Garden City: Doubleday, 1969), pp. 163-207. Apparent changes since the mid-sixties, when these statistics were gathered, invite substantive reflection.

3

CHANGES IN PERSONS AND COMMUNITIES THROUGH EDUCATIONAL MINISTRY

Education must, then, be not only a process that transmits culture but also one that provides alternative views of the world and strengthens the will to explore them.

—Jerome Bruner

Education is nothing more
than the polishing
of each single link
in the great chain
that binds humanity together
and gives it unity.

—Johann Heinrich Pestalozzi

The secret of education lies in respecting the pupil.

—Ralph Waldo Emerson

A good education is not so much one which prepares a man to succeed in the world, as one which enables him to sustain failure.

—Bernard Iddings Bell

There is only one subject-matter for education,
and that is life in all its manifestations.

—Alfred North Whitehead

ON CARING

Whenever educational ministry happens, we must pay attention to individual persons and to the communities in which they live. In this section William Koppe deals with people in relation to the congregation and Jack White adds a look at the pastor's role in the larger community of which the congregation is a part.

Koppe, a research expert in religious behavior, makes some direct suggestions for developing and using congregational life as a powerful factor in helping individuals make sense out of their world. He picks up the growth theme described in *How Persons Grow in Christian Community*, and shows how each phase of individual growth calls for an appropriate and different response. On the basis of Koppe's Pragmatic Life Perspectives concept, educational leaders can begin to design and carry out more effective classroom and congregational activities. Koppe's four phases are useful ways to evaluate development and growth of persons and to weigh and direct congregational educational efforts.

Koppe, through his careful research work in the Lutheran Longitudinal Study, has picked up the subtleties of education and congregational life. He recognizes the necessity to have both flexibility and stability present to help a variety of people work hard at building their life perspectives.

He has a meaningful concept of education, and is willing to test it and relate it to field settings. Supported by a growing body of research data, Koppe continues to investigate implications for educational ministry.

White writes out of his twelve years' experience in parish ministry and his six years' experience in teaching students about church and community issues. He takes a focused look at specific activities of a pastor who pays careful attention to the community in which a congregation is located. He describes the opportunities for theological dialogue in the midst of crucial societal issues; the use of statistics to teach us more about ourselves and our world; the value of participation in planned change efforts; and some ways to help people build contracts to further our life together. The interdependence of life provides the framework for these opportunities. White broadens the usual conceptualization of the pastor's educational role to include a social ministry.

White's portrayal is a paradigm for looking at a variety of ways the pastor can be a learner and a teacher *within* and *without* the congregation itself. In describing the pastor's role in the community, White lays the groundwork for perceiving the ministry of the laity as primarily taking place in the world. This ministry is interactional rather than reactional. He is no advocate of either clerical or theological imperialism, but he tries to show the importance of the pastoral role and the myriad ways the church can teach and, perhaps more important, learn from the community in order to serve it more fully in Christ's name.

ARE CONGREGATIONS GOOD "SOIL" FOR EDUCATIONAL MINISTRY?

William A. Koppe

Pastors perceive their roles in the educational ministry of their congregations generally in terms of pedagogical assignments, such as catechetical instruction and adult education, administrative chores, which may be delegated to others, and concerns for leadership training. In other words, they think in terms of educational processes. Thoughts about the context for learning are often restricted to provision of adequate space and equipment. In part, these attitudes come from the concepts they have of education.

In the minds of many, education is predicated on a belief that learning essentially is remembering concepts or attitudes. Its processes are often oriented toward workshops for teachers, leader's guides, pupil's books, and other educational paraphernalia designed to transfer learnings from teachers to learners. Even "discovery" methods are often designed to induce students to discover what a teacher could have told them in the first place. The emphasis seems to be that learners are "caused" to learn by forces outside of themselves. If, for example, we can keep learners "captive" in the community of a congregation, it is assumed they will come to identify with that community. Forces such as imitation, habits, and some direct teaching will, presumably, cause a learner to be brought up in the way he should go.

In this view, learners are assumed to be basically passive products of educational ministry, provided they can be kept interested in participating in congregational programs. Congregations are judged *prima facie* to be "good soil" for educational ministry. This opinion, however, is far from unanimous. Dr. C. Richard Evenson, for example, stated:

> Every educational effort takes place in some kind of community. In every case there is at least the interaction of teacher and learner. . . .

> Since the learning is to result in identifying with the community, it is surely implied that the learning takes place in the full context of that community. To the extent that the community lacks the characteristics with which its youth should be able to identify, the definition becomes a set of objectives for the adult Christian community to achieve. . . .[1]

> After all, if adults want to bring youth to identify with the adult Christian community, it assumes that this adult community is something with which it is worthwhile to identify.[2]

The fact of the matter is that learners in any situation seek out that kind of information which will help give meaning to their lives. They tend to identify with those persons, groups, cultures, and congregations which provide resources. Of course, the learners themselves determine whether or not those resources are helpful.

The pastors who join with their congregations to inspire learners to identify with the life and mission of the congregation must recognize that learners are far from passive receptacles for teachers' wisdom or clay for the educational potters' wheels. Learners are active seekers for nutrients in the culture and groups that make up the soil in which they are growing.

Pastors, better than any other congregational members, are in a position to assess the total educational ministry of the congregation in terms of the many diverse resources available for learners. Better than any other persons, they are able to recognize the many ways in which learners may find meaningful involvements important to them as well as to their congregations. Pastors can recognize how identification with the life and mission of the church contributes to the individual's search for personal identity.

At least two research findings are instructive. There is a growing body of evidence that learners learn best those materials and concepts which contribute to their search for meaning in life. There is also evidence that youth's level of involvement in a congregation, or their tendency to drop out of its life, depends on the same search for meaning. As the strategical leaders in congregational ministry, pastors have the greatest opportunities to be sensitive to diverse situations in congregational life which may become resources for those who are searching for meaning.

The Soil for Christian Growth

The individual has played an important part in determining what he is now. And what he may become tomorrow is equally dependent upon the use he makes of the opportunities and resources that may open for him today. He is a unique personality and meets experience in his own way. Attempts to "handle" him without recognition of his own contribution to the total outcome may backfire.[3]

Just as the roots of the vine search out the best nutrients available in the soil and find substitutes when a favored element is absent, so persons search out resources and guidance for life from those available. Just as the vine will die if it cannot find the necessary nutrients, so persons will abandon an area of growth if there are no acceptable resources to feed upon. If we limit ourselves to discussing educational ministry, four growth phases provide us with a way of looking at congregational programs and lifestyles as resources for learning. These phases have been uncovered in the Lutheran Longitudinal Study and are related to the concept of Pragmatic Life Perspectives. This concept refers to the way individuals interact with their world in terms of their personal interpretation of that world.[4] Let's look at these four phases:

1. *The Perspective-Applying Phase.* At any period in life, persons operate on the basis of Pragmatic Life Perspectives. As long as they feel relatively confident, and as long as their experiences make reasonable sense in the light of those perspectives, they may make only minor revisions in their lives which do not affect their general point of view. They feel confident to live life as they see it.

2. *The Unstable Perspective Phase.* When too many personal life experiences are not consistent with their Pragmatic Life Perspectives, persons lose confidence in their abilities to cope with these experiences on their own. At this time, they seek to stabilize their lives by depending on those who, in their opinions, will provide them with security, skills, and information. They will tend to choose those institutions and authoritative resources which present to them images of being the most likely to help them to make sense of their lives.

3. *The Perspective-Rebuilding Phase.* As long as they lack faith in their own abilities to interpret life, persons will depend on the resources of the persons and institutions they trust for security, skills, and information. With that trust, they will submit to discipline and even learn in areas remote to their immediate concerns. However, their immediate concerns—the problems they could not solve in life—are still primary. The more directly resource persons and leaders deal with these concerns, the more likely they are to be influential in the lives of learners.

4. *The Reality-Testing Phase.* As they become more secure in their reinterpretation of life—their revised Pragmatic Life Perspectives—

persons then will feel the need to test these perspectives, incorporating them into their total lifestyles. Persons then may grow confident enough to depend again upon their own interpretations of life and to enter another perspective-applying phase.

The Growth of Hopes, Dreams, and Potentials

When persons are relatively satisfied with their Pragmatic Life Perspectives, that is, when they feel most able to cope with life as they are living it, they are most likely to expose themselves to new experiences. In this perspective-applying phase they have two concerns. First, they are likely to be testing the limits of their capabilities and to be assessing responses to their actions. Second, they are likely to be looking beyond their present limitations, projecting what could happen if the limitations were not there. That is, they are in a position to dare to dream of ultimate solutions to world problems, as they understand them, unhampered by the crushing boundaries of reality.

This is a time for making plans and for acting on those plans. It is a time for doing what seems worth doing *from the learner's point of view.* Can persons operating at this phase of life find the nutrients in congregations on which to grow?

According to the Lutheran Longitudinal Study, there are three basic qualities which promote growth at this phase. The first is the most obvious: those congregations which are involved in many diverse activities are likely to be the ones which provide action settings. It is true that it is easy for a pastor to stimulate a wide variety of action projects in a large congregation, where those who wish to test and apply their Pragmatic Life Perspectives find many outlets. But it is also true that large congregations tend to select the most talented members to serve in all "important" roles, so that the moderately endowed are likely to surrender to mediocrity. The pastor who is overly impressed with his competently led and successful activities may overlook those who have become religious spectators. As a matter of fact, large congregations will survey their programs to make sure that even "Charlie Brown"[5] has successful experiences in his areas of concern.

If a small congregation is to be good soil for applying Pragmatic Life Perspectives, its pastor and leaders must draw upon all available talent to carry on any corporate activities. It is, however, too easy for small congregations to settle into simplistic lifestyles because only a few are willing or because all "important" activities are delegated to the pastor.

Pastors need to help their small congregations reevaluate their mission as a congregation at this time and in this place, such that they place demands on all members in areas which are important to the membership.

The second quality follows from the first. Congregations which foster growth during the perspective-applying phase tend to involve many lay persons at all levels of operation. This means five-year-olds and fifteen-year-olds as well as "mature" adults. The worlds of childhood and adulthood must be meshed more effectively so children may both learn about and try on a variety of grown-up experiences; and so adults may share their children's dreams, thoughts, joys, disappointments, and playfulness.

Teenagers, for example, do not become involved in the life and mission of the church as often either when someone else plans for them or when they are turned loose to do their own planning. Those congregations in which youth and adults together, with open communication, plan activities important to both yield a higher level of perspective-applying behavior.

The third quality is vision. It is characteristic of those who are *growing* in Christian community that they are extending themselves beyond their present capabilities. If a congregation limits its mission to what can be done *now* and predicates its activities only on the traditions and habits of the past, its routines will be easily learned even by the youngest members. Christian education materials which explain why we do what we do add little to an interpretation of life, and certainly involve no opportunities to try out the existing Pragmatic Life Perspectives or to push beyond their limitations. Perhaps pastors need not feel they must be the source of all criteria for congregational activity.

Congregations in which pastors lead members to evaluate continually their missions as a Christian group and in which leaders are encouraged to dare to dream beyond the limitations of the present are more likely to stimulate members to reach beyond their grasp and to develop a growing need for the skills, knowledge, and other resources necessary to make at least some of the dreams come true.

In part, then, pastors lead their congregations to become good soil for Christian education when they encourage members to be involved actively in many tasks *they* consider to be important. It also happens when pastors make sure that lay persons have a prominent role in determining policies and activities and when members are encouraged to dare to dream dreams for themselves, for their congregation, and for their community.

The Growth of Confidence

When persons lose confidence that their Pragmatic Life Perspectives can make sense of life as they perceive it, they are likely to seek stability and predictability on the one hand, and sources of authoritative information on the other. This is the second, or unstable perspective, phase. One of the characteristics of persons at this phase is that they find themselves involved in a number of experiences to which they cannot respond. One kind of response is to try to shut out these experiences, to simplify life.

If a congregation is to be good Christian education soil for those in this phase, there are five qualities which it must manifest. These five important qualities work together for a single objective: to give persons the confidence that the church and its congregations will indeed be a help in arriving at a more satisfactory understanding of life, particularly in areas of current questioning.

1. *Challenge*. The first quality of a congregation which will promote growth at this level is that its activities challenge members beyond existing understandings. Those who can easily cope with all the church has to offer will feel little need to seek skills or resources beyond those they possess. It is very well to dream dreams when no action is required. Short-range attempts to implement these dreams, however, may bring one face-to-face with the reality of limitations.

2. *Support*. Problem-solving cannot take place without the frustration which grows from being challenged beyond one's capacities. But the congregation which would be good soil for religious growth will not ignore these frustrations. Its leaders will be continually open to listen to the concerns of learners and to be a support group. There is a risk, of course, that some members will fall back on easy answers based on partial understandings. It may be, too, that only some members of a congregation can play this supportive role while pointing learners toward systematic sources of help. Pastors are often in a position to recognize and to encourage these persons in these roles.

3. *An Image of Competence*. The third quality is perhaps the most vital of the five. A congregation will be perceived as an authoritative resource only to the extent that it projects an accurate image of its capability to deal with the areas which disturb the learner. It is important to recognize that this image may be culturally defined in such a way that adults and youth may overlook the potentialities of the congregation unless a special effort is made to make this image prominent. It is equally important to recognize that persons will not necessarily turn to the church even if the church is the most appropriate place to turn. Particularly in cities, youth and adults have many sources of skill and information. The church may be avoided by those who are suspicious that it may be

hypercritical and over-eager to control, to give final answers, or to recruit paying members.

A number of research projects are building a body of evidence that persons are not looking for entertaining or cop-out religious experiences. Those who are searching for meaning in life are concerned with more profound religious questions than we have formerly suspected. However, if the image a congregation projects is irrelevant to the concerns of learners, they will turn elsewhere. Therefore, both the image and the program will have to be sensitive to the religious questions being asked if the congregation is to be perceived as a help in time of confusion.

4. *Stability*. Most persons with unstable life perspectives crave a degree of environmental stability and predictability. Some have called this the major contribution a congregation can make. Roger Barker, the educational researcher, suggested that new learnings are acquired more effectively in a small town because the change stands out in relief to the highly predictable lifestyle. When an individual is not in a position to operate from a relatively stable perspective of his own, he has a need for stable environmental supports and will even tolerate considerable discipline to get it. Both second- and seventh-graders are more likely to be restless to the point of becoming behavior problems when the disciplinary routines are absent.

5. *Authoritative—Not Authoritarian*. The fifth quality of a congregation which is good soil for educational ministry at this phase is that it is based more on being authoritative and genuine and less on being authoritarian. Pastors who have a ready answer to the wrong questions, or who in effect tell the learner that his questions are unimportant, are likely to frighten learners into real or psychological escape.

Researchers in religious education are frequently surprised to discover that youth and adults persistently request that the church meet needs it already serves. This strange finding can only be explained in terms of communication. Either youth do not really want what they are requesting, or the image of the church is presented in a way that youth do not recognize them as an authoritative resource.

In review then, for those who have an unstable perspective on life, a congregation will be good soil for educational ministry when it presents challenge moderated by an understanding support, an accurate image of its offerings in the eyes of the learner, and both stable routines and an expectancy that it will supply authoritative help without authoritarian control.

The Growth of Knowledge

Those who have selected the church as a resource for learning to cope with life are usually willing, or even eager, to accept disciplines required by educators. In this perspective-rebuilding phase learners have two basic needs. First, they need to reduce the unsure areas of their lives to what is predictable. Second, they are concerned with reconstructing their Pragmatic Life Perspectives, particularly in areas where they have been frustrated. At this point, it is necessary to remind ourselves that hardly anyone *consciously* would recognize that his Pragmatic Life Perspectives are inadequate nor would he *consciously* set out to overcome his frustrations. Few, if any, would be able to describe logically the need to know. Some may even be surprised that they are now interested in things that formerly bored or even irritated them.

First-graders and junior high school youth are remarkably alike in at least one characteristic. Both tend to want instruction and information which leave little room for interpretation. For the most part, they are frustrated with life's loose ends and confused by them. They want to know what they can count on. Doubts expressed by seventh- and eighth-graders are often a rejection of ideas which leave too much unexplained. Their expression is often an appeal for what is basic and unambiguous.

If a congregation is to be good soil for educational ministry, it must provide stability for those who have lost their way. It must provide a stable base free of challenge so that energies will be freed for new learning. This is in direct contrast to the suggestion earlier that a congregation must provide challenge for those who are able to operate independently. For the pastor, it means being sensitive to differences in needs of individuals at different age levels and being ready to select and to train leaders with that same sensitivity.

Given a base of security supported by predictable routines, those who have lost faith in their Pragmatic Life Perspectives are usually ready to submit to those who seem to have something to teach. Well organized and practical teachings of "what is," "how to," and "for what reason" are likely to be accepted eagerly, assuming that common sense is exercised regarding the impact of teaching on learners. Goldman made this point when he discussed the teaching of the Bible:

> Bible-centred religious education emphasizes that the Bible must be taught because it *is* thè Bible. Child-centred religious education, however, focuses upon the fact that it is the child as a growing person who should be our central concern. Where some parts of the Bible may answer his needs at a certain stage of his development these should be used.[6]

This is not a time to take advantage of a person's pliability to lay pet lectures on him. It is as important to learn the learner as to learn the material.

The whole attitude of concern for persons—for individuals who are trying to find their way through life—requires tireless leadership in a congregation. It is not as important that its members pattern their lives to fit institutional routine as it is that they create an atmosphere of mutual involvement in one another's lives. Only then does specific information take on meaning for those who seek it.

This attitude has two desirable by-products. Those who have become disenchanted with their life perspectives often are in periods of healthy doubting. Teachers and pastors who focus first on the individual are likely to find ways to search with learners for new bases of understandings which recognize doubts as rejections of concepts which should be put away with other childish things. The second by-product is that person-centered educational ministry is unlikely to find itself trapped in telling people what they already know. "Tell Me the Old, Old Story" provides a sort of emotional bubble bath which, perhaps, contributes to the security-base for some. Those searching for information to make sense of life, however, are not ready to be told what they already know.

Pastors may well look into their leadership training procedures. Do they focus on the individual or do they tend to teach gimmicks to manipulate persons into lockstep religion?

There is little doubt that, when persons have turned to the congregation as a source of new knowledge to build their life perspectives, they also develop an evaluation of the congregation's response to their need. If they seek the congregation once, will they seek it again? Have they found nutrients in this soil?

The Growth of Witness

The reality-testing phase, the last in the series, is crucial. Given information, concepts, and new ways to organize perspectives, most healthy persons grow increasingly impatient to put new perspectives to the test. Of course, over-dependent persons are just as hesitant to break free of the comfort of living a life organized by others as independent persons are over-anxious to "go it on their own." One thing is sure: unless a learner takes the risk of testing his newly formed Pragmatic Life Perspectives, he can never really internalize what he has learned. He can never make it his own. If his hesitance to try his wings is too great, he may never verify what he has learned and settle for the partial identity growing from over-dependence.

The pastor's role is obvious in at least one sense. If study without the tests of reality lead nowhere, pastors constantly need to be aware of those who are becoming too comfortable in dependent roles, and to prod them to take specific actions following their learnings. Pastors may be fortunate to have specialized leaders who can help individuals to state their own positions and then encourage them to "go it on their own."

Educational ministry is incomplete unless it leads to independent action. Pilots are never really qualified to fly until they take their first solo flights with no one to back them up. Real consolidation of religious growth comes about more often by failure than by being rescued.

It would almost appear as if a congregation cannot become good soil for educational ministry simply by doubling the water and the fertilizer. In some way, those who are to live and grow in Christian communities, those who are to identify with the total life and ministry of the church, must be deprived of their crutches and encouraged to take up their beds and walk.

In Restrospect

The role of the pastor in educational ministry would be a simple one were it limited to the structured—controlled events scheduled as classes and sermons. The fact of the matter is that a congregation with a healthy educational ministry tends to be a kaleidoscopic hodgepodge. Strommen and his associates, in *A Study of Generations*, suggested, "You can assume that for members of a congregation today, a constant requirement is to accept diversity and to use times of tension as times of opportunity."[7] Tension, indeed, may be one of the best indications of growth.

You may think that educational ministry is a four-ring circus in which one is never sure of exactly which ring is which. Indeed it is! If life in a congregation becomes too well-organized, one can seriously question whether educational ministry has any chance to occur. If, on the other hand, one finds challenges, frustrations, problem-solving, reality-testing, and dreamers dreaming even impractical dreams, one can be sure of the presence of nutrients for educational ministry.

NOTES

1. C. Richard Evenson, "The Purpose of Confirmation Education," in *Confirmation and Education*, ed. W. Kent Gilbert, Yearbooks in Christian Education, vol. I (Philadelphia: Fortress Press, 1969), p. 39.

2. *Ibid.*, p. 38.

3. Lawrence C. Little, *Foundations for a Philosophy of Christian Education* (Nashville: Abingdon Press, 1962), p. 179.

4. For in-depth discussion of this matter, see W. A. Koppe, *How Persons Grow in Christian Community*, Yearbooks in Christian Education, vol. IV. (Philadelphia: Fortress Press, 1973).

5. A Charles Schulz cartoon character in *Peanuts* who is a perpetual loser.

6. Ronald Goldman, *Religious Thinking from Childhood to Adolescence* (London: Kegan Paul, 1964), p. 230.

7. Merton P. Strommen et al., *A Study of Generations* (Minneapolis: Augsburg Publishing House, 1972), p. 286.

LEARNING AND TEACHING IN THE COMMUNITY

Andrew J. White

"You clergy think I have nothing to do but to heed your call to meetings," said a lay leader of the congregation to his pastor. "My ministry is important, too. I have people counting on me at my work as well as at my church!"

A "ministry" of the laity? Of course, and baptized Christians are called upon to identify and exercise that ministry in all segments of their life. How will pastors help persons in the identification and implementation of that ministry? This chapter deals with the preliminaries to that issue. Clergy who are able to exercise their ordained ministry in the community as well as in the congregation will be better able to help ministry happen in the lives of their parishioners.

The thesis, then, is that educational ministry is richer when pastors focus also on opportunities to teach and learn within the community. This is not an argument for the neglect of the parish, but for an inclusive ministry.

Pastoral and educational ministry should be inclusive ministries. Inclusive ministry is ministry to persons who are in need of God's gracious word, but it is also a ministry to those persons in the light of the social settings in which they find themselves.

In our society individuals are interdependent and rely on a wide variety of persons and organization for goods and services. Values and lifestyles are formed in great part by associations. Pastors ignore these influences only at peril to their inclusive ministry.

Pastors should take their communities seriously. They should learn from their communities about the needs of people, how to be better citizens themselves, how to program their own congregations for increased service to persons, and how to apply their own faith where they live. Pastors should also teach in the community. The community needs the gospel preached. It needs increased attention to justice for all. It needs sensitive organizations, like the congregation, attending to human need.

In their teaching and learning, pastors are both like and unlike other persons. Like other Christians they are to be the very best citizens they can be. They work for justice, mercy, and reconciliation among people who must live together despite their estrangements. They are different in that they know themselves to be called under the discipline of the word of God. They are to represent the gospel before humanity as all believing Christians are to do, but they also have been set apart and called by the church to be its representative. As such, they are to lead their congregations. Let pastors and congregations, then, be the representatives of the word in the midst of the human structures in which they find themselves.

What are the structures of society which touch the lives of each of us? They are many and varied. We are part of a family. We live in a neighborhood. We attend schools, or did. We use banks, supermarkets, and subways. We live under multiple governments and belong to various voluntary associations. What forms the structures take and the kinds of policies they operate under tend to influence the shape of our lives. To engage in a full pastoral ministry means, therefore, to take seriously that we are social beings who are a part of, and rely upon, the structures which operate in our communities.

The pastor of the local congregation is a community actor and his or her role is not a walk-on part. He needs to see himself playing a central part in the drama of the place where he lives. In many ways he is an example helping the laity develop their own ministries in their places of life. This is an awesome challenge.

One way to handle the challenge is for the pastor to become an educator in the community. The term *educator* is used in the sense of a learner-teacher, not as an intellectual imperialist.

Theory of the Community

The difference between being educators in the community and being simply residents lies in the ability of pastors to conceptualize their activity in the light of some adequate theory of the community and act with some sense of direction. One such theory, as presented by Roland L. Warren (*The Community in America* [Chicago: Rand-McNally & Co., 1963]), has vertical and horizontal dimensions. Warren developed his theory because the traditional way of thinking about communities is no longer adequate and because the health of many communities has been deteriorating.

Traditionally the community was seen as a limited geographical area with definite, ascertainable boundaries. Now, however, communities overlap and governmental and quasi-governmental units are organized on functional bases to deliver educational services, fire protection, transportation, and the like. Also, many people live in one community and earn a living in another. Theory is required to explain and to aid the planning of relevant programs by churchmen. One cannot ignore the increased orientation of local people and institutions to regional and national systems, to cite one example of a phenomenon which requires explanation for the sake of sensible mission strategy.

The "community problem" likewise cries out for substantive theory to assist in the development of solutions. That problem is not a singular problem. There are many critical concerns, such as urban blight, indebtedness of the community, lack of housing, poor schools, crime, the problems of the aged, need for industrial development, inadequate transportation, delinquency, and traffic congestion.

Pastors have their own "theological theory" to bring to the task, but if they ignore the current sociological conceptions of the community, they may be addressing the gospel to towns that are unreal and to people who are so beset with problems that they cannot hear easily. Warren can help pastors identify their actual communities with realistic acknowledgement of local problems. On this no-nonsense basis, they can deal more directly with their tasks as representatives of the word.

The Vertical Dimension

First, the vertical dimension. Most local institutions, agencies, and individuals receive their satisfactions from being a part of an extra-community system. The manager of a local food market affiliated with a national chain receives his rewards from the chain. With high volume sales and well-satisfied customers he may, in time, expect and receive promotion to a larger outlet of the company. The branch bank manager, likewise, may find herself rewarded with a vice presidency on that day when promotions are in order, if her branch reflects the growth pattern expected and the efficiency required of the branch by the organization.

The pastor of the local congregation is also a branch manager of sorts. Certainly the system which guided him into the ministry, supervised his education, shepherded his call, and eventually may attempt to help him relocate in another congregation, is extra-community in its orientation.

In all of these examples of the vertical orientation of society's members, the local community should not be denied or diminished.

n fact, all of the example systems depend upon and exist to serve he people who live in the local community. There has been a endency, however, to give higher priority to those vertical systems vhich most directly relate to the interest and self-interest of the ndividual. This is the case certainly for corporations that employ arge numbers of persons and demand loyalty to the organization n return for pay. It is also the tendency of voluntary associations. To enhance communication, to increase efficiency, and sometimes o promote ideology, it has become the vogue in American society o organize people into networks of associations which, though ooted in the local community, find corporate meaning beyond it. These extra-community oriented associations may take the spotlight off the local community.

Certainly the denomination is a classic expression of this reality which cuts through our society. In the denomination the local church affiliates with a larger judicatory and finds itself sub-divided into conference, or district, or cluster. The larger judicatory (synod or district) is but one part of the national church, which itself has functions and structures appropriate to it. It is conceivable that pastors could become so involved in tasks related to the vertical organization that they might not invest much energy in the local community in which the congregation is situated.

The Horizontal Dimension

By contrast, the horizontal dimension reminds us that no organization's local unit, no matter how strongly integrated into the extra-community system, can function long in disregard of the impact that its behavior makes on other units in the locality. The horizontal dimension declares that there are locality-relevant functions. These may be called maintenance functions, for they consist of all the things, formal and informal, that local units do to maintain a relationship to each other. These may be generalized as production-distribution-consumption, socialization, social control, social participation, and mutual support. Practically speaking, this means that the people who live in a given community must deal with each other to provide food, professional services, teaching of the young in school, police protection, churches for worship and other voluntary associations for other purposes, and finally hospitals and the like.

The interdependency of life in the local community may seem so obvious as to be boring; however, in recent years excitement and anxiety over interdependent behavior has arisen. In the mid- to late-sixties the so-called urban riots (or rebellions, depending upon your perspective) were physical threats of major proportion. The disruptions in one part of a community affected other parts. Anyone who tried to pass National Guard roadblocks set up on familiar corners became aware of urban interdependency. More recently, threats of polluted water and poisonous air, less militant, but equally lethal, have brought home the lesson of the symbiotic nature of human life.

When understood correctly, the horizontal and vertical dimensions of our culture are inextricably connected. What here has been styled the vertical system can serve to help the individual attain identity. For example, when one says, "I am a Lutheran," that may be shorthand for a history, a confessional stance, and an identification with a particular voluntary association. Together the members of such a vertical system are able to pyramid their resources into sizable proportions. They are able to develop group pride in group projects. However, to what end is this? Luther was appalled at the thought of the church of Christ becoming known as Luther's church and thus confusing ends and means. To be sure, human structures can become ends. The prayer against this goes, "Help us to worship God and use things instead of worshiping things and using God." The resources of the vertical systems can be put to work for the good of people in the horizontal places called communities. There the "mosaic of worlds that touch but do not interpenetrate," as urban society has been described, challenges pastors to lead in making concrete love for all humanity in response to God's gracious act in Christ.

Many pastors spend their energy in developing the congregation which they serve. Certainly that is what they are to do, but if they ignore the community, then the result may be contrary to the values that they preach, particularly the call for men to be brothers and to assume one another's burdens.

Let us use a quite secular person and his office to illustrate the challenge before pastors to be educators in their communities. The figure is the city manager. He is by definition an actor in the horizontal community. He is employed to serve the people of his community regardless of their vertical attachments. He may not be a professional theologian, but he deals with value questions constantly. He is one who must deal with data. He is a manager, and thus a planner of change. He is expected to build contracts so that people of diversity can live together. Let us look at the following scenarios as they might be played out in any community.

Learning and Teaching Through Theological Dialogue

"How can people do things like that to one another?" the city manager demanded of the pastor as he shoved the daily police report across his desk for the pastor to see. Scanning the list of arrests and incident reports the pastor read, "Assault with deadly weapon, rape, assault, armed robbery, assault with deadly weapon," and so on. The list was very long.

"It gets worse every day," the manager said, "and the worst are the domestic quarrels. See this one on line sixteen? That's a wife's complaint. He pulled a knife on her and cut her up. If the neighbors hadn't heard her screaming and called my guys, she'd be dead. As it is, she's at Huron Hospital disfigured for life. They're pumping blood into her to replace all that on her kitchen floor, and when he gets out from behind bars he may finish the job he started last night.

"Where will it all end? This damn town's changing so fast I don't know where to begin to get us out of the mess. If only it was like it used to be. I'm an engineer and they hired me to run this city efficiently. I know every sewer line under every street. I know every pot hole on the surface of the streets before they open up. I know in July how much salt we will need to keep the streets open through the next winter. But I don't know what to do with people who act like animals."

Then he looked the pastor in the eye and said, "You're a Christian preacher. How in God's name can you tolerate, or even explain, that list to me?"

The pastor resisted the temptation to give a quick answer since his friend had long before made very clear that in his own field he despised the flip and shallow. He did not want or expect that from the man of faith either. The first time the pastor walked into his office he expected naivete, but no more.

Shortly after the city manager was asked to step up to the job of managing the city, the pastor had walked in to meet him, to offer himself for future service, and to indicate his interest in the affairs of the community. The manager was not a member of the pastor's congregation and never became one.

Later the pastor heard, "You were the first preacher in my forty years of government service to come in without wanting something from me. All the others wanted a tree cut down from church property, special trash collections, parking considerations at the meters in front of the churches, or they wanted to get traffic tickets fixed."

After two years of the manager's tenure a pattern had developed in the relationship. Usually the pastor went to him, since the manager's job kept him near his desk in city hall at least ten hours a day with numerous night meetings to boot. The pastor would go to the outer office, greet his secretary, and Helen would say, "The boss is busy now. It'll be quite a long time," in which case the pastor seldom would wait. In a few minutes with Helen he could find out the nature of the current pressures on "the boss" and, in a sense, on all in the city, though few knew because not that many asked. More and more often Helen would say, "He's busy, but it won't be long I know he wants you to wait." On a few occasions she would say "Am I glad to see you, come on in."

One particular morning the city manager exercised a privilege which was his all along. He called the pastor and asked, "Can you come in this morning? We've got a problem and maybe you can help." When he asked how the pastor could explain the list of cuttings, brutalities, and human indignities to fellow human beings on the day's blotter, he could have been giving the descriptive urban checklist which he and the pastor were learning together:

- The city—particularly its housing stock—was aging;
- Increasing numbers of renters were utilizing apartments and homes owned by absentee landholders;
- Property was noticeably deteriorating in some areas of the city
- The average income-educational levels of the city residents were going down;
- Racial panic was a reality;
- The style of crime was changing; incidents were increasing.

These and other factors were very important. The city manager and the pastor spent many hours on these items, but whatever the pastor might know about those urban characteristics, the insights of the Christian faith were important too, and on that morning the manager had called because he wanted to know how the Christian pastor could explain man's inhumanity to man.

Distortions of Human Life

The basic Christian truth continues to be that God acted in a decisive way for humankind through the man Jesus. The primary task of being faithful is to offer living testimony with one's whole life that he believes Jesus is the Son of God who died for the sins of all people. In response to such a gracious God, that which otherwise would be impossible (living in harmony with one's fellow human beings) becomes possible. But the police blotter does not reflect humanity's response in faith to a living God. It reflects human hatred and brutality, the distortion of human life.

The police blotter is but one way to measure the fact of sin. The willful acts that are represented there are indicative of the way sin-filled persons operate. They set themselves in opposition to their God and assert what they want. The late Paul Scherer, homiletician of note, in a reference to one of Job's speeches said that Job's problem was not that he could not find God, but that he could not find the kind of God he was looking for. That suggests that humanity is trying to construct God in its own image and, of course, it is, however audacious that may be.

The urban community of our time provides a kaleidoscope of sin made operational. Take the day's police blotter the pastor was shown by the city manager. First on the list was assault with a deadly weapon. Perhaps the actual case was a little man trying to be bigger than he really was. The club, the knife, the gun, and a wide variety of such deadly weapons may serve the psychological needs of some egos. The little man bolstering his ego with artificial means has provided humankind with tragedy and comedy intertwined.

One memorable scene from Charles Chaplin's classic film *The Great Dictator* (1940) comes to mind. The great dictator whose logo was the double cross (xx) invited the neighboring dictator to his place to discuss a treaty. Neither man (prototypes of Hitler and Mussolini) trusted the other. The great dictator's advisors urged him to keep his "friend" in a subordinate position at all times through the negotiation. In brilliant Chaplinesque slapstick, the high point of the matter was reached with each dictator in a barber chair, the old-fashioned kind with a hand lever to regulate the height, maneuvering each in turn to a position looking down on the other. The comedy flowed from the absurdity of the situation and the exaggerated height of the two chairs. The tragedy was in the reality that grown men behave like spoiled children in quite serious attempts to get on top of one another.

The Reality of Sin

Who knows why a person grabs for the deadly weapon? Actually it may be only in the given instance that one can explain it. The pastor had available to him a theory (call it "a theory of sin") which could enable him to know, to expect, and even to explain why in a given instance on the blotter an inhuman act of brutality took place.

What about the city manager? By admission he was out of his field of expertise ("I'm an engineer."). He longed for an explanation ("How in God's name can you . . . explain?") He was no professional theologian, but he had a theology. Basically he saw human beings as good. He thus had no way to explain brutality. There was no room for ambiguity in human behavior.

The city manager may have seen people trying to assert themselves over others. By an inductive learning process he may even have put together a partial explanation for human aggression ("that's the way it is"). The pastor here had the opportunity to talk with the manager about sin and the phenomena that result from it. He coul also suggest the need for checks against that aggression. Gun con trols, for example, are likely to be resisted by the person without sophisticated notion of sin. Certainly such knowledge will not insur favorable opinion for gun controls, but at least a view of humankin that takes sin seriously will suggest a rationale for the law to b utilized in human relationships.

Teaching and Learning

The pastor stood to be a learner as well as a teacher in this situa tion. He could learn about the people of the city and their problems He could be challenged to a deeper appreciation for their needs The city manager could teach him that life needs to be dealt wit in a straightforward way with the tools at hand. Joseph Sittler i reputed to have said once that *Gunsmoke* is the most theologicall sound TV show on the air. His reason was Matt Dillon's (Marshal o Dodge City) acceptance of himself as a human being and doin without pretension what he had to do with the means God ha made available to him. In any event, the city manager was not dis abled by his inability to comprehend the events around him. H had a job to do.

A second item on the blotter of crimes for the day was rape The actual case might have been that of two strapping youn toughs out on the town spying a pert young nurse coming off dut at Huron Hospital. It was an easy matter to trail her through the dar lot to her car, drive with her to the nearly deserted park, and hav "fun" at her expense.

One way sin shows itself is in the search for gratification a another's expense. We human beings use each other, but in s doing we de-personalize. Here the woman was not seen as a whol person with feelings and rights of her own. She became an "it," a body to use, abuse, and cast aside after the moment of "pleasure."

The city manager felt revulsion toward "those animals." Even Billy Graham, in a hasty moment, urged castration for alleged criminals like these. The pastor's opportunity here may be to recall Graham's hasty retreat. The pastor might ask about the woman's well-being. Has she been forgotten in the fit of anger directed at the males? Has anyone looked into the possibility that the men are sorry?

No easy answers here, but the pastor may find it helpful to raise questions of theological significance in connection with overt, blatant crime to learn and teach about sin, which is a condition of all of human life. These questions might bring to the surface the "eye for an eye" feelings within us, the need for compassion, the possibility of confession, and the reality of God's absolution on those who repent.

What about the pastor himself? Has he become the "court theologian"? Is he a prophet or a chaplain? As these questions imply, there is the risk that the pastor's association with the city official will be co-optive and will lead him to compromise. To be instructive may be a risk that he will have to take. Will his congregation be supportive of his time and effort outside the program controlled by the church? Hopefully no narrow view of the pastor's role will prevail. He is about inclusive ministry that takes seriously all human experience and tries to address that experience with the gospel of Jesus Christ.

By struggling with his own ministry in the community, it is most likely that he will gain appreciation of the struggle of his parishioners to apply their own faith to their life experiences.

Analyzing Statistics

The city government is required by law to record much data. The crimes discussed above are recorded, analyzed, and reported to the judicial-correctional system which carries on after the executive arm finishes its tasks. The city officials count the various licenses they issue, the number of people who use the municipal parks, pools, and rinks. They estimate how many firemen, building inspectors, water meter readers, and school crossing guards they will require. All of the decisions implicit in these items must be based on the careful analysis of reliable data. They are also based on values which may be explicit but more often are not dealt with openly.

The criteria upon which decisions are based should be of great interest to the pastor in the community. Does the city want to be efficient? Fiscally sound? Racially integrated? Humane? Beautiful? What about the congregation the pastor serves? What are its values, and thus the criteria upon which it will base its decisions? In a time when great value seems to be placed on the quantification of data, the pastor may wish to balance that with qualitative questions such as these.

The balance between quantity and quality urged here is needed in the church itself. It has become increasingly popular in the church itself to try to quantify for the sake of goal-setting and evaluation. Program budgeting and planning has resulted in some congregations, synods, and whole denominations gearing up for a relatively new way of decision-making: project by project. In this format the planners are required to identify and detail a specific project, locating it within the larger social framework. Theoretically, quantifying objectives, identifying criteria for evaluation, and adding a time dimension will allow for more precise measurements of effectiveness and efficiency. That's all fine if effectiveness and efficiency are the ends to be achieved.

As educators in the community, as well as in the church, pastors can bring to statistical analysis a concern for the persons who are represented by cold statistics. Pastors can ask themselves and others to select statistics on the basis of which they can contribute information about relationship and potential relationship.

For example, many church councils are interested in how many pastoral calls their clergy have made since the last meeting. It would be more appropriate for the pastors to lead them to inquire about "meaningful contacts." These are not recorded mechanically but can be charted only after the planners have some common understanding of what a meaningful contact is. The very criterion itself encourages the planners to relate to each other. Likewise, "How many were in church last month?" gives way to "Who worshiped and who did not, and why?" "How many groups used the building?" may become "What groups, doing what, were here last month? Was the building serving the needs of the community?" In other words, statistics are not used well if they only call attention to numbers. Similarly, these kinds of questions can be used in the community.

The city manager identified above called the pastor one day in anguish over the false security produced by statistics. Trouble broke out in the streets in the adjacent town. Looting and fire damage accompanied rampaging street gangs. One of the phone calls the manager received the next morning was an expression of thanks for the efficient, well-disciplined city police force, which the caller assumed had protected him from the problems of the next town.

The pastor heard, "How can people be so naïve and trusting? My police force is set at 65 men. We are five short because of retirements and resignations. Four men called in sick that day. The chief and twenty-two others were on duty from 7:00 A.M. to 4:00 P.M. and another twenty-two—from 3:00 P.M. to midnight. When the riot broke out over there I had eleven men on duty. One captain was in charge; a lieutenant was standing by for emergency service and supervision; one man was jailer; another was at the desk to answer the phone; two detectives were upstairs trying to solve a murder and a patrolman was assigned to help them; and four men were out in two patrol cars trying to cover three square miles of streets!"

Yes, the city was safe that night, but the pastor and the city manager knew that the police played a very small role in that. The pastor knew from the Bible that war horses, chariots, and weapons are not adequate objects for faith. The modern equivalents are no better. It was appropriate for the pastor to ask what did make the city safe that night. The answer, that the lifestyle of the community was peaceful, leads right to another question. How can that peaceful style of living be encouraged? Do the neighbors know each other? Do they care about each other? Can the city help the people become acquainted? The pastor's own values and faith commitment will color the questions he asks, of course.

Statistics can be helpful in understanding the nature of the community and in raising questions for the community to deal with. One example should make the point that pastors can use data to help them be inquisitive educators in their communities.

Age-Sex Pyramid

Simple, yet potentially revealing for statistical analysis, is the age-sex pyramid. This is a device which can help the user gain insight into the composition of a given community with regard to two significant variables: age and sex. The pyramid is made up of horizontal bar graphs, each of which represents a particular age group, extending to the right and left of a vertical line. Normally the extension of the bar to the right represents female persons in the particular age group and the extension to the left represents male persons in the same age group.

The actual age-sex pyramid for the U.S.A. according to the 1970 census appears on page 164.

Suppose that this pyramid were not based on the total U.S. population but rather represented the figures for the three census tracts immediately surrounding a congregation called Reformation Church.

One might be impressed by the percent of aged people in the population, particularly women. Are those same percentages reflected in the membership of the congregation? Are there adequate programs available to meet the needs of the elderly in the community? Such questions allow the pastor to teach and learn. They lead to even more specific questions: How adequate are the health care delivery systems in the community? Do the elderly have adequate housing and transportation? Do the supermarkets cater to the needs of the elderly? Theological questions also follow: Do the elderly find meaning to life? Do they worship? How do they act as "little Christs" to others?

Another part of the age-sex pyramid that should catch the eye of the educator in the community is the relatively small number of

THE AGE-SEX PYRAMID

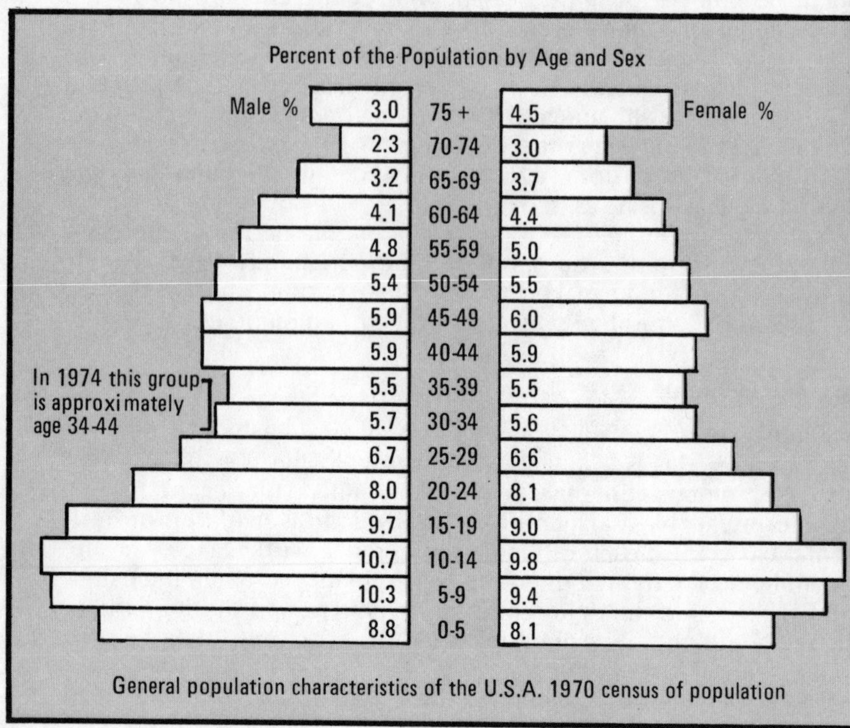

General population characteristics of the U.S.A. 1970 census of population

persons between ages 30 and 40. Remembering that these data reflect 1970, the reader in 1974 should remember that these persons would now be ages 34 to 44. These are highly productive years for most persons. These statistics suggest that in 1974 the lowest number of persons in the middle years of life were between ages 39 and 44. Many industries are beginning to forecast a severe leadership crisis for the next decade. They are short of middle-management persons who can be groomed for executive positions. Many a firm has found it necessary to retain high-priced consultants, many of whom had opted for early retirement, to assist the inexperienced and young in gaining management experience, but without risking the organizational stability.

The church also faces this leadership crisis since the potential pool of leaders is small for them, too. In the local congregation, older leaders who begin to feel that they should step aside for younger persons may discover that there are few persons who will logically assume leadership. The problem is compounded in the churches because they have often experienced a lessening of interest and participation of persons who are in their twenties. Whereas industry has begun to advance to younger persons into leadership positions and has provided experienced consultants to help them, the churches traditionally have lacked numbers of the very group that seems to be industry's solution.

In a time which seems to call for innovation and risk-taking, the churches should deal with an aging leadership. For the good of both the church and the community, the pastor as educator might ask: What are we doing to recruit and train leaders for tomorrow? Can we risk giving heavier responsibility to those who are younger than those we have been accustomed to trust?

Those large numbers of persons in the late teens and twenties also speak loudly. If it is true that Reformation Church and perhaps other congregations have not successfully reached or held on to the youth in their formative years, then use of the sex-age pyramid might reveal the actual challenge which is before the churches. A pyramid for the congregation parallel to the community's chart would reveal significant differences and could suggest programmatic responses.

If the pyramid was, in fact, a representation of Reformation's community profile, the pastor as educator might be asking: Are the needs of youth being met? Where are the values being formed? Are families doing their job? Are the institutions and churches making any impact? Difficult questions, to be sure, but the questions of an educator.

Finally we would need to look at the lowest age ranges. True, there are many children, but the remarkable drop in birth rates in recent years forebodes marked changes in the local community. As early as October, 1971, the U.S. Census Bureau declared the highly touted population bomb defused! As a result many communities are experiencing empty classrooms for the first time in decades. Some colleges are crying for students to fill their overbuilt dormitories. The teaching profession suffers from an oversupply in some sectors of the country. The pastor might raise questions about the quality of public education and ask whether such a time is not ripe for the qualitative improvement of our educational systems.

The community-oriented educator who serves as pastor of Reformation will also keep a careful eye on other things, such as the racial characteristics of the community and the number of women given significant positions of responsibility. Behind numbers are people who are brothers and sisters. The pastor will lead in raising to consciousness the humanizing behaviors that could mark social interaction and the justice which should be a part of the world.

Statistics can be confusing. They need to be questioned. They are, after all, simply tools to simulate real situations. By means of statistics one can construct a model whose characteristics can be studied in order to make reasonable estimates of things in the world which would otherwise be difficult to measure.

Changing Values

The bias of the particular reporter of statistics or the receiver of them can influence which statistics are given weight. Some persons will point to numbers of persons on welfare rolls and will assume that all persons on welfare are cheaters who are living off taxes paid by others. The pastor can teach by insisting on clarification of the numbers. How many persons represented the statistics are elderly, blind, crippled, and unable to work? It is true that some cultures have chosen to allow the infirm to starve, but compassion has been pressed by those holding Christian values.

Our western culture has appropriated some of those values, but they do change from time to time. When the Social Security Act was adopted in the 1930s, a specific value was written into the law, namely, that children would be better off if their mothers were to remain in the home to care for them. The Aid to Dependent Children provisions of that law were based on such a value. In recent years that value has been challenged by those who feel that mothers who apply for such welfare aid are not doing the best thing for their children. Thus many would encourage the mother with children to work and leave the children with others.

What is the issue here? Is it welfare cheating or is it a genuine shift in the values with formerly undergirded the law of the land? It is incumbent upon pastors to press for clarification. They should get behind the statistics, using them as means, not ends. As they do so, they will find that data give concrete examples to deal with in preaching and teaching. Pastors who are familiar with their communities will not avoid issues simply because they are complex. They will expand their ministry from personal problems to include the environmental causes of them.

Martin Marty is fond of telling seminary students that they must "serve two masters." He is not defying Scripture, just arguing that pastors are healthier persons when they broaden their interests. The congregation is served better then too. The data of the community offer infinite possibilities for the broadening of the interests of pastors. Pastoral concern of the type described above will also provide many ways for the congregation to follow its pastor into the community with concern that can be translated into mission strategy.

Planned Change

> "When you're preachin' the word of God you don't give a ——— about the world, do you?" The answer to this question of a Boston waitress is, "Yes, you certainly do!"

One of the serious problems pastors are required to deal with is the conviction of many persons that the church has no business engaging in social action in the community. Jeffrey Hadden's research convinced him that there was a great cleavage in the church (*The Gathering Storm in the Churches* [Garden City: Doubleday, 1969]). He found Christians divided, with most laity believing that the clergy should stay in their pulpits and not become involved with social issues. By contrast, those who have studied theology carefully see the relationship between God's love in creation, redemption, and sanctification and argue for a holistic view of God's continued concern for his whole world. They further see the world as humanity's assigned arena for witness to faith and service to all persons.

The theological dialogue in which pastors participate in their communities will center in concrete problems of which they become aware. Community problems are perceived differently by individuals, but usually some common definition of the problem emerges. Those people who shape the statement of the problems are quite powerful, though their power is often granted to them by default rather than by intent. The problem statement dictates what will be worked on and has implicit in it a variety of possible solutions. Since defining problems and proposing solutions are basic planning functions, we can call all those who do these things planners. Pastors will want to identify the planners in their communities. Often they will find persons in city hall who hold the title "planner."

The city manager also served as the chairman of the city's planning commission and as the chairman of the Board of Zoning Appeal. The city charter thus gave him a great deal of power as the convener of those bodies which had control over man-made changes in the city.

An oversimplified cartoon hanging above the manager's desk depicted a man pushing a large rock. The cartoon asks, "Are you a pusher or a rock?" Some persons try to change their communities to meet their own values. Other persons are sedentary, and perhaps unmovable, ignoring the values which undergird their lives. They may be ignorant of their values, or they may not know how to make them operational.

In his *City of God*, Augustine pondered how it was possible for people to display such loyalty to the earthly city, Rome, when the City of God was available as a more worthy object of human dedication and devotion. The city was seen as a vision, an ideal setting with perfect relationships. Augustine's problem was how such a vision could be made operational.

It is not necessary to push such an argument to the extreme position which suggests that humankind will bring in the Kingdom of God on earth in order for the elements of such a vision to be utilized as criteria to judge present human behavior. Pastors as educators can help persons in the community label aspects of such a vision. They have the opportunity to help those they talk with reflect on the quality of life and the nature of the relationships that are shared in the community. The vision itself should provide guides for next steps. Pastors, and others, can ask, "Is what we propose in harmony with our values and the vision which we have constructed for our community?"

The manager's city had a master plan because at one time planners were presumptuous enough to think they could plan for now and tomorrow. Elaborate scale models were constructed and charts with multi-colored splotches and codes were printed. The master plan was the tool of both the Planning Commission and the Board of Zoning Appeals. When a new usage for a particular plot of land was proposed, or when a zoning variance was sought, the color and code on the charts quickly gave the commission and the board the information they thought they needed. If the proposed building conformed to the way the planners had conceived of the use of the land at the time of the master planning, then permits would be granted. If not, then the answer would be negative.

Given his theological orientation, the pastor might ask who the planner was. Was he all-wise? Have circumstances changed? What do the residents of the area have to say about it? Have people been remembered? Is justice being achieved?

Some odd things have happened in communities in the name of justice. Black people, poor people, and Jews have been kept out of some communities by zoning procedures. One technique has backfired in some places. It is the practice of requiring oversized lots for home construction. Often an acre or more has been required. Schools, sewers, and other services have caused a financial crisis. Large lots have tended to attract large families, and hence school needs have expanded. The need for adequate sewage disposal has required massive installation costs to be borne by each home owner through assessments, not only on the basic lines, but also in the feeder lines across all that acreage. The same added cost pertains to every service which is piped or wired to the house. In recent years the isolated homes have also been invitations to crime. The price of exclusiveness has risen dramatically.

In this age of town houses, condominiums, and apartments, second looks are being taken at such zoning practices. The pressures for new housing will continue to mount as the large numbers of teenagers move into their twenties in the next decade and as they marry and establish their own homes. Many a city manager sees the added revenue brought to the city from the taxes of the high rise. He may see also the different kinds of services required of the city. He probably is leading the way toward more flexibility in planning. He is learning that it is difficult to plan for future generations.

Pastors might try to bring to the surface the basic feelings and views held by the community's planners about the capacity of tomorrow's leaders. It is natural to worry about the abilities of those coming after to carry on as well as today's leaders. It is also presumptuous to assume that no one will be gifted by God in the future. Pastors' theology could guard against triumphalism in the community as well as in the church.

Some pastors will not be able to spend the time directly in finding and working with the community's planners. They may prefer to train the laity to ask the kinds of questions that Christian theology should bring to the planners. Discussions and studies in the local congregation on community problem identification and solution could help in this. What is important is that we realize how values held by planners are central to community problem-solving. Surely Christians will not want such planning to go on without their values being considered.

Planning is not easy. John DeBoer has pointed out that there are both research and planning tasks associated with the various steps in decision-making.[1] When a problem is identified, research into the assumptions and past policies should enable planners to outline the dimensions of the problem and suggest goals. When a broad goal is articulated, research on resources and models available should enable planners to identify alternative ways to proceed. When a choice is made as to the direction or way the problem is to be solved, then research can show the costs, the manpower needs, and the necessary timetable for planners to develop the alternative chosen into a detailed action plan. When such a plan is adopted, then the research task is to review the process and analyse any new developments so that planners can evaluate and recommend their responses. They can amend their action or terminate it.

Two idea systems that have dominated change thinking for some generations have been identified by Kenneth Benne, Warren Bennis, and Robert Chin (*The Planning of Change*, 2d ed. [New York: Holt, Rinehart, and Winston, Inc., 1969]). They have called the two counterposed ideas "the law of nonintervention and the law of radical intervention." Both of these are questionable to the Christian in their extreme form. One is based on natural law and ignores human stewardship of God's world. The other is based on conflict and struggle which ignores human responsibility to fellow human beings.

Planned change, one form of which is outlined above, seems to be a feasible alternative. It is intentional and experimental. It is people utilizing their given resources, harnessing energy and technology to work at solving the problems of individuals and their societies. It ought not be imperialistic. It is of temporal significance but not of ultimate value. It should be open to criticism and judgment. Any particular planned change does not have salvatory significance, but it may be extremely important. The Christian can exercise his or her own best judgment.

Working Together

Planned change requires collaboration among a wide variety of community actors. Benne, Bennis, and Chin argue that collaboration is a *sine qua non* of effective planned change. For the pastor the question of collaboration is: Will I compromise what I stand for if I work together with those who do not hold or even deny my faith? Christian pastors hold dearly to the scandal of particularity seen most clearly in the life, death, and resurrection of Jesus Christ. They wonder how their fraternization with non-believers or non-evangelicals will be viewed. Lutherans have attempted to deal with that problem by official position statements. One of these was the Evangelical Principle of the LCA. The Executive Council of that body said (August, 1962): "The evangelical principle means that official relationship with interchurch agencies will be established only with such agencies as are composed exclusively of churches which confess Jesus Christ as divine Lord and Savior."[2] The context of this principle was participation of congregations in city, county, and area councils of churches.

An issue in many communities in the late fifties and sixties revolved around Unitarian participation in local councils of churches. Lutherans refused to be allied with Unitarians in such councils and insisted on the evangelical confession of the Lordship of Jesus Christ by all members bodies before joining. This principle was operative long before the action cited above. That action simply continued the practices of the merging churches which formed the LCA. The centrality of Christ, the scandal if you will, was thus of crucial significance on the question of inter-church relationships.

Within the commission which drafted the LCA Manifesto of 1966, there was some debate over this evangelical principle. The principle was not challenged per se, but the application of it by individual congregations in their particular communities was questioned. The charge was that some pastors and congregations were using the principle to avoid cooperative efforts with others in the community. In particular it was said that some were avoiding involvement in efforts to achieve racial justice by misuse of the principle. In direct response to that charge, Proposition Eight of The Manifesto called upon each congregation "to lift its voice in concord and to work in concert with forces for good, cooperating with church and other groups participating in activities that promote justice, relieve misery, and reconcile the estranged."[3]

The clarification provided by Proposition Eight is an example of the best of the two-kingdom ethic at work. While inter-church organizations should be constituted only by those who share a common confession of faith in Christ because presumably they exist to expound and promote that confession, associations that work solely for justice are quite another thing. There is no theological bar to Lutheran participation in such efforts.

Pastors in the community can give guidance on such matters. Their task is to bring their best theological resources to bear on questions in the particular case. They ask: What are we planning for? (To what end?) and how are we planning? (with what means?) As educators in the community they will try to lead their fellow Christians to take responsibility for their community. Pastors avoid the triumphalism of dictating to the world its form and mores, but they will work energetically for justice and will be living witnesses to God by word and lifestyle.

The members of the congregation struggle daily with similar problems in their offices, homes, and community organizations. By their own involvement in community ministry, pastors can gain experience vital for enabling the ministries of their people in such situations.

Contract Building

Individuals recruited to the profession of city manager often have not been prepared to deal with people. That is changing, of course, but until recently such managers usually were sought among the engineering professions. After all, a manager was to be a technician bringing to city government the goals of efficiency and productivity directly from industry. If big business could successfully solve its production and distribution problems, then surely the city could adapt the methods to its own tasks. But the city is made up of people, all of whom are in some sense the boss. Among all the diversified people are conflicting ideas and values. They need to be reconciled.

Once many in the church thought that a simple transference of loyalty from church system to community would solve many issues. We became aware of our own heavy focus on our church system to the exclusion of what was going on around us. A mass of muckraking literature appeared beginning about fifteen years ago. We read with glee Berger's *Noise of Solemn Assemblies*, Berton's *The Comfortable Pew*, and the most memorable of all, Winter's *The Suburban Captivity of the Churches*. Each of these fine books made a contribution, but the overarching effect was a ganging up on the church. For a number of years we were hypercritical. The present-day cynicism within the church about hierarchical structures may flow as much from the impact of the literature as from the evils which the literature attacked.

Contract-Building Skills

Now a shift has been made. Church systems are beginning to accept responsibility for communities. It is said that today more dollars are being given to the church than ever before, but most of those dollars are remaining in local hands. This is evidence of pressure to serve the community. It is not unlike the pressures on the city manager to deal directly with the people of his city rather than serve them through distant offices and departments. This shift to the local community can be viewed as a very positive development highlighting the particular needs of particular people.

The manager has found he must focus on services to particular people who not only want services, but also want to be recognized as significant actors within the city. That insistence could result in a renewal of individualism promoting isolationism or, as the pastor might see it, the result could be a new opportunity to acknowledge humanity's dependent state.

Interdependency is the better way to see human nature today. It is the lesson being taught by the environmental crisis and by urban living. Pastors as educators have their opportunity to call attention to the qualitative dimension of our interdependencies, but to do so they must learn about the nature of the expanding urban life which marks our culture. A role for them is that of contract-builder.

In our society the organization of life may be depicted as a series of concentric circles. The smaller the circle, the greater the probability of face-to-face, or primary, relationship. The larger the circle, the greater the probability of anonymity, isolation, and loneliness that attend secondary relationships. Folkways and mores function as controls in the primary relationship circles, whereas formal controls like the police, regulations, and courts mark the more complex urban societal rings.

At the center of the smallest circle, the household offers maximum face-to-face opportunities to relate. When households overlap in their activity, a somewhat larger circle of relationships called the neighborhood is formed. Interhousehold friendship and visiting patterns take place in the neighborhood; so do car pools and koffeeklatches, providing communication links. The neighborhood offers the households small-scale order, mutual aid, and friendship beyond the home.

Beyond the neighborhood, larger units appear in a vast array. Among the names we may give to these are ward, councilmanic district, or suburb. Whatever the name officially, they may be called "communities of limited liability," as Scott Greer and others have noted.[4] Few persons risk all that they have for such a community. With increased mobility persons grow shallow social roots. If the job is changed or if the neighborhood deteriorates, most people give little thought to the ward they live in. They simply move on.

There are even larger circles of organized life: the city, the metropolis, the state, the nation, the world. Most of these seem unmanageable to the average citizen. Apathy thus marks our society. Life is touched by hordes of strangers. They drive buses, collect tolls, pass laws, service vending machines, and the like. Who can know them all, or care about them all?

The issue for pastors should not be simply how many relationships there are, but the nature of the contracts which different persons have with others. Contract-building is a skill important to develop. At every level of social interaction contracts are important. Some contracts are explicit and detailed. Other contracts are implied and vague. Most are not in legal language, but consist of expectations that one may have of another.

What pastors may make clear is that all contracts require a degree of intentionality. Regardless of who initiates the covenant or of the possible one-sidedness, the parties need to agree for a contract to be binding.

Human beings tend to enter into contracts either for defense from a common threat or for the achievement of some superordinate goal. These two reasons represent points on a continuum and, of course, motives are often mixed.

Contracts based on a perception of a common enemy are the easiest to effect. Forts, castles, and compacts have been constructed for common defense. In our time we have seen NATO and SEATO.

At the hearings of the Select Committee of the U.S. Senate investigating the Watergate break-in, we see evidence of a paranoiac fear of enemies.

One of the weaknesses of alliances built on the perception of a common enemy is that with the removal of the enemy the contract is ended. That may not be bad unless institutional paranoia takes over and new enemies are contrived for the sake of maintaining the relationship. More stable are contracts that grow from common goals. These are also more difficult to effect, since in any community these days interests are diverse.

Community Organization and Community Development

Let us distinguish these two major integrating forces by the terms *community organization* and *community development*. It is not exactly precise to label community organization as an effort to build contracts as a defense from common enemies. Likewise, it is somewhat limiting to utilize the term community development to attempt to find and act upon common goals, but the tendency identified with each is accurate. Pastors in the community may be leaders in either of these two efforts. In each case they would be helping persons who happen to live in the same community establish contracts with one another.

The most famous slogan associated with community organization efforts is that of the late Saul Alinsky: "Rub raw the sores of discontent." What Alinsky knew from his experience was that there are many malcontents in every community, and in order to change a situation those discontented persons need to be identified and unified around a common problem. The organizer sent in by Alinsky was always instructed first to be a student of the community watching carefully for signs of discontent.

Pastors who pay attention to the voices of the community can also pick up such signals. Of course, if they ignore the cries or the symptoms of social pain, the voices of the community may become silent in their presence. Few persons want to reveal their problems to unsympathetic persons who might possibly be from the enemy camp. On the other hand, they gladly speak to one who seems to represent hope for change of the condition.

Pastors who help coalesce community persons for the purpose of improving social conditions, and do so by labeling someone "the enemy," may soon have deep spiritual problems to deal with. Take the case of Don Strong, pastor-organizer. One set of cries Don heard clearly was from residents of a slum tenement. The roof leaked and generally the conditions were so poor that numerous code violations were on file at city hall. Don organized the residents and helped them file official complaints. He was even able to guide them to a successful rent strike. The deeply felt anger seemed to explode in the numerous meetings. The owner, out of fear for his safety, negotiated through his attorney and would not set foot on the property. Don thought little of this until after the conflict presumably was over. The tenants had won. The repairs were made, but amidst the victory celebration Don heard the clear threat to the owner's safety, "If that bastard ever so much as shows his face here, I'll kill him."

How does one undo the conflict which served to surface and solve an injustice? That was apparently never a problem for Alinsky, but it is for pastors. Their assignment includes the reconciliation of enemies. It is "both/and" for pastors in community organization. They must work for the elimination of injustice and for the reconciliation of persons.

Community development efforts, by contrast, may be undramatic and painfully slow. Since perceiving a need by oneself is more motivating than having someone else label the need, a major task of community development is to increase individuals' perceptions of the need for change. One way for this to happen is to use the "go and see how someone else is handling it" style of learning. We in the church are notorious for keeping our successes to ourselves.

The case of Fred Salt may illuminate community development. He found himself the pastor in an economically depressed rural town. The young got out as fast as they could. There was no pride and little vision. Fred knew that the task would take time and that an initial success was necessary. He saw no enemies to fight, since the enemy was in fact in the psyche of every resident of the community.

The project that he found to spark some new life was a tennis court. Land was found in the public park. Sod was removed and the underlying clay made ready. Old fencing was found and a donor came forward with part of the new fencing required. The service club promised to pay for the rest. Volunteer labor appeared at his urging, and Fred promised to give tennis lessons two days a week all summer. It wasn't long before a town meeting was called to discuss the next project and the development of the community was underway. A new spirit began to prevail.

Two terms have been used here, community organization and community development. Actually what has been said is not to be construed as definitive of either process. The examples served only to highlight two kinds of contract-building efforts which pastors in the community may find helpful.

A subordinate art of contract-building is negotiation. The Scholarship, Education and Defense Fund for Racial Equality (164 Madison Ave., New York, N.Y. 10016) put forward some simple rules for negotiation some years ago. These included strategies and ideas for getting ready to negotiate for consideration by pastors who would be educators in their communities. Such pastors probably will find themselves in contact with persons and groups of persons who have labeled problems and have identified persons in power positions who presumably have some ability to affect the conditions which require correction. These rules can help pastors relate in a meaningful way.

Art of Negotiating

Negotiators need to demonstrate to their opposites that substantial community support is behind whatever they are asking for. They need to have collected all the information required for the strongest possible case. They also need to have provided for clear communication with those they represent so that inevitable compromises can be judged acceptable by the body represented.

In actual negotiations, begin by describing the situation which you wish to change and upon which your demands are based. Anger should be in the facts and not in the negotiator's voice or behavior. One person should be the spokesman, but others can be called upon to discuss matters of which they have special knowledge. One should never argue with teammates in public. Unity is important for a negotiation team.

Negotiators should not allow themselves to be sidetracked to discussions unrelated to the purpose of the meeting. If something unforseen occurs, simply ask for a recess to re-group the team. A negotiator should never conclude a session by saying, "That's a deal," but owes it to the group that sent him to say, "I'll report this to my supporters." The limit is to say, "I'll recommend approval of our understanding."

Instruction in the art of negotiation can be a significant service performed by pastors. They thus can help maintain the dignity and mutual respect of persons for one another. They can, by this means, promote honest representation and integrity among all parties and encourage persons to take each other seriously.

How does one become a contract-builder? The answer begins with genuine caring for all of God's people in the community and continues with tangible efforts to know them personally. It includes identifying their needs and helping them express themselves. These efforts, like planned change, are temporal. Of course all efforts by human beings are that. Only God effects ultimate objectives. Among fellow human beings is precisely where we are called upon to be the representatives of God's own word.

Once again, let us emphasize the conviction that both pastoral and educational ministries are inclusive ministries and are carried out in the community and in the church by men and women who know themselves to be called as representatives of God's word and his church. Hopefully every pastor will serve as an example through personal involvement with the local community, and these involvements will instill greater appreciation of the ministries parishioners can perform.

The concept of pastor-educators as both teachers and learners is a challenge to them to be open to new insights even as they witness to the faith which has been handed down to them. This is a clear route toward making pastoral and educational ministries more effective.

NOTES

1. John DeBoer, *Let's Plan* (Philadelphia: United Church Press, 1970).

2. Minutes of the Second Biennial Convention of the Lutheran Church in America (Philadelphia: Board of Publication, 1964), p. 231.

3. Donald R. Pichaske, *A Study of The Manifesto* (Philadelphia: Board of Publication of the Lutheran Church in America, 1967), p. 205.

4. Scott Greer, *Emerging City* (Glencoe: The Free Press, 1962).

4

ORGANIZING FOR ENABLING

Of the best rulers
The people only know they exist
The next best they love and praise
The next they fear
And the next they revile.
. . . But of the best when their task
is accomplished, their work done
The people all remark, "We have done
it ourselves."

—Lao-Tse

A most important part of the teacher's role is to communicate to students his own valuing of learning. Teachers motivate young people by their own motivations. Learners learn to like to learn from teachers who exhibit the intellectual accomplishment of regularly acquiring and acting on new knowledge.

—C. Glen Hass

A living faith can be inspired
only within a community that has hope.
The adage that where there is life, there is hope
might better be reversed to read
that where there is hope, there is life.

—Philip H. Phenix

Young people hate grown-ups for many reasons. One of the reasons is that they feel grown-ups' minds are fixed and limited. Whenever they meet a man or a woman who does not always say what they expect, who tells them novel stories about strange aspects of the world, who throws unexpected lights on what they sadly know as ordinary dull life, who seems as completely alive, sensitive, energetic, and zestful as they themselves, they usually admire him or her.

—Gilbert Highet

ON ORGANIZING

What does organization development have to say to the church's educational ministry? Are there ways to bring about change in the church and beyond which make use of the ideals and resources which people in congregations are currently not utilizing? Bob Bacher and Norm Wegmeyer suggest ways of answering those kinds of questions.

Bacher walks us through a short course on why congregation development should be a starting place for renewal and how that development can be effected. His educational position, a provocative application of Paulo Freire and biblical points of view, emphasizes that action or reflection taken alone as goals or means finally results in arrested development. Building on recent awareness of the power of institutions over our capacity to think and act profoundly, Bacher sets the stage for a presentation of the "outside-in" approach to change. He looks at this approach to change critically and gives a convincing argument for congregational change through a reflective, action-oriented, participative program.

Bacher summarizes his research and practice in congregation renewal and describes the important variables and products of congregation development which make up a rudimentary theory of change. One form of this theory is being tested now in the national ALC/LCA Parish Life and Ministry Project.

Conflict, consensus, and theological discernment provide other topics for Bacher. He uses Rollo May and the Blake-Mouton Managerial Grid © as additional resources. As the churches move toward recovery of congregational life, this chapter appears to be "must" reading.

Norm Wegmeyer pursues the pastor's leadership role more specifically. He takes an overview of Paul's writings and work and makes observations that suggest that Paul took his leadership role seriously. In this unconventional look at Paul, Wegmeyer at the same time presents a check-list of criteria for effective leadership. The leadership style Wegmeyer proposes is an excellent summary of current research in the field and pastors looking for such a review will find this helpful.

Wegmeyer also points out five areas of a congregation's education program where pastors can make significant contributions. Wegmeyer provides useful suggestions on the pastor's role in goal-setting, decision-making, enlistment involvement, leadership development, and evaluation.

The discussion of leadership development may be potentially the most helpful since it provides an almost manual-like approach to leadership training. Some will find this approach useful in evaluating or designing leadership programs. Being aware of differences among people in previous training, personal needs, and potential tasks means programming will have to be more flexible and varied than we have sometimes thought. This presentation is a step in that direction.

Regretfully, the discussion on evaluation in educational ministry programming is only suggestive. When thorough evaluation is an accepted part of the church's work, we can begin to build better models. Clearly, Wegmeyer wants to leave us with an openness to tough evaluation and the gains that will bring.

EDUCATIONAL MINISTRY AND CONGREGATIONAL DEVELOPMENT

Robert N. Bacher

Recently, a Lutheran seminary conducted a survey of parish pastors' continuing education needs. "Christian Education" was the next to last choice! Other items, such as "Dealing with Conflict in the Parish," "Making Worship Alive," and "Current Theology," headed the list. This could mean that pastors feel their educational ministry activities are in good shape. However, we believe this ranking illustrates the low image pastors have of educational ministry. Whatever pastors think Christian education is, they're not much interested in improving their abilities to make it more effective. Too many other elements of parish life are more important. Unfortunately, theological students also tend to share this opinion.

To those who think that educational ministry is of little importance, the essays in this volume are saying, "Wait a minute, not so fast." Maybe educational ministry is a handle for the development of a congregation as a living instrument for God's mission today and the years to come. Maybe it all depends on how we look at educational ministry.

A Subservient Activity

Education in the churches is a *subservient* activity. Education is not an end in itself; it serves something else. Educational activities are engaged in *because* they contribute to the achieving of other purposes. In other words, the Sunday school is a strategy, not a goal. But the moment educational activities are seen as subservient to larger and broader purposes, the question is raised, "What other purposes?" The underlying issue which most of the previous articles in this volume are struggling with is: education for what? This subservient view of education in the churches should not be so surprising unless we have been naïve about the overall education enterprise in society. For example, most of us are painfully aware of the way our schools perpetuate a societal view of black people as inferior because of systematic exclusion of the contributions of black people to the shaping of American history. Recently, a sociologist described the school as one of the sources of illusion of equality in our society. The school is a "nursery for endless striving," a place where the vacuous dream of equality of opportunity is perpetuated *ad nauseum,*[1] and reality is ignored.

A Brazilian adult educator, Paulo Freire, described the servant role of education in this way:

> A rigid and oppressive social structure necessarily influences the institutions of child rearing and education within that structure. These institutions pattern their action after the style of the structure, and transmit the myths of the latter. Homes and schools (from nurseries to universities) exist not in the abstract, but in time and space.[2]

Considering education in its subservient role also leads to another conclusion. Education may assert itself as a vital force in today's society and the life of the church as it asserts and exercises its *critical* function. Educational endeavors should be the very ones which ask, "Why?" and "Why not?" This would guard our churches and our society against jumping on band wagons, sloganeering, faddism, uncritical acceptance of supposed "truths," in short, a kind of willy-nilly consumerism toward life itself. Much would be gained if educational efforts attempted to be the very occasions for reflective, critical looks at what is happening to us all. While education, then, is serving larger purposes, it also must be a critic of those purposes.

If we look at education as subservient to other purposes (education for what?), we must consider three related topics: the nature of knowing, institutional influence on knowing, and the supposed neutrality of education.

The Nature of Knowing

What is knowing? Clue number 1: The Old Testament Hebrews evidently understood no split in the nature of knowing, that is, a separation between thinking and acting, as illustrated by the Hebrew word *vadah* for knowing. *Vadah* signifies a unity of feeling, knowing, and acting. To know something is like knowing someone, you encounter him or her, you participate in that which is known.

Clue number 2: In the New Testament, three words are needed to describe wisdom adequately: *sophia,* which sees the ultimate truths of God; *phronesis,* which sees what ought to be done in any given situation; and *sunesis*, which is discriminating, critical wisdom that can assess and evaluate possible courses of action. Knowing in a New Testament sense involves not only the vision to know God, but also the practical knowledge needed to turn that vision into action with the sound judgment to determine what course of action will best achieve the aim.[3]

These clues suggest that a pathway to a dynamic use of educational ministry in our churches is to assume that it has to do with both thought or reflection *and* action. This means that those occasions in congregational life labeled educational precisely have to do with reflection *on action* rather than reflection on reflection.

A good biblical word for the twin foci of action and reflection is *praxis*. We need praxis in our churches. Pastors need praxis; lay persons need praxis. What is it? Paulo Freire's definition describes the nature of praxis in a fashion close to the biblical understanding of the Word.

> As we attempt to analyze dialogue as a human phenomenon, we discover something which is the essence of dialogue itself: the word. But the word is more than just an instrument which makes dialogue possible; accordingly, we must seek its constitutive elements. Within the word we find two dimensions, reflection and action, in such radical interaction that if one is sacrificed—even in part—the other immediately suffers. There is no true word that is not at the same time a praxis. Thus, to speak a true word is to transform the world.
>
> An unauthentic word, one which is unable to transform reality, results when dichotomy is imposed upon its constitutive elements. When a word is deprived of its dimension of action, reflection automatically suffers as well; and the word is changed into idle chatter, into verbalism, into an alienated and alienating "blah." It becomes an empty word, one which cannot denounce the world, for denunciation is impossible without a commitment to transform, and there is no transformation without action.
>
> On the other hand, if action is emphasized exclusively, to the detriment of reflection, the word is converted into activism. The latter—action for action's sake—negates the true praxis and makes dialogue impossible. Either dichotomy, by creating unauthentic forms of existence, creates also unauthentic forms of thought, which reinforce the original dichotomy.
>
> Human existence cannot be silent, nor can it be nourished by false words, but only by true words, with which men transform the world. To exist, humanly, is to name the world, to change it. Once named, the world in its turn reappears to the namers as a problem and requires of them a new naming. Men are not built in silence, but in word, in work, in action-reflection.

> But while to say the true word—which is work, which is praxis—is to transform the world, saying that word is not the privilege of some few men, but the right of every man. Consequently, no one can say a true word alone—nor can he say it for another, in a prescriptive act which robs others of their words.[4]

There are similar calls to a discovery of praxis coming from such diverse areas of endeavor as theology,[5] business corporations,[6] and sociology.[7] By raising the question of the unity between reflection and action, we are developing an active stance toward learning which suggests more use of participatory methods in Christian education, action *on* the world and reflection on that action.

In this light, it is possible to interpret the various definitions of educational ministry which are emerging.[8] Consider the Central Objective for Educational Ministry in the Parish, developed jointly by The ALC and the LCA:

> The central objective for educational ministry in The American Lutheran Church and the Lutheran Church in America shall be to assist persons to perceive, respond to, and participate in God's continuing activity and revelation, particularly in Jesus Christ, in the human and Christian communities as they deal with their continual life involvements of being a person, relating to persons and groups, and living in society, culture, and the physical universe.[9]

To implement praxis related to this kind of objective it is necessary to get rid of the notion that to know is, therefore, to act.

To distinguish between knowledge as information and knowledge as awareness is also useful. Knowledge as information means information is stored or located somewhere and is retrievable. Storing or locating information is the function of libraries, computers, and memory banks. Right now, these are the best ways of coping with the exponential growth of knowledge. On the other hand, knowledge as awareness means that it in some fashion has the potentiality for action. Awareness implies I have knowledge in a form and shape that is mine and I can move on it. This kind of knowledge truly *in-forms* me and is not just available to me in some objective, abstract fashion. I act and I know; I know and I act. Or even more accurately—*we* act and we know; we know and we act. No one really *knows* alone.

Institutional Influence on Knowing

If the concept of praxis is desirable, there is also the question of praxis where and by whom. In other words, praxis does not take place in a vacuum, but rather within the context of some institution such as a local congregation.

In his book, *Where Faith Begins*, C. Ellis Nelson advocates that we:

> . . . remove from our minds the notion that the communication of the Christian faith is directly dependent upon any instructional agencies or methods and fix in our minds that faith is fostered by a community of believers, usually a congregation. Instruction is a necessary part of the life of the congregation, but instruction must be related to the life of the congregation.[10]

Similarly, in the examination of confirmation ministry (Yearbook in Christian Education I), C. Richard Evenson proposed:

> . . . that the whole Christian community be seen as the focus of confirmation education. . . . To the extent that the community lacks the characteristics with which its youth should be able to identify, the definition becomes a set of objectives for the adult Christian community to achieve.[11]

In the Lutheran Longitudinal Study, William Koppe sought to identify the major sources of influence in the life of growing children related to their faith and life. He emphasized the teaching aspect and the congregation's total life. His findings suggest that "the congregation must be continually involved in clarifying its mission, priorities, and goals. . . . It must then act as a resource to help them (the children) to achieve their purposes and goals."[12] The point seems clear. The development of the life and ministry of the congregation is an authentic subject for examination.[13] This area will be explored in more depth later.

Supposed Neutrality of Educational Efforts

Seeing education as a servant of larger purposes not only raises the issues of praxis and institutional influences, but prompts other questions. What kind of society is it that we work toward? How does commitment to that society or lack of it influence the ways we attempt to educate? Usually, Christian educators do not deal with these questions to any large extent. There is some kind of assumption that these questions are for "social action types" and have little, if anything, to do with educational ministry. Yet, the Christian faith has a deep concern for the pursuit of justice among people and nations. But this concern becomes an illusion if each pastor-educator is not wrestling in his own heart and mind with ways of sensitizing people to the need of societal change that supports justice for all persons.

The record, according to a recent historical study of the Sunday school, is not good. In 1832, the American Sunday School Union sent its agents westward with specific instructions, such as: "On the delicate question of slavery, abstain from all remarks; much injury may result from an indiscrete observation."[14] Or, there was the "selling" of Sunday school as a "good thing," supported by such slave-owner testimonials as:

> Some years ago my people were a very insubordinate people; it was very hard to get along with them, and the severest measures had to be used; but a few years ago missionary work was begun—the work of the catechism; preachers had to teach as we teach in Sunday school; their instructions were largely catechetical; and now I go to sleep every night with the sound of the songs and prayers . . . ringing in my ears, and I have now no use for any of the measures that were used before.[15]

Examples such as these led Robert W. Lynn and Elliot Wright to conclude: ". . . The maintenance of racial separation, which equals racism, was by word and deed nurtured by the Sunday school in periods when strides towards racial interaction could have been most beneficial."[16]

On the other hand, there were and are other instances, however uncharacteristic, where Christian education activities broke through this supposed neutrality. For example, in 1859 a Sunday school superintendent from Oberlin, Ohio, was jailed for two months in Cleveland for work with the Underground Railroad. Children of the Oberlin Sabbath School Association, all 400 of them, not only visited the jail but filled it up. Four days after they went home, their superintendent was released.[17]

Perhaps Joseph Williamson had the most straightforward way of making the point: "The first principle is that learning how to live is a larger and more urgent matter than learning how to know."[18] Because this is true, it is necessary for education to be in touch with its commitments toward societal change, and give up any notion of supposed neutrality.

CONCEPTS OF CONGREGATIONAL DEVELOPMENT

Since the influence of institutions on what we do and know is so pervasive and powerful, there is a need to reflect on institutional dynamics. One institution, the congregation, its dynamics and development, is a major concern.

Biblical Perspectives

To deal with the importance of viewing a congregation as an organization and some of the themes involved in congregation development and change, we start not with organizational, but with biblical perspectives. In his study, *Images of the Church in the New Testament*, Paul S. Minear detailed more than 80 minor and major images of the church (such as the body of Christ, unleavened bread, people of God, God's planting, or wedding feast) in the New Testament. Further, he described the role these images played in church and societal life. Though it was not evidently the primary purpose of his study, Minear provided a sound basis for congregational life and ministry development. Minear characterized the images of the church in the New Testament with certain key features:

> They are obviously communal. The formation and use of the images causes us to consider how we need each other. We will not produce, evidently, images to stir the mind and heart in our separateness but in our communal-ness.
>
> Images . . . will not often arise from the acute insight or the clever tongue of one individual alone, for even the greatest poet relies upon a poetic tradition. More often they will be the possession of a community whose commerce over the centuries with the given reality has produced an intensive repertoire of effective images.[19]
>
> We have seen reason to believe that church images exert their pristine power only when they are the genuine product of a vital communal imagination and when that imagination uses them to correct its own self-understanding, as a confession of its sin in not conforming to those images.[20]

Further, Minear pointed out that these biblical images of the church have specific purposes:

- To invoke imagination about what is possible and desirable;
- To stimulate critical analysis;
- To comprehend contradition between the desired and possible, and what is now present;
- To take action to remove contradictions.

> The image of unleavened bread thus bridged the new and the old . . . and at the same time articulated the eschatological character of the communal life. We may also note that the image was presumed to have imperative force; Paul appeals to it as the basis for handling a difficult disciplinary problem. The congregation must now do what it has not yet done. It must become what it is: the unleavened bread.[21]
>
> They (the apostles) were continually made aware, by treason within the church, of the need for more profound self-understanding on the part of particular congregations. The images we have thus far reviewed contribute to that self-understanding by inviting Christians to perceive

what happens in what happens. What actually happens when they as the church happen to eat together?[22]

The analogy presents us not so much with a picture to be visualized by the eyes, as with a continuing communal story in which all are engaged. Or, to put it in another way, the readers are invited, not to imagine a letter with its envelope and its address, but to recall the forces that have been at work in their own hearts and to accept their resulting responsibility.[23]

And the images are disposable. This means they are not truth-for-all-time. They come into being to serve a purpose. They are used; they are revised and replaced. Some images may remain vital longer than others, but all in all, the desired result is not interaction with the image itself but through the image with the reality behind it.

In the New Testament, we observe no sentimental fascination for the images themselves, such as a preacher or poet feels for a symbol of his own devising. The overarching interest is that reality toward which they all point (the triune God).[24]

Minear's insights suggest that a congregation needs to be involved in developing its possibilities, assessing where it is now, "recalling the forces at work," "to perceive what happens in what happens;" then it must identify the contradictions between its possibilities and its actualities. Throughout this process, the congregation should be reminding itself always that it is not making itself in its own image but in the image of the triune God, and it should be undertaking actions to remove those contradictions. Also, to keep the process ongoing the congregation needs regular communal renewing and updating of the pictures of itself. Minear's view of New Testament images offers *a basis for parish development*: to strive towards conversion of communal imagination.

An increasing number of congregations seem to be benefiting from following this conception of parish development.[25, 26] One experimental program in this area is the Parish Life and Ministry Development Project of the ALC and the LCA. About 200 congregations in the two churches began a process of planning and implementation. This process includes an intensive look at where they are, where they would like to go, and the translations of those desires into specific goals. Information about the congregation and its goals is then shared with synod/district and churchwide agency personnel working with the congregation to identify resources for achieving the congregation's goals. The results of this "partnership" approach to parish development will be reported later. The project design is described in detail elsewhere.[27] Our purpose here will be to identify some of the underlying concepts which help account for the fact that there is an increase among congregations in undertaking a communal search for potentialities, actualities, contradictions, and actions in a refreshing and recycling way. This kind of activity unleashes sources of energy, vitality, and commitment because such processes are expressive of the way institutions can develop and renew themselves.

We see five essential themes operative in congregations today and which will most likely be with us for the near future. These themes are:

A. Basic *assumptions* about congregation development.
B. Three *variables* of development in congregations.
C. The *products* of development: a theory of change.
D. The *intentional* parish relating mission and people.
E. Biblical/theological *discernment* of congregation development.

A. Basic Assumptions About Congregation Development

Congregations who engage in a planning/implementation effort have made a decision, conscious or not so conscious, that they will not move forward by only changing the hearts and heads of their members. In other words, an approach to change has been adopted which moves beyond individual growth and change. This is significant. This approach to change could be called a cultural approach, although the term is not completely satisfactory. Cultural does not refer to fine arts such as music, painting, or sculpture. Rather, cultural describes the process which attempts to create a culture, a holistic, total corporateness, a *connection* of people in their time and place. Daniel Callahan's definition is helpful: "A culture consists of people working for common ends, sharing some binding visions, agreeing on some values to be shared."[28] Perhaps the best way to get at this is to describe the two kinds of basic changes which are possible.

The first kind of change and the one usually more familiar to us can be called "inside-out." This individualistic approach assumes that the most important kind of change which can occur happens inside the individual, a reshaping and movement of that person's beliefs, attitudes, values, and perceptions. Powered by internal, personal modifications, this kind of change can move out into the environment of the individual and begin to change things there.

The second kind of change, which we are identifying as a cultural approach, can be called "outside-in." This approach assumes that with some development and change in the environment of the individual, the change experience begins to move inside the individual and results in some changes in individual attitudes, values, and beliefs.

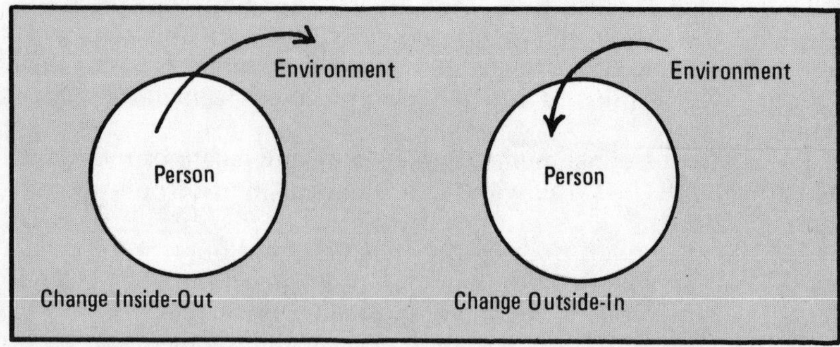

Change Inside-Out

There are some very eloquent spokesmen for both points of view. The inside-out approach:

First there is Will D. Campbell, a Baptist minister, who works with and speaks out for the poor, white person of the South. Somehow he bridges the aspirations of the poor Southern black person as well as the poor Southern white. He has done such things as conduct kitchen Eucharists in the home of Ku Klux Klan members. He writes about his disdain for institutions and politics. Political action and institutional change efforts lead to the illusion that doing is being:

> . . . Whatever institutional reordering may be demanded because we trusted in deceptive words will not spring from sociological analyses and projections, but from a renewal, a repentence, a "right-wising" that takes place within the fellowship of those individuals who proclaim Jesus Christ as Lord, and ourselves as your servants, for Jesus sake![29]

This point of view needs to be taken seriously because it reminds us that too often the church lets the "world" write the whole agenda, which means, for most of us, letting partisan-oriented politicians and governmental agencies define the issues. Campbell is imploring that we not neglect: (a) the revolutionizing of people's hearts with the gospel's radical meaning of love, and (b) the church's participation in defining the issues and problems. For our purposes here, we list Campbell as an advocate of inside-out change in that for him the changing of hearts is primary and the "one thing needful."

Similarly, Charles Reich, in *The Greening of America*,[30] evangelizes for the position that a radical transformation of consciousness is already going on in the hearts and minds of those people now under the age of 30. Through them, love, healing, joy, peace, and trust will abound. Such an achievement will come about naturally and internally, and there need not be any corresponding use of politics or strategies of change in institutions or society.

While Reich's message runs the risk of creating a passive, let-it-happen response among people, it does highlight the significance of consciousness change. How many governmental, volunteer, and church programs for social change become ruined precisely because of the oversight that social change *is* related to individual consciousness change and that, in fact, most long-term change is sustained because there was a "mind change" in individuals? Reich seems to have captured the ennui of most liberals resulting from the over-expectation of social programs in the 1960s.

Third, Carl Braaten, professor of systematic theology of the Lutheran School of Theology in Chicago, in his book, *Christ and Counter-Christ,* is seeking to restore an appreciation of the great Apocalyptic themes of biblical faith. Braaten counsels:

> St. Paul said, "Have this mind in you which you have in Christ Jesus." Find out where your head is at, get smart. Minds do not become liberated in mass, but one by one. Seize yourself; get hold of your instincts, feelings, imagination, or you're doomed to be just a quantum in a mass techological society. In the present situation, the revolution will have to become more religious than political. Politics is helpless in the face of the mass techno-society. Revolutionary changes in political structures do not reach down to the infra-structures of personal reality. In a society of material satiety, what is there for the individual whose alienation is at bottom a sickness of the soul, sin, cynicism, despair? In our society it is the children of the affluent, who have not personally suffered the miseries of poverty, legal injustice, cultural deprivation, who are searching for a therapy of soul, that a political revolution cannot provide.[31]

As Campbell reminds us of the need for individual transformation by the radical meaning of the gospel, and Reich reports what he sees as individual transformation in youth culture, Braaten too is skeptical of only political and structural change, because the individual is too likely to remain untouched. He also passionately pleads for each of us to get our heads on straight so that we are aware of where we are going.

And fourth, as the book of Proverbs says it, "Keep your heart with all vigilance, for from it flow the springs of life" (Proverbs 4:23).

According to these exponents, congregations with an emphasis on *corporate* response are wasting their time because they are monkeying around with the institution.

Changes Outside-in

But maybe these congregations know something.

Some spokesmen for outside-in change:

First there is Amitai Etzioni, whose efforts over the years as a sociologist and researcher at Columbia University, and his participation in many governmental and institutional programs of change have led him to exclaim that we might as well be honest. While all the very American rhetoric supporting individual change is certainly impressive, the actual record is something else. Using such examples as changing people's smoking habits or developing safer drivers on the roads or getting addicts off heroin, he concludes that it may be more hopeful to change the environment around us than to *start* by changing basic individual attitudes. Just one example from a cost effectiveness point of view: it costs $88,000 per life to attempt to improve driver behavior through driver education, while (using 1971 figures of 59,220 Americans killed on the highways) it required $87.00 per life for the use of seat belts. Yet we continue to emphasize driver education while strong laws for car safety (which are already on the books) are rarely enforced with car makers.[32]

Second, Jesse Jackson of Operation Breadbasket in Chicago proclaims:

> I don't believe you can change the hearts of a lot of tyrants, but you can change the economic alternatives under which they make decisions. When the executive of a large company sees minuses appear on his computer where he once saw pluses, his conduct changes even though his attitudes might not change measurably. You don't strive for love between institutions; you strive for love between individuals and justice between institutions. Sometimes justice has its own way of creating, if not love, at least respect.[33]

Third, Jerome Bruner in the field of education suggests that most of basic human development has not occurred or even been started by changes in attitude but rather through external development of tools. Changing the environment works back toward change in the individual. Thus Bruner advocates working with learning environments around individuals, rather than focusing first on individual attitudinal change.[34]

This conclusion has led him recently to speak of the need for "a community of learning" in schools and all educational enterprises whereby a supportive communal situation is fostered.[35] From recent research, he cites the increase in scholastic performance, self-worth, and pride among children tutored by older children and the very substantial increase of those same qualities among those doing the tutoring. Cross-age tutoring may be one handle for forming communities of learning which are supportive, challenging *environments* in which individuals may grow.

Fourth, Joseph Wold, a Lutheran missionary, and others in Liberia report the disasters of trying to work with individual conversions in that country. Operating out of at least one strand of missionary tradition, they have moved toward working with the decision-making structures of the village which they enter and in which they live, and have reported dynamic results as measured by adult baptisms and number of confirmands.[36]

Fifth is Daniel Callahan, who asks questions about one of the largest societal problems we have today—biological ethics, relating to such things as organ transplants, genetic engineering, prolongation of life, and behavior controlled by psychosurgery. He notes that individual solutions and individual decision-making about these issues will never be enough; we must be about the creation of a culture in which values and beliefs are present to handle these kinds of problems. He points to the *limits* of individual decision-making:

> One function of a culture is to make up for our deficiencies and private wisdom, to take some of the burden of truth-seeking off individual shoulders, to save us from going to the mat on each and every question, to allow us to know things with our feelings which we do not know by philosophical standards in our heads. To be sure, every individual will have to seek the truth at some time. But he should not have to do it alone and should not always have to do it. The culture should assist him.[37]

Which approach, the individual or the cultural, offers the best handles for the creation and sustenance of God-responsive life in our congregations? Both, of course. The weakness of the outside-in approach is that it may not finally result in transformed individuals who are able to live on their own with a minimum of environmental support. On the other hand, the weakness of the inside-out approach is that while individuals get "turned on," they are generally unable to put their growth into practice, and not much really happens in the way of institutional or societal change. However, while affirming both approaches, it is quite a different question to ask, "Where do we start?"

We are advocating starting with the cultural approach to change in the development of our parishes. Congregations need to set about deliberately affecting the connections between people: people working together for common ends, developing some visions among us which help bind us together, and identifying some of the values which we can share.

Advantages of the Cultural Approach

But you may want to ask, "So what?" What are some of the differences this kind of cultural approach to change might make in congregations?

One difference would be more parish planning. There would be more struggling with the purpose of why we exist, more dealing with short-term goals (statements of what we're trying to accomplish), more identification of specific resources, and more emphasis on mutual decision-making. Time would be spent on projecting the life of the congregation into the future, more gathering of facts about ourselves and our community, more setting of priorities. A lot of this data would be written down so members could refer to it and use it to make decisions in committees, task forces, and church councils.

Second, congregations using the cultural approach would be faced with the necessity of learning how to use conflict. Conflict is often a result of attempting to make corporate decisions and responses; some members leave and others come because they are attracted to what the congregation is trying to do. We need to learn how to fight like Christians in the church, to indicate our dissatisfactions and our disagreements, but to stay with each other, to fight and return for another day, to say at times, "I don't really agree with this direction, but you have convinced me that it has value, and therefore I will support this decision." A strong case could be made for the fact that many of our parish activities, including worship, emphasize only an individual experience. We deliberately separate poeple as if to say, "We will avoid conflict and disagreement by keeping everyone in their separate little boxes, smiling at each other across the barriers, and acting as if all is well." Yet there is good evidence that when conflict is dealt with in organizations it is a major source of creativity.[38, 39] When conflict is confessed, if you will, it is one of the primary sources of new ideas, fresh insights, and energy to get things done.

A third difference which a cultural approach to change makes is that preaching is drastically affected. Preaching becomes a moment for parish development and not only individual development.

The illustrations a preacher uses to explain a sermon theme are usually the clue. Generally, many sermonic illustrations tend to rely either on nature or person-to-person examples to "symbolize" what God is like or what Christ means or what the Holy Spirit is doing. The last sunset that was seen and the last counseling case that was held are often sources of examples. But preaching from a cultural change point of view becomes reporting and interpreting what the

Holy Spirit is doing in and through that congregation, that total people of God in that time and place.

Difficulties

We should also identify some of the difficulties pastors and congregations are having with this kind of cultural approach to change. We can identify four. First of all, there is the unfamiliarity with a corporate language of faith and piety. This is what Martin Marty calls the "difficult jump" from the language of individual piety to the language of corporate congregational life and action. When it comes to individual-centered language, such as "dying to sin and rising to new life in Christ" (Romans 6), we feel at home. But to speak of the dying to the old and a projecting and fulfilling of the new: the death and birth connected with corporate congregational activity, the words fall strange on our ears.[40] If congregations are going to be more alive and responsive in our day and in the years to come, we will need to develop and be at home with faith language which speaks about us corporately.

Second, attitudes towards parish administration will need to be altered considerably. "Very few souls are saved by committee meetings" is a commonly heard phrase. This seems to imply that the group gatherings in congregations somehow don't quite measure up as a religious activity, while individual soul winning does. Yet surely what is put under the label of administration provides some of the best opportunities for applying the cultural approach to change in the parish. An expansion of thinking is needed to care for the congregation as an organization, as an activity worthy of the efforts and energies of lay people and pastors.

Digging a little deeper, we need to look at Lutheran attitudes toward organizational matters. Our position seems to have been that only the gospel is required and that we are not "hung up" like Episcopalians or Presbyterians who refer to their organizational structure in their name. With us, "organizational things" are a matter of indifference, we are free to change them, to make them more responsive to the needs of the gospel in our day. Now that sounds like a mandate of freedom in the area of organizational matters. However, these words over and over again may have led us to believe that only the content of the gospel is important, and that the way we go about doing things, the way we organize ourselves, and the way we make decisions are really *not* important.

It is not the same thing to say that organizational things can be changed and that we are free from any specific form, and to conclude that organizational matters do not count. Contrast the percentage of time spent in a seminary curriculum on the content of the gospel with the percentage of time spent on getting ready to be a parish pastor. This is an indication of where priorities lie at the present time, although some seminaries are changing their curricula.

Fourth, pastors and congregations are having trouble using organizational concepts and techniques. Since many of the terms and ideas come from business and industry, they do not seem applicable to the life of the church. Maybe the freedom with which Moses adopted secular ideas for his own purposes could offer encouragement to those who are hesitant. According to many Old Testament scholars, the structure, language, and the basic idea of *covenant* was lifted bodily by Moses from the thoroughly secular concept of a treaty between sovereign powers.[41] In other words, Moses (and others with him) adapted a secular format to their religious responses. Scholars can trace verse-by-verse direct parallels of biblical covenants with existing international treaties of the day. To read about covenants in the Scripture is, perhaps, to assume the idea dropped out of heaven into the minds of leaders such as Moses. But this was not the concept originated. When it comes to organizational matters, let us be free as Moses to pick and choose ideas, formats, and structures which allow us to be about our mission.

Benefits

Finally, then, what are some of the benefits to be derived from this cultural approach to change?

1. We will again gain some words and symbols for common reference and communication. Four Youth Staffers from the LCA Youth Staff Project drove across the United States together. In a matter of seven days, they developed an internal language of their own which made it difficult for anyone not sharing their experience to understand what they were talking about. They could produce with one word instant understanding, communication, and laughter without having to explain anything at all. They formed a temporary culture with its own symbols and communicative devices. Through the development of purpose statements and goals and the constant lifting up of the total corporate situation in sermon and liturgy, words and symbols are provided which are necessary for congregational people to communicate among themselves and then, in turn, to interpret that identity to people outside their ranks.

Are there symbols, verbal and visual, in your congregation which have instant communication value and do not even need to be explained? If such symbols exist, there is good evidence that the congregation has potential for understanding a cultural approach to its own development and renewal.

2. With a cultural approach to change, we absorb unwitting learning and knowing. In his book, *The Triumph of the Therapeutic*,[42] Philip Rieff comments that "a culture survives principally . . . by the power of its institutions to bind and loose men in the conduct of their affairs with reasons which sink so deeply into the self that they become commonly and explicitly understood." Thus the important dynamics of a culture may be in the "unwitting" part of it. It appears to us that we have laid too much stress on each individual "going to the mat" on each and every question. We have talked of "meaning" and "decision-making" and have forgotten that a lot of knowing and learning happens not so consciously. There are some things I just know as an American because I am part of an American culture. Surely there are things I just know and can act on as a Christian because I am part of the church. There is the story about the response of the old woman, who after listening to a sermon by Karl Barth, was asked what she thought of it, and replied, "I didn't understand a word he said, but he made God great." With supports around us, with the feeling that we're not going it alone, with people available for checking things out, with some mystery left in our worship, maybe we will learn and know things at a level which just is not available by isolating individuals and attempting to pour the content of the gospel into their heads and hearts. We gain unwitting learning and knowing. To keep unwitting knowing from deteriorating into unexamined assumptions and even overt stupidities, there should be times for critical examination and self-conscious evaluation (perhaps the annual congregational meeting is intended to be such a time).

3. Eventually, we would gain synergy in our efforts. Synergy most simply stated is two plus two is more than four; the total efforts produced cannot be explained by just adding up individual efforts. Something new, something more, something extra is produced as people work together. It's the kind of result that comes from some athletic endeavors. Because of a *team* relationship, the efforts of each member rub off so they produce something more and greater than any individual could be capable of. Sometimes knowledge is brought to consciousness (which was there all the time but would have remained hidden) as people clash and support each other. There is a tremendous scene in the film *Twelve Angry Men* where, as twelve men seek to reach a jury decision involving the life of a young man accused of murder, the men, suddenly, because they are not seeking to smooth out their differences but to activate them, arrive at a new insight about a fact in the case. The insight was present in the memory of many of the twelve people, but was brought to life only in their interaction. They remembered

collectively. They could have forgotten individually. "Do this to remember me," said Jesus. It may be that there are many understandings, perspectives, and insights actually hidden from our consciousness that lie within us all. How will we bring these out? In our individual prayer closets? Probably not. But as we clash and interact with each other, someone will say, "Yes, I remember now. But only as we talked did we discover this we knew all along." Synergy, two plus two is more than four, is one of the benefits of the cultural approach to change in our congregations.

4. Also, we would gain new ways to connect up our circles of culture. Taking a cultural approach to change means that we would not only attempt to develop one group of Christians in one place together, but we would begin to ask broader questions about interlocking cultures—for example, other congregations in the community, the clustering idea of congregations, the relationship between the congregation and the synod/district or the congregation, the synod/district, and churchwide agencies of denominations. In other words, as we learn to live out common aims and visions and values, we will find more cooperation with others more productive.

We have described an approach to congregational life and development labeled cultural. We identified some differences it can make, as well as some of the difficulties and benefits.

But how does it work? The next sections will describe some of the variables in such efforts for change and an understanding of some of the dynamics of congregational change.[43]

B. Three Variables of Development in Congregations

A monumental report of the Commission on the Nature and Mission of the Congregation was adopted by the 1966 Convention of the Lutheran Church in America at Kansas City. Why did this report not have a great effect on congregations? More especially, why did not that part of the report known as The Manifesto: God's Call to the Church in Each Place, along with the accompanying study book and the congregational planning guide, not result in hundreds, if not thousands, of highly developed and renewing congregations in the LCA? The report seemed to be sound theologically. It was the product of good thinking. And it was articulated well. Why did it have so little effect? One answer to this question, and it forms the basic thesis of this section, is that the report itself and the efforts to implement it did not take into account enough of the key variables in the development of a parish. Therefore, with a few exceptions, the content of The Manifesto never became part of the bloodstreams of congregations in an operational way.

The question becomes, "What are the crucial aspects in a congregation that, if effectively developed, would result in a renewed and renewing congregation?" We see three important variables in a congregation's life. They are: congregational climate, congregational tasks, and congregational logic. The assumption is that a focus of energy, effort, thinking, and human and financial resources on these variables produces development.

DEVELOPMENTAL VARIBLES

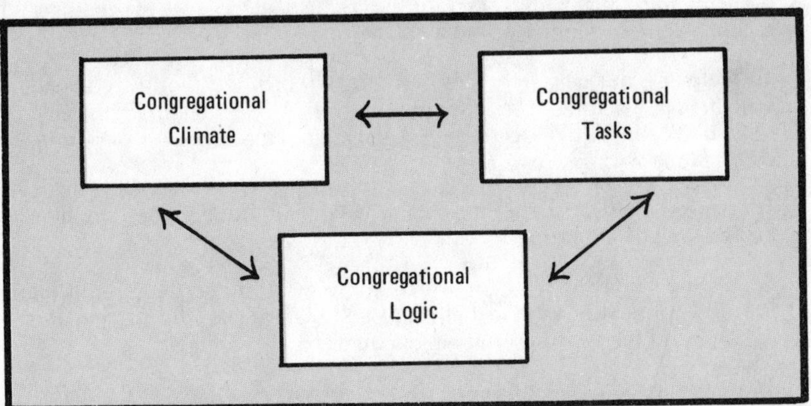

Congregational Climate

Congregational climate is defined as those processes through which a congregation operates, how it does things. In the literature of organizational theory and development, this is sometimes called the behavioral climate. For example, what is the quality of communication in the congregation? Is information flowing freely up and down and sideways, or is it consciously or unconsciously distorted and withheld when it would assist in sound decision-making? How is conflict handled? Is its existence denied? Is it smoothed over quickly when it arises, or is it dealt with in a confrontative and problem-solving manner? Is candor present? Do people speak out their minds and hearts in constructive ways, or do they do almost anything not to speak the truth in love? Is critique (systematic evaluation) a valued part of the congregation's way of doing things? Are activities regularly evaluated? Is an attempt made to learn from what has been done in order to improve what will be done in the future? These four—communication, conflict, candor, and critique—are factors which make up the congregational climate.

Congregational Tasks

Congregational tasks are the activities related to the actual doing of the ministry and mission of the congregation—for example, worship, study, social ministry, and membership recruitment. These and others are the actual mission tasks which The Manifesto describes so well as a way of translating ideals into practical courses of effective action:

> To lift its (the congregation's) voice in concord and to work in concert with forces for good, cooperating with church and other groups participating in activities that promote justice, relieve misery, and reconcile the estranged.
>
> To welcome the new light shed on God's word and world by sound scholarship. To strive to deepen the inner life of its members through regular worship, the Sacrament of the Altar, the study of Scripture, meditation, and prayer.
>
> To appreciate its rich heritage of worship and to be open to new expressions of adoration of God.
>
> To be the family of God in which those who suffer the bruises of life find some support and help, the complacent are stirred, and the creative and the venturesome are encouraged.
>
> To equip its members through a deepened understanding of the Christian faith to perform their ministries in the experiences of daily life, at work and at leisure, in family and neighborhood, and as responsible citizens.
>
> To seek, welcome, and involve in its fellowship all men without regard to race, status, or background.[44]

Congregational Logic

Congregational logic has to do with what the congregation thinks of itself, how it defines its mission. How has it defined its mission in the past, how does it see its mission in the present, and how does it project its mission in the future? A dictionary definition of *logic* is "reasons or sound sense, as in utterances or actions, convincing force." A congregation's logic is its theology—explicit and implicit—and its values—what is important. A sound congregational logic exists when congregational leaders have reached agreements about the nature of the congregation's mission, about its short- and long-term objectives related to the resources it has or can develop, about its "audience"—who it is trying to reach—about its structures and policies, and about its development requirements for growth over the long haul. These agreements are generally written down, and changes in them are tested, altered, and acted on by many of the congregational members. The resulting document testifies to dynamic convictions of a pilgrim people in a changing world.

To develop a congregation means to change all three of these aspects of a congregation's life in a positive direction. To neglect one or two aspects means that development will not occur. For example, many efforts in the past have attempted to get a congregation to engage in some self-examination and planning related to its tasks. Without really affecting its logic and its climate, this effort can be predicted as one which will certainly fail. In some situations there have been attempts to build up the congregation's logic (for example, its theological understanding). However, if the behavioral conditions and the translation of the logic into specific congregational tasks were not sound, then little or no development occurred. Equally dangerous is the attempt to affect only the congregational climate by improving communications or, through small groups, improving people's relationships with each other, without really touching the definition of mission or its implementation.

One pastor reported how he and the leaders in his congregation had worked toward building relationships among themselves, only to fail miserably when they sought to define their mission because they fell back on precedents and past practices. In the terms of these developmental variables, he and his congregational leaders were able to affect the congregational climate, which did have some effect on congregational logic. Another pastor describes the diligent fashion in which he and a special task force used The Manifesto, the study book, and the congregational planning guide, only to have the resulting recommendations come to naught within the church council. Why? Again in the terms of the three variables, they were able to develop some understanding of congregational logic. However, because they had not dealt with climate, they were unable to affect directly the congregational tasks.

The diagram on p. 204 illustrates how two of the most well-known processes, improving communication and instituting sound planning practices, relate to these three variables. Improving communication means that people in the congregation are sharing relevant information with each other so that together they work toward implementing their mission. This means the climate is sound and they have something to communicate about: their logic, their mission, their reason for being. Planning procedures relate to the establishment of a vision of what can be (logic), and the setting and implementing of specific goals related to the fulfillment of that vision.

PROCESSES AFFECTING DEVELOPMENTAL VARIBLES

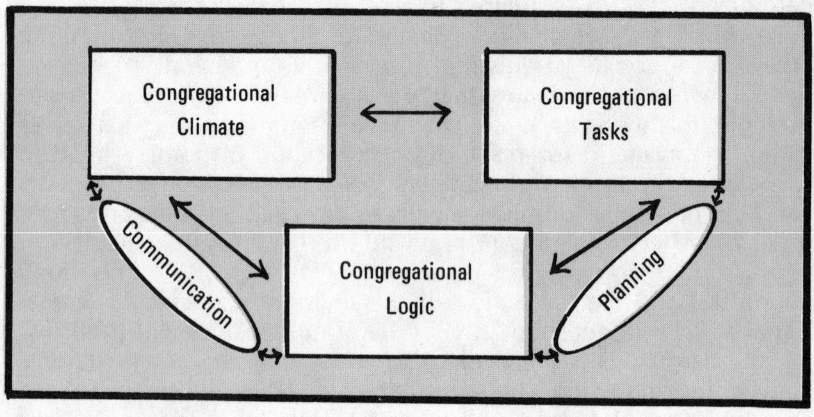

C. The Products of Congregation Development:
A Theory of Change

In the cultural approach, once the congregational logic, tasks, and climate are examined, there are three *products* which must be involved if a development approach to a congregation is to be achieved. They are:

The production of gaps between what should exist in a congregation and what actually does.

Assumptions about change, especially those held by the leaders of a congregation, are some of the keys to parish development. There seem to be three options. *Evolutionary* approaches emphasize change by encouraging making small incremental deviations from the status quo. While continuity is maintained in the midst of change, too little change is made quickly enough to anticipate the future. Accompanying evolutionary change is usually the feeling of being one or several steps too late. According to recent organizational research, most organizations seem to rely on evolutionary assumptions for their development.[45] *Revolutionary* approaches emphasize the failures of the evolutionary approach and are employed by persons frustrated by the oh-so-painful small bits of movement. They focus on breaking with what is and bringing in what is new and fresh. This leads to a "someone wins—someone loses" situation. Frequently, however, people who resist revolutionary changes can force a deadlock. Then nothing happens. *Planned or intentional change*, sometimes called development, has become more possible through new-found concepts and methods. Briefly, it means that a congregation must project an idea of where it wants to go. Its ideal, its potential, must be expressed, and then its people must develop pictures of where things actually are in order to motivate any desire to change. To produce an ideal description without attention to the actual may be nice as an intellectual project in imagining, but it does not produce change. On the other hand, to produce an awareness of the actual without the ideal is to engage in a kind of "so what" operation and does not produce change either. When both occur, then the contradictions between the ideal and the actual appear, and people become motivated to work on the contradictions. Recall the purpose of images of the church in the New Testament as described by Paul Minear, mentioned earlier. The images invoke the possible and encourage critical analysis for the determination of how things are. Then contradictions appear between the way things are, and the images and the contradictions can be worked on.

Pathways to close the gaps must be produced.

As contradictions or gaps are identified these contradictions can be translated into specific barriers to be overcome. The contradictions are raw material for tasks to be undertaken, for goals to be achieved. Pathways to accomplish these ends must be developed.

Energy is produced in people so they set about closing the gaps.

Energizing people is probably the most neglected of the three development products. There seem to be at least three sources of this kind of energy to get things done. First, there is the energy that comes from projecting the ideal, from identifying what the potential of the existing situation is. An excitement is induced which attacks the roots of fatalism and apathy. It is an attitude that says, "We can do something. We can have an effect. We can be potent in acting in our present situation as we begin to see what the potentials and possibilities are."

Second, energy is available from the handling of conflict. If conflict is not dealt with and confronted at least to the point that it is not immobilizing the persons involved, then much energy is used up in adjusting internally to a conflict situation by denying it or explaining it away as not important. However, as conflict and its sources are externalized, there is usually a thrust of energy for getting on with the job.

Third, energy seems to result from authentic dialogue. Freire writes, "The naming of the world, through which men constantly recreate that world, cannot be an act of arrogance. Dialogue, as the encounter of men addressed to the common task of learning and acting, is broken if the parties (or one of them) lack humility. How can I dialogue if I always project ignorance onto others and never perceive my own?"[46] Parish development happens as dialogue is activated, as members of congregations are treated as fellow subjects, not as objects to carry out a parish program. Again in Minear's terms, this is a *communal* search for potentialities, actualities, contradictions, and actions.[47] Parish development is not an individual quest by a pastor or a few elite members, but must engage as many of the members as possible.

D. The Intentional Parish: Relating Mission and People

The fourth theme relating to the development of parishes is that to a degree some of the people need to reach a consensus on mission for the congregation. See the written example of a congregation's consensus on mission and goals on page 207.

The existence of such a statement on paper does not, of course, guarantee that anything has or will happen. However, by reading between the lines it is possible to feel the drops of sweat and tears and perhaps even (symbolically) blood that go with such efforts at consensus on mission. In other words, this statement is the product of struggle. It is the result of the difficult process of trying to reach some logical, passionate implementation of the cultural approach to development and change by coming to some agreements on purpose and reason for being, and then the day-by-day working out of such purpose.

Is it really so important to reach these kinds of agreements, this kind of consensus on mission? It is worth the creation of conflict, the departure of some members as well as the reception/inception of others because they are attracted to a congregation which attempts to have a consensus on mission? We think so. And we would like to explore in some detail why we think it is important and why the struggle is worth it.

Person and Purpose

It is helpful to begin by examining some ways of looking at an individual which illustrate the importance of deciding on a mission, of having an intentional life; then the same process can be followed in analyzing the organization's needs.

A contemporary view of the individual built on long standing traditions and insights is that a person is a consciousness of two elements, love and will. This analysis is developed in Rollo May's *Love and Will*. May is a prominent psychoanalyst. His friendship with Paul Tillich has made him eager to deal with the deeply religious nature of persons as well as their psychological make-up.

CONGREGATIONAL GOAL SHEET

Name of congregation (SAMPLE)

Location ____________

Fill out a separate goal sheet for each of your important ministry goals whether or not you desire suggestions for implementation programs or resources from the pilot test office. Distribute copies as follows:

White copy: Send in with profile report form   Yellow copy: Give to center support team   Pink copy: Keep

1. OUR GOAL IS TO . . .
Develop an Area Shepherding Plan by the end of 1973

2. What we hope to accomplish by this goal is to. . .
- be able to minister more immediately to the spiritual and physical needs of both members and non-members.
- reactivate some inactive members.
- provide for shut-in visitation.

3. We see this goal relating to ministry area A.

4. What we are already doing that relates to this goal (present related programs and activities):
- Community canvass, 1971
- Some cottage stewardship meetings in 1972
- Have instituted a congregational telephone network.

5. Our present leadership needs and potentials relating to this goal:
- Present council members already live in strategic location in community
- Several new members are interested in working on a shepherding plan but would need to be trained.

6. The specific age or interest group(s) to which this goal relates most directly:
Family units in various neighborhoods

7. The settings, schedules, situations, and other areas in which we seem to have the greatest potential for acheiving this goal (You may use numbers to indicate settings. See Section VIII). 3, 4, 6, 23
We hope to be able to make things happen "out there" in neighborhoods rather than back here at the church.

8. We will feel that we have made progress toward this goal when:
- Some inactive members are activated
- shut-ins are visited regularly
- Contact with 10 or so new families have been made.

9. Major obstacles we see in implementing this goal:
- many of our members are elderly
- people don't like to go out after dark

10. Check one: We would X would not ___ like recommendations for the implementing of this goal.

11. We have the following local resources we plan to use in implementing this goal:
- Neighboring congregation which already has a shepherding plan in operation, a good Evangelism Committee.

May asserted that every person's task is to unite love and will. They are not united automatically by biological growth, but must be fused through conscious development. Love without will becomes sentimental and experimental. Will without love becomes manipulation:

> The old myths and symbols by which we oriented ourselves are gone, anxiety is rampant; we cling to each other and try to persuade ourselves that what we feel is love; we do not will because we are afraid that if we choose one thing or one person we'll lose the other, and we are too insecure to take the chance. The bottom then drops out of the conjunctive emotions and processes—of which love and will are the two foremost examples. The individual is forced to turn inward, he becomes obsessed with the new form of the problem of identity, namely, Even-if-I-know-who-I-am, I-have-no-significance. I am unable to influence others. The next step is apathy. And the step following that is violence. For no human being can stand the perpetually numbing experience of his own powerlessness.[48]

May described the love which blocks will and the will which blocks love. He identified apathy as the absence of both. The presence of the unity of love and will, on the other hand, he called care.

LOVE AND WILL

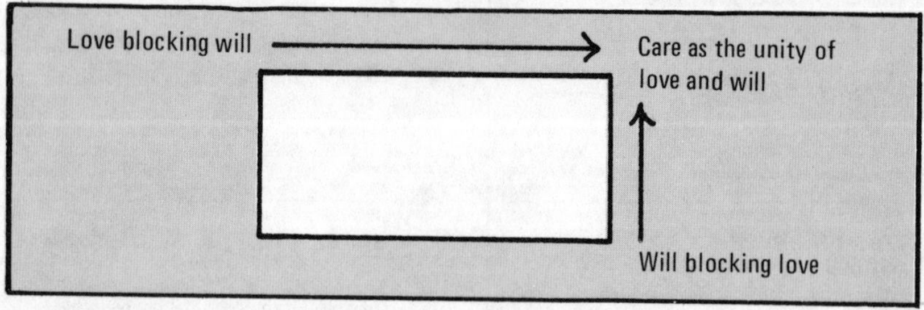

Contrary to much thinking of our day, it may not be that we have so much of a *love* problem. Although we do have that, we also have a very great *will* problem. It may be that we should develop liturgies which not only have prayer responses, such as, "Lord, teach us to love," but also, "Lord, teach us to will."

As can be seen in the diagram, the task is to activate in a maximum way both the capacities of love and will, not to pit them against each other.

Let's describe the role of will. It seems to operate by two processes—negation and fantasy. Will negates those situations in which the person feels strangled and constricted. Will destroys the first freedom, the original union (Adam and Eve in the Garden or cutting the apron strings of Mom and Dad), not to fight everything forever, although some of us never stop at that stage, but to activate choice —which woman or man to love, which groups to devote oneself to, which vocations to undertake. Negation, however, is not enough.

Fantasy must also be activated as an act of imagination. Rollo May used the word *fantasy* not to mean something unreal to which we escape, but as its original meaning, *phantastikous*, "able to represent, to make visible." Fantasy, then, is a language of the total self, communicating, offering itself, trying things on for size. It is the language of "I wish/I will," the projection and imagination of the self into the situation. Fantasy approximates and draws reality into the self and then pushes reality to a new depth. Again, recall the similarities of Minear's discussion of the role of images of the church in the New Testament as conceivers of possibilities, exercises in the imagination accompanied by identifying contradictions between what should be and what is. There is also similarity to the organizational concept of producing an ideal description of where the organization should be going, in contrast with where it is now.

Creative Organization

So much for the person. What about an organization? What May has done for the person, Robert Blake and Jane Mouton have done for the organization; they have defined an organization as a creative union of people and purpose. Putting these two dimensions together in a Grid © fashion they come up with the analysis shown on the following page.

By adding a scale of 1 to 9 to each axis of the Grid, which indicates that a concern is neither totally absent nor totally present but exists in degrees, it is possible to describe five different responses to the problem of developing a creative union between people and purposes. For example, in the lower right corner of the Grid is the 9, 1 position. This is an all-out drive to achieve purpose, to be concerned for what happens. In the upper left corner the 1, 9 position is an all-out concern for people's well-being, maintaining harmony among people. Likewise, a minimum degree of concern for either purpose is represented by the lower left hand corner, 1, 1. The 5, 5 position represents a kind of half-way point, a kind of compromise approach. The 9, 9 position, upper right hand corner, represents an all-out concern for people and purpose.[49]

Similar to May's assertion that we need an activation of the will, this organizational approach stresses the identification and fulfill-

THE MANAGERIAL GRID

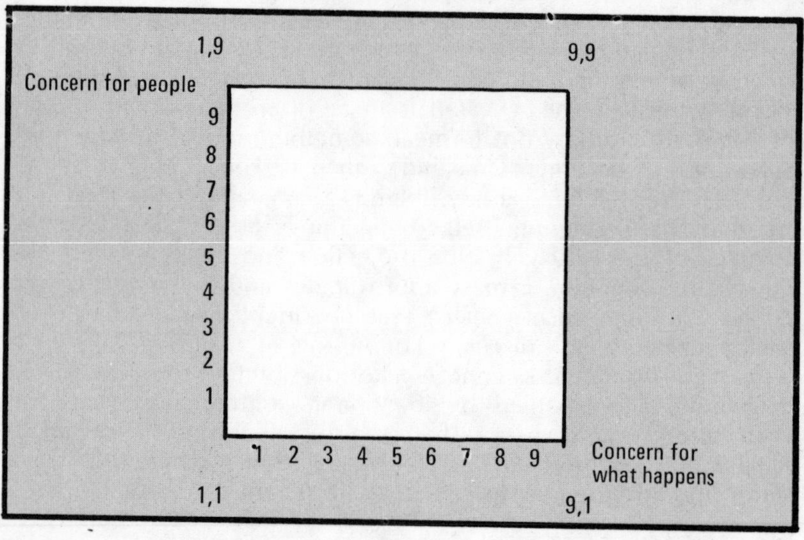

ment of the purpose of the organization that is more than just meeting the needs of the people in it. Perhaps two examples will help. When Peter Townsend took over Avis Rent-A-Car, he discovered a lot of people sitting around doing little or nothing. Many nonproducing people on the payroll did not contribute to, in his view, what an organization needed. People, he felt, who were not needed should be notified that they were out of a job, but he also gave them one year's salary to find a new position. He assumed that, ultimately, people are not helped by being retained in an organization when they are not really contributing to the fulfillment of the purpose. On the other hand, he cared for them individually by giving them financial security for finding new work.[50]

In a similar vein, Robert Keach, using the Old Testament story of Gideon gathering volunteers to go against the Midianites, exclaimed, "No member should be allowed to drop out of church until every effort is made to communicate with him and to love him. Nonetheless, once a minister and a group of people decide that they exist for a mission in God's world, then nothing should deter them from acting on this theological assumption."[51] On the other hand, "Clergymen are a group of people who, on the whole, seem to need a lot of acceptance and love. A man may choose the ministry because his connection to a congregation will provide him with support, attention, and the feeling of being needed. The ministry has been built on the premise that a clergyman will talk and act so as to make his parishioners happy and satisfied. This assumption puts him in an impossible bind."[52]

The reason, then, it is important and worth the struggle and risk to achieve a consensus on mission is that it releases energy and motivation for persons in organizations to accomplish a union of love and will, a unity of care both for people and for mission. This is the sense of mission that takes the congregation way beyond current talk about meeting the needs of people which is, after all, a rather weak expression unless these needs are identified specifically, such as: the need to influence, to exert will, to achieve purpose. The congregation will not be developed out of love *or* will but love *and* will; it will not develop on concern for people *or* purpose but concern for people *and* purpose. A consensus on mission is desirable because it attempts to reach to the depths of who we are as people and as organizations.

A consensus on mission seems to have three qualities.

A Genuine Consensus

It is a genuine consensus and not something else. For example, it is not a search for unanimity, complete agreement. There seems to be a lot of confusion around about what consensus is. Describing the need for a consensus of values within a society, John W. Gardner wrote: "Everyone does not have to agree in order for the consensus to be effective. It is only necessary that there be rough agreement among a substantial portion of those men and women whose intelligence, vigor, awareness, and a sense of responsibility mark them as shapers of the community purpose."[53]

From decision-making theory it is possible to describe how a consensus is achieved as two conditions are met: (a) understanding—everyone within the decision-making body feels that he has had the opportunity to make clear his own position and to understand the position of others; and (b) influence—that is, each person had the opportunity, and the time to influence others even though he may not have succeeded. Thus, a person may agree to a consensus, that is, buy into it, even though there is disagreement with the decision made or direction determined. Nevertheless, the individual can say something like, "I have had the chance to understand and be understood—I have had the chance to influence and be influenced. Therefore, since the rest of you feel this way, I will go this way, too. Come hell or high water, I will stand behind the decision. That is, I will not bad mouth it when I am away talking to someone else."

Achievement of a consensus takes time. Usually, it will not be achieved overnight. It involves a lot of struggle and hard work, many attempts at communication and influence among the people involved. One congregation took one year with a group of nine people meeting for breakfast every other week at 7:30 A.M. in a local restaurant to hammer out their eleven-line purpose statement and their theological and sociological assumptions. Only then did they submit the final statement to the whole congregation. Yet once a consensus is reached, it is not good for all time. It must be kept fresh and ongoing. Some congregations use their purpose and planning document as an integral part of their classes for new members. They also use it to develop a budget each year. The annual meeting, then, becomes a decision-making time, dealing not only with the budget but also with reviewing their whole purpose, assumptions, and goals. The various committees and task forces serving throughout the year are a means of providing feedback for continually revising the consensus, especially as it exists in its written form.

Capability for "Stretching"

The second quality of a consensus on mission is that it has in it some "stretching" capability. It is a projection into the future, a statement of possibility, a statement of the "not yet." It is a longing for something not now in existence. It is not just a statement of what now exists, of what is, of where we are, and analysis of our situation. This stretching quality is the key to organizational change and drives us very deeply into an understanding of our faith and theology.

Carl Braaten chided the Christian church for being locked into "too slow" a change process. Braaten called for the frequent and intensive use of our imaginations, our buying into the Kingdom of God "not yet," so that when some vision of the future becomes operative in our minds and hearts it will help us to learn what to say no to now. Profoundly he wrote, "I don't believe that a person can say 'no' unless he has captured an alternative with his imagination."[54] Thus, for Braaten, transcendence, which belongs at the heart of our spirituality, was an expression of the not-yet-realized-future of God, which is always coming upon us. This needs to be accompanied by a negation, a no-saying, which he believed to be a most releasing, freeing, activity enabling us not to be caught up in saying yes all the time, a kind of over-positivism toward ourselves and the issues around us. This parallels closely Rollo May's understanding about the nature of a person as a union of love and will, namely, the will has to be fed on fantasy to conceive possibilities to work back from, learning how to say no and yes to the achievement of these possibilities and dreams projected into the future. Christ is coming, Braaten pointed out, and that should stir us.

To get congregations dreaming about possibilities, there are certain helpful techniques, such as: writing mission statements; doing Bible study on images of the church in the New Testament; and imagining that you are a group of people who just got off a bus in the community and, as there are no churches present, your job is to create the kind of church you would like to see there.

Middle Range Level

The third quality of a consensus on mission is that it is of a middle range level. This means that it does not deal, on the one hand, with surface activities, nor, on the other hand, does it spell out the deep implications for each person. This is an important point. When recorded on paper, a statement of mission cannot have in it all the very personal things related to their faith and life that "turn individuals on." After all, a consensus is a set of agreements on some common ends, some unifying visions, some values to be shared. It is not a statement directing each of us to do our own thing in isolation and separation. There is a danger, then, in pushing for the statement to be *too* personal, just as there is a danger in allowing the statement to be so shallow, so general, so non-offending that nothing is really said. Thus, it is important that there be a quality of middle-rangeness to a consensus on mission.

One of the major themes of parish development is intentionality. Congregations need help in becoming intentional in their activities and ministries. They need to develop useful procedures for marking down and recording for themselves as well as others what they intend to do as the people of God. In this way, they can avoid the twin dangers of drifting into the future and thereby being completely subject to it in a reactive kind of way. Also they can avoid a kind of intentionality that is so narrow that it aims at only achievement of one thing and runs roughshod over people in the process. An intentional congregation is one which is working out a synthesis of mission and people. Here, people continue to seek to maintain a union of love and will. They are trying to be in the 9,9 corner of the Grid—concern for people and purpose. Such a congregation is, in some sense at least, attempting to fulfill the prayer of the Liturgy of Thanksgiving of the celebration of Holy Communion: ". . . Make of one will those whom thou hast fed with one heavenly food" (*Service Book and Hymnal*, p. 39).

How do you ground the life and ministry of a parish thoroughly in biblical and theological categories?

E. Biblical/Theological Discernment of Congregation Development

During a weekend retreat, some congregational decision-makers tried to make sense of data gathered from fellow members and their community, and to project their corporate life ahead for a year by formulating goals. At the close of the retreat, the pastor, pondering the broken bread and poured wine of their Eucharist together, spoke about the struggle of their attempts to know who they are as a congregation and to act on that knowledge. He described the broken remnants of their efforts and the joy of their life together. In this way, he was discerning the moment biblically and theologically and inviting others to comment. They did. They spoke of specifics. They confessed; they forgave; they gave thanks. They prayed for each other, for their efforts, for their community and congregation. They left not just with newsprint sheets full of data summaries and analyses, together with a series of congregational goals for presentation at the upcoming annual meeting, but with *a religious interpretation of all they had done together*. They had *discernment*.

Another pastor used the theological analysis of Robert Benne's *Wandering in the Wilderness*,[55] in his annual report to the congregation. He reviewed the history of the parish, assessed its present moment, and projected its future. He noted the years of the 1950s in the congregation as the time when things looked good. The parish was growing numerically and financially; optimism was rampant. He described the shattering advent of the 1960s, in which "everything nailed down became unstuck." He outlined the racial difficulties of the congregation and the disagreement of congregational members over civil rights and black power. He recalled the varying opinions and commitments related to the war in Vietnam. The pastor wrote, "If the sixties were our exodus from the secure bondage of the fifties, then the seventies will no doubt turn out to be our wilderness experience." He then listed the challenges he felt the congregation was facing at the present and would be facing in the next few years. Finally, he reported the attempts to identify what the congregation was about, where it was going. In conclusion, he asked the same question as the Israelites in the wilderness, "Did the Lord bring us here to die in aimless wandering?" He *discerned* the meaning of the moment in explicit biblical/theological categories.

These two examples could be expanded quickly to hundreds if not thousands. What they represent is the recurring need for parish life and ministry development to be accompanied simultaneously by biblical/theological discernment. There are no magical planning or organizational processes for the revitalization of a congregation that do not need a strong sense of interpretation, celebration, and the giving of meaning. Such tools must always be in the company of "moments of meaning." Not only the pastor, but lay people as well, should be able to do this. Unfortunately, if the pastor cannot or will not do it, lay people will find it difficult to do.

This theme of discernment is akin to the role of theology as critique developed by such theologians as Paul Tillich, and Richard and Reinhold Niebuhr. They first asked what is happening, and then how we could understand and ground what is happening in the symbols of Christian faith.

Dual Responsibility

Fritz Buri put it another way. He made a claim for a dual responsibility, namely, a responsibility for the world and a responsibility for revelation. Christian theology arises out of revelation in Jesus Christ. We must, always, be reflecting on and realizing our indebtedness to that origin. We must also be aware that the salvation revealed in Christ applies to the whole world. There is responsibility for enabling this revelation to be heard and understood by the world. The tension produced for the nature and task of Christian theology is to keep both responsibilities related. "Instead of insisting on the purity of doctrine in the face of a deaf world and maneuvering itself into the situation of a voice crying in the wilderness, this theology should consider the fact that it itself becomes aware of revelation only in the form of a theology of a certain time and it understands revelation only from the point of view of its own time."[56] On the other hand, "Christ could become so humanized that in him we no longer have to do with God and His Kingdom but only with man and his world."[57] This dual role of the place of theology (revelation and world) is a major assumption behind parish development.

This does not mean that we have to get all our "gospel stuff" straight before we can become a congregation. It does mean, however, that we need to develop Christian discernment of what's going on, of taking to the depth the material of our everyday congregational life and ministry.

Thus, parish development has two tasks before it: to engage in processes that will enable a congregation to examine, express, and implement the reason for its existence, and to be continually discerning theologically and biblically why we are doing all of this and what it has to do with our relationship to God. Such a congregation is developing not only know-how, but also "know-why."

ALC/LCA Project in Parish Life and Ministry Development

One example of a denominationally-based effort in congregation development is the Parish Life and Ministry Development Project of

The American Lutheran Church and Lutheran Church in America. The four features of the project are:

A. It focuses on the congregation as a worshiping, learning, witnessing, and serving body of Christians. We have just come through a few years of stringent criticism of the parish and the announcement of its non-renewability by some voices. It appears that the time is ripe for an increased application of energies and resources in the parish by the church in its international, national, regional, and congregational parts. Not to think and act now and in the next few years may be to have passed up a *kairos* point in history related to congregational development. By adopting this focus, the pilot project is not suggesting that there are not other valid forms of ministry, most of which in fact are supported financially and prayerfully by congregations themselves, such as world-wide ministries, certain social actions, and educational efforts as seminaries and church-related colleges. This project, however, focuses on the local congregation. The project also recognizes that such functions as worshiping and learning need also to be related to such external activities as witnessing and serving.

B. The project is a symbiotic endeavor. Symbiosis is defined as "two organisms of different kinds living in intimate union and to the benefit of both." This project is a symbiosis not of two but of three entities, namely the congregation, the synod/district, and the appropriate churchwide agencies. The pilot attempts to build a partnership between these three entities for the "benefit of all." The project attempts to establish means of working together, rather than play off these various appropriate roles. The project is saying in its very design that it is possible to develop a kind of tyranny and arrogance on the part of one of these entities in looking at the other two. Our goal, then, is a symbiotic relationship.

There is another kind of symbiotic feature to the pilot project. It has to do with the symbiosis between people and machine, in this case a computer. The use of this kind of "partner" leads to the description of another feature of the project.

C. The project is a socio-technical venture. The creation of man-machine cooperative systems are described quite adequately and eloquently in John G. Kemeny's little paperback book, *Man and the Computer* (New York: Charles Scribner's Sons, 1972). Rather than seeing the computer as an enemy to be approached in fear and awe, Dr. Kemeny presents a case for a large percentage of society coming to use computers in an everyday and practical way. This pilot test is such a venture. Specifically, (1) the project attempts to identify and assist the kind of *persons* in congregations, in synod/districts, and in churchwide agencies who can do parish development and assist others in doing it. The findings of the project should indicate to a congregation something about the equipping of its pastor and people to do parish development and also should provide information to synod/districts and churchwide agencies about the kind of skills needed by staff persons in working in parish development. Such findings are the *social* part of this venture. (2) In addition, the computer will be used for the storage, search, and transmission of knowledge about resources to the local congregation in response to information and goals they have submitted about themselves. This is the technical part of the venture. In some sense this can be seen as a crude forerunner of a kind of retrieval system which eventually could place a terminal mode of a computer in every congregation, or at least close by so that a pastor or lay leader could sit down at such a terminal and engage the computer in conversation in identifying the available resources related to a particular need and situation. Such an approach with individual students has been used at Dartmouth College for several years now and is not out of the realm of possibility in the next decade for denominations and their congregations.

D. The project makes use of the social and behavioral sciences especially as they relate to the concepts and techniques of planning, training, consultation, and organizational and learning theory. The last two decades have seen the development of a wealth of approaches on such subjects as data gathering and analysis, decision-making, interpersonal communication, dealing with conflict, developing organizational models, and short-term and long-range planning. The project seeks to incorporate—in fact, to test out—new combinations of these approaches.

NOTES

1. Murray Milner, Jr., *The Illusion of Equality* (San Francisco: Jossey-Bass, Inc., 1972), pp. 21-31.

2. Paulo Freire, *Pedagogy of the Oppressed* (New York: Herder and Herder, 1972), p. 152.

3. William Barclay, *More New Testament Words* (New York: Harper and Brothers, 1958), pp. 146-155.

4. Freire, *Pedagogy of the Oppressed*, pp. 75-76.

5. Bernard J. F. Lonergan, S. J., *Method in Theology* (New York: Herder and Herder, 1972), pp. 9-20.

6. H. Ignor Ansoff, *Corporate Strategy* (New York: McGraw-Hill, 1965), pp. 15-18.

7. Alvin W. Gouldner, *The Coming Crisis of Western Sociology* (New York: Basic Books, Inc., 1970), pp. 488-502.

8. C. Ellis Nelson, "Is Church Education Something Particular?" *Religious Education*, Jan.-Feb. 1972, pp. 5-16. Respondents' articles, pp. 16-41.

9. "A Central Objective for Educational Ministry in the Parish: ALC and LCA," in *Foundations for Educational Ministry*, ed. C. Richard Evenson, Yearbooks in Christian Education, vol. III (Philadelphia: Fortress Press, 1971), p. 301.

10. C. Ellis Nelson, *Where Faith Begins* (Richmond: John Knox Press, 1967), p. 183.

11. C. Richard Evenson, "The Purpose of Confirmation Education," in *Confirmation and Education*, ed. W. Kent Gilbert, Yearbooks in Christian Education, vol. I (Philadelphia: Fortress Press, 1969) p. 39.

12. William Koppe, *How Persons Grow in Christian Community*, (Philadelphia: Fortress Press, 1973), p. 184.

13. John H. Westerhoff, III, ed., *A Colloquy on Christian Education* (Philadelphia: United Church Press, 1972), pp. 80-90.

14. Robert W. Lynn and Elliott Wright, *The Big Little School* (New York: Harper & Row, 1971), p. 20.

15. *Ibid.*, p. 36.

16. *Ibid.*, p. xii.

17. *Ibid.*, p. 37.

18. Joseph Williamson, "A Pedagogy for Christians," in *A Colloquy on Christian Education*, ed. John Westerhoff, III (Philadelphia: United Church Press, 1972), p. 32.

19. Paul S. Minear, *Images of the Church in the New Testament* (Philadelphia: Westminster, 1965), p. 23.

20. *Ibid.*, p. 258.

21. *Ibid.*, p. 36.

22. *Ibid.*, p. 41.

23. *Ibid.*, p. 32.

24. *Ibid.*, p. 223.

25. Richard L. Keach, *The Purple Pulpit* (Valley Forge: Judson Press, 1971), pp. 37-44.

26. Carl T. Uehling, "Every Year They Sign Up or Sign Out," *The Lutheran*, October 18, 1972.

27. "ALC/LCA Parish Life and Ministry Development Pilot Test: An Introduction," Pilot Test Office, 422 S. Fifth Street, Minneapolis, Minnesota 55415, and 2900 Queen Lane, Philadelphia, Pennsylvania, 19129. See also pp. 215-17 in this article.

28. Daniel Callahan, "Living with the New Biology," *The Center*, July/August, 1972, pp. 4-12.

29. Will D. Campbell and James Y. Holloway, *Up to Our Steeples in Politics* (New York: Paulist Press, 1970), p. 36.

30. Charles A. Reich, *The Greening of America* (New York: Random House, 1970).

31. Carl E. Braaten, *Christ and Counter-Christ* (Philadelphia: Fortress Press, 1972), pp. 114-115.

32. Amitai Etzioni, "Human Beings Are Not Very Easy to Change After All," *Saturday Review*, June 3, 1972, pp. 45-47.

33. Herman Ahrens, "Jesse Jackson: The Past Is Over," *Youth*, September, 1972, p. 22.

34. Jerome S. Bruner, "Education as Social Invention," *Contemporary Educational Psychology*, ed. Richard M. Jones (New York: Harper & Row, 1966), pp. 28-43.

35. Jerome S. Bruner, "On the Community of Learning," *Saturday Review of Education*, March, 1973, pp. 21-24.

36. Joseph Wold, Special Issue of *World Encounter*, October, 1966, Division for World Mission and Ecumenism, Lutheran Church in America.

37. Callahan, "Living with the New Biology," p. 5.

38. Robert R. Blake, Herbert A. Shepard, and Jane S. Mouton, *Managing Intergroup Conflict in Industry* (Houston: Gulf Publishing Co., 1964).

39. Keach, *Purple Pulpit*, pp. 81-101.

40. Martin E. Marty, *Death and Birth of the Parish* (Saint Louis: Concordia, 1964), pp. 7-8.

41. Delbert R. Hillers, *Covenant: The History of a Biblical Idea* (Baltimore: The Johns Hopkins Press, 1969), pp. 25-45.

42. Philip Rieff, *The Triumph of the Therapeutic* (New York: Harper & Row, 1968).

43. The next two sections were originally described in a paper by Robert N. Bacher and Jean Bozeman, Assistant Professor of Religious Education, Lutheran School of Theology at Chicago.

44. "Report of the Commission on the Nature and Mission of the Congregation," in *A Study Book on The Manifesto*, ed. Donald R. Pichaske (Philadelphia: Board of Publication of the Lutheran Church in America, 1967), p. 205.

45. Robert R. Blake and Jane Srygley Mouton, *Corporate Excellence Through Grid Organization Development* (Houston: Gulf Publishing Co., 1968) pp. 12-66, 230-240.

46. Freire, *Pedagogy of the Oppressed*, p. 78.

47. Minear, *Images of the Church in the New Testament*, p. 250.

48. Rollo May, *Love and Will* (New York: W. W. Norton and Co., 1969), pp. 13-14.

49. Robert R. Blake and Jane S. Mouton, *The Managerial Grid* (Houston: Gulf Publishing Co., 1964).

50. Peter Townsend, *Up the Organization* (New York: Alfred A. Knopf, 1970), pp. 45-46.

51. Keach, *Purple Pulpit*, p. 88.

52. *Ibid.*, p. 94.

53. John W. Gardner, *Self-Renewal: The Individual and the Innovative Society* (New York: Harper Colophon Books, 1965), p. 117.

54. Braaten, *Christ and Counter-Christ*, p. 87.

55. Robert Benne, *Wandering in the Wilderness* (Philadelphia: Fortress Press, 1972), pp. 1-5.

56. Fritz Buri, *How Can We Still Speak Responsibly of God?* (Philadelphia: Fortress Press, 1968), p. 2.

57. *Ibid.*, p. 3.

THE PASTOR'S LEADERSHIP ROLE

Norman Wegmeyer

Probably there has been more self-conscious study, experimentation, and written material on organizations in the last 50 years than in all previous history. Why, then, look to the Bible for guidance in areas it doesn't seem to be concerned with, such as organization development and the way groups work? Even though one could find some proof passages or some examples of organizational efforts in Scripture, what value would they have for a very different, more complex twentieth century?

No doubt these questions and concerns are valid. It will not do to try to find a few appropriate passages to bless our efforts about what seem the more mundane matters of organizing. Nor should we try to pattern our styles of organizing on the way it was done in Bible times. But it is helpful to look to the Bible for guidance and illustration of how the church functioned.

EXAMPLE OF THE APOSTLE PAUL

The New Testament provides a glimpse of how Paul operated as pastor and offers some interesting clues for administration. Even if Paul's style was not always clearly apparent, he was conscious of his role as an administrator and he worried about it. For instance, the Book of Acts describes how Paul grew restive after his first missionary journey. Finally he said to his traveling companion, Barnabas, "Come, let us return and visit the brethren in every city where we proclaimed the word of the Lord, and see how they are" (Acts 15:36).

There is an interesting translation of 2 Corinthians 4:1 in the Jerusalem Bible: "Since we have by an act of mercy been entrusted with this work of administration, there is no weakening on our part." *Administration* seems a good choice for the Greek word *diakonos*. Generally *diakonos* is translated as *ministry*. The word *deacon* developed from *diakonos*. In the early church, a deacon was an assistant to the bishop, evidently with many responsibilities in the area of administering and organizing.

Paul's letters to the church in Corinth provide a few insights into his style of working with people and some principles for administration. The most instructive way to get these Scriptural clues would be to read 1 and 2 Corinthians thoroughly and carefully, with a sharp eye on how Paul operated. Here we'll simply suggest some items we feel are evident and point to some passages for examples. These will be stated in a form to highlight Paul's style, and also to provide guidance for those who are church administrators.

1. Respecting Persons

A statement becomes a cliché because it is said too often. However, it may be said often because it is so profoundly true. This is certainly the case with "respecting persons." This is one of the bedrock principles of working with groups in organization development.

The apostle Paul had his troubles with the Corinthians. Sometimes his correspondence openly demonstrated his anger and disgust; at other times his feelings seemed to be just below the surface of his words. But throughout his letters he maintained a consistent respect for persons. It was shown in ways such as these:

Remembering That All Are Children of God

This was especially evident in Paul's concern for the "weaker brother for whom Christ died," (1 Corinthians 8:11). It seemed inconceivable to Paul that he should take advantage of some personal privileges if they were detrimental to another person. His ready remembrance that Christ also died for the brother kept him from abusing or using the other person.

Confidence in and Encouragement of Persons

Praise, admiration, thanks, encouragement for other people were not strange to Paul. His letters often expressed these sentiments:

> There is really no need for me to write you about the help being sent to God's people in Judea. In know that you are willing to help, and I have boasted of you to the people in Macedonia. 'The brothers in Greece,' I said, 'have been ready to help since last year.' Your eagerness has stirred up most of them (2 Corinthians 9:1, 2, Today's English Version).

I am so sure of you, I take such pride in you! In all our troubles I am still full of courage, I am running over with joy (2 Corinthians 7:4, TEV).

Dealing with People at Their Level

Sometimes it is a put-down to be willing to "deal with people at their level." But it may also reflect an honest effort to respect persons. There are suggestions in the Corinthian letters that Paul attempted to work with people in this way.

When I came to you, my brothers, to preach God's secret truth to you, I did not use long words and great learning (1 Corinthians 2:1, TEV).

Answering some criticisms about himself, he detailed what he felt were his rights if he wished to claim them, yet he suffered many things because of his determination to "become all things to all men" (1 Corinthians 9:22).

For the pastor, respecting persons cannot be overemphasized. It includes the ever-present challenge to listen—really listen. It suggests that the administrator acts on a belief that people do have opinions, ideas, and suggestions which are valid and worthwhile. It urges the leader to avoid falling into the trap of playing favorites.

2. Maintaining Honest, Open Communication

Honesty—openness—communication. These are three constantly recurring words in organization development literature. No doubt they are mentioned often because they are a scarce commodity, or at least they are difficult to maintain. The problem of honest, open communication is not a new issue, ushered in with the complex twentieth century. Paul's letters to the Corinthians indicate that he had to contend with a large communication gap. Much of the undertone of the letters reveals an effort to deal with some issues that had been misunderstood. Many passages have the tone of "Well, you have been quoting me as saying . . . but now let me set you straight." The fact that there were communication problems does not detract from the rather remarkable way in which Paul communicated with his congregations.

Speaking Frankly, Honestly, Clearly

He said he would be open in all that he said. From all evidence he did just that—and invited others to do the same.

This is what we are proud of: our conscience assures us that our lives in this world, and especially our relations with you, have been ruled

> by God-given frankness and sincerity, by the power of God's grace, and not by human wisdom. We write to you only what you can read and understand (2 Corinthians 1:12-13, TEV).

Making His Position Known: Not Playing Games

Paul could not be called wishy-washy. He did not mince words, nor did he appear to say things for effect or to curry favor. We have indications that the Corinthians wrote to Pastor Paul to learn his feelings and solicit his advice—and he gave it freely and honestly. Whether the problems concerned factions or lawsuits, immorality or the place of women in the church, food offered to idols or the conduct of the worship service, the members of this early Christian community knew exactly where Paul stood. When one reads his letters, one gets the impression of a sincere man, honestly explaining what he believes.

Having a Healthy, Realistic Self-image

A healthy, realistic self-image evidently did not come easily for Paul. On the one hand, he seemed to have doubts about his ability, his looks, his speech, and other personal characteristics. On the other hand, he was given to boasting. He alluded to boasting more than twenty times in his second letter to the Corinthians, and every time with some apology. No doubt some of these extreme feelings were called forth because his ministry had been challenged and he had been severely criticized behind his back.

Yet, one senses that he was a remarkably mature man with a healthy, realistic self-image. He was self-confident, but willing to be corrected. He was rational and courageous, but unafraid to show his emotions and his great need for other people.

> All these promises are made to us, by dear friends. So then, let us purify ourselves from everything that makes body or soul unclean, and let us be completely holy, by living in the fear of God. Make room for us in your hearts. We have done wrong to no one, we have ruined no one, nor tried to take advantage of anyone. I do not say this to condemn you; for as I have said before, you are so dear to us that we are together always, whether we live or die (2 Corinthians 7:1-3, TEV).

> I wrote you with a greatly troubled and distressed heart, and with many tears, not to make you sad, but to make you realize how much I love you all (2 Corinthians 2:4, TEV).

Yet when he was challenged, he did not hesitate to stand up for his own honor.

> I do not think that I am the least bit inferior to those very special "apostles" of yours! Perhaps I am an amateur in speaking, but certainly not in knowledge; we have made this clear to you at all times and in all conditions (2 Corinthians 11:5-6, TEV).

The ministry is one of the most difficult occupations for a person to maintain his honesty. To maintain a façade of unreality, to avoid honest emotion, is not only inviting to the pastor, but is often expected by the congregation.

Do pastors share their honest thoughts or display honest emotions of anger, ecstasy, dejection, or gratitude? Some do. But many temper their true feelings to conform to the image which they think is expected of them.

Of course, our thoughts and emotions must be controlled, but it is most conducive to good administration if the leader is as honest and candid as possible so that playing games is not necessary.

Presumably, as a Christian, a pastor will be rejoicing, reconciling, admitting failure, forgiving failure, praising, freely acknowledging his weaknesses and dependence. How tempting to believe that to administer is to play the role of the controlled, always cool, always right person! And how wrong! The administrator must maintain honest, open communication. Communication usually gets clogged up and distorted when filtered through the masks of unreality.

3. Sharing Leadership

Modern studies in leadership and organization development have emphasized situational or functional leadership. This is in contrast to older theories of "leadership qualities," which suggested that some persons are born leaders and others are followers. Functional leadership means that within a given group there are the needed abilities to perform the needed leadership roles. So at various times in a given meeting at church, the "leader" may be the speaker, janitor, musician, cook, or anyone else.

This kind of leadership thinking is very much in harmony with Paul's thinking. His analogy of the church as the body of Christ (1 Corinthians 12:12-27) is a keen description of functional or shared leadership.

> For just as the body is one and has many members, and all the members of the body, though many, are one body, so it is with Christ (1 Corinthians 12:12).

> We are not trying to dictate to you what you must believe, because you stand firm in the faith. Instead, we are working with you for your own happiness (2 Corinthians 1:24, TEV).

The way Paul worked is also an example of his belief that we must share leadership. He traveled from place to place, not staying long at any, but soon turning the responsibilities over to the local people. Evidently he did not feel everything would stop if he did not stay around to keep the wheels turning.

It is rare for the pastor to want to bear the whole burden of maintaining the life of the parish. At least some pastors seem to be given to complaining that church members don't carry enough of the load. But sometimes the problem is that administrators forget that sharing the leadership means sharing initiative and decision-making power. We would do well to emulate both Paul's words and actions by simply trusting that people do have varied gifts—they can make decisions and carry them out, and they are interested. This is being demonstrated today by more and more congregations which are putting the concept of shared leadership to work.

4. Using Conflict Creatively

Likely Paul was not consciously aware of the creative value of conflict, and he sought to reduce or eliminate it many times. But he was not adverse to participating in it if need be. He was not afraid of a good fight if he felt there were some things that needed to be aired openly.

> Some of you have become proud, thinking that I would not be coming to visit you. If the Lord is willing, however, I will come to you soon, and then I will find out for myself what these proud ones can do, and not just what they can say. For the Kingdom of God is not a matter of words, but of power. Which do you prefer? Shall I come to you with a whip, or with a heart of love and gentleness? (1 Corinthians 4:18-21, TEV).

> I want to tell you who have sinned in the past, and all the others; I said it before, during my second visit to you, but I will say it again now that I am away: the next time I come nobody will escape punishment (2 Corinthians 13:2, TEV).

But he did not relish a fight just for the excitement. There was always a purpose—that the gospel be proclaimed, that persons be helped to grow in grace and love. On one occasion he realized that his words had caused some anguish, but he was not sorry, because he felt it did some good.

> For even if that letter of mine made you sad, I am not sorry I wrote it. I could have been sorry about it when I saw that the letter made you sad for a while. But now I am happy—not because I made you sad,

> but because your sadness made you change your ways. That sadness was used by God, and so we caused you no harm (2 Corinthians 7:8-9, TEV).

In this matter of conflict, as well as in other matters, Paul's relationship with Christ was his balance wheel. Like a gyroscope, his "looking to Christ" kept him on an even keel in the stormy encounters of his life. If conflict honored Christ, it was worth the struggle; if it dishonored him, it was better to make peace. But Christ, not peace, was the ultimate good.

It is amazing how zealous Christians are to maintain some sort of peace, and yet how often conflict breaks out in the church. The challenge to the pastor as administrator is to know how to handle conflict and use it creatively for the glory of God. Conflict has its roots in a very precious gift of God—individual choice, opinion, and abilities. If this can be kept in mind, it may help pastors avoid viewing conflict as totally bad or a nuisance.

Conflict is often a touchy subject for pastors. On the one hand, there are those who seem to thrive on it, and feel they are not being sufficiently prophetic if all seems to be going smoothly. On the other hand, some pastors seem deathly afraid of conflict and expend much of their energy pouring oil on troubled waters. Both extremes may be needed occasionally, but neither is healthy as a continuing policy. Openly airing conflicting views is necessary to maintain the health of the body. It can stimulate creative thought release built-up tension, and pave the way for fruitful decision and action.

5. Performing Various Appropriate Roles

Performing various appropriate roles may seem to be a catch-all category. Actually it deals with an important part of administration. The administrator must perform many roles, be equipped to do them effectively, and use good judgment in deciding when to do what. Here are a few examples of these roles:

Questioner/Challenger

To question traditions or commonly accepted practices in the light of the gospel—Paul felt this was his prerogative as a leader:

> If one of you has a dispute with a brother, how dare he go before heathen judges, instead of letting God's people settle the matter? Don't you know that God's people will judge the world? Well, then, if you are to judge the world, aren't you capable of judging small matters? (1 Corinthians 6:1-2, TEV).

Teacher/Information Giver

Frequently Paul felt compelled to explain difficult matters of faith, such as the resurrection of the body. Paul's letters provide examples:

> So is it with the resurrection of the dead. What is sown is perishable, what is raised is imperishable. It is sown in dishonor, it is raised in glory. It is sown in weakness, it is raised in power. It is sown in a physical body, it is raised a spiritual body. If there is a physical body, there is also a spiritual body (1 Corinthians 15:42-44).

Admonisher

Paul could come straight to the point:

> Be alert, stand firm in the faith, be brave, be strong. Do all your work in love (1 Corinthians 16:13-14, TEV).

Encourager

The apostle was ever ready to strengthen his co-workers and fellow believers:

> So then, my dear brothers, stand firm and steady. Keep busy always in your work for the Lord, since you know that nothing you do in the Lord's service is ever without value (1 Corinthians 15:58, TEV).

Goal Setter

Paul shared a vision of some long-range purposes:

> It is love, then, that you should strive for. Set your hearts on spiritual gifts, especially the gift of speaking God's message (1 Corinthians 14:1, TEV).

He also suggested some specific, measurable goals, such as the collection of money for the needy:

> I am not laying down any rules. But by showing how eager others are to help, I am trying to find out how real your own love is (2 Corinthians 8:8, TEV).

> Now the matter about the money to be raised to help God's people in Judea: you must do what I told the churches in Galatia to do. Every Sunday each of you must put aside some money, in proportion to what he has earned, and save it up so there will be no need to collect the money when I come. After I come I shall send the men you have approved with letters of introduction, to take your gifts to Jerusalem (1 Corinthians 16:1-3, TEV).

Mediator

When word came that someone in the congregation had caused trouble, Paul had some healing words of advice:

> Now, however, you should forgive him and encourage him, to keep him from becoming so sad as to give up completely. Let him know, then, I beg you, that you really do love him (2 Corinthians 2:7-8, TEV).

To identify these various roles may seem superfluous to the pastor who is accustomed to being a jack-of-all-trades. However, the challenge of the list is not only that as educators and administrators, pastors do things, but also that they should be equipped to do them, and that they should exercise good judgment in knowing what to do when.

One of the most important things for a manager is the use of his time. For pastors, this is crucial. This means being keenly aware of such factors as:

- Personal abilities and limitations
- The abilities and limitations of others
- The needs of the situation
- The goals

The decision must be made whether it is wiser to ask questions, give information, admonish, encourage, or do some other thing. Granted that one's working style is not easy to change, it would still be useful to devise a simple list of some key roles and deliberately try some new ones or cut back on some which seem to be exercised too readily. Better still would be the effort to enlist the group(s) you work with in helping you determine the kind of leadership needed.

The matter of becoming equipped to perform more adequately the various roles moves into the area of career development. One way in which pastors might help each other in developing new professional insights and skills is through the "case method." It is described in some detail in James D. Glasse's *Putting It Together in the Parish.*[1] Basically, it is a disciplined system whereby a person describes a "case" to some of his colleagues who then help the presenter think through his handling of it. Both the description of the case and the discussion of it follow some clearly worked out plans. It evidently has been unusually helpful to pastors in developing their professional skills.

In reflecting on these characteristics of Paul's operational style, the simplest, most useful piece of advice to the pastor as an educator and an administrator would seem to be, "Go and do thou likewise." Even a quick review of organization development and group work literature indicates that these things, so characteristic of Paul, must be evident in the life of a good administrator. The pastor as educational administrator should evaluate his own style of administering and determine the implications for his own "ad-ministry."

THE EDUCATIONAL ADMINISTRATIVE TASK

The pastor, as chief administrative officer in the educational program of a congregation, can make significant contributions in a number of areas, such as: (1) goal-setting; (2) decision-making; (3) enlistment involvement; (4) leadership development; (5) evaluation.

1. Goal-Setting

The pastor has a key role in goal-setting for a congregation's educational ministry. He is the designated leader, and usually his call gives him responsibility in directing the educational program of the congregation. Whether he likes it or not, he cannot and should not avoid this role. Regardless of their competency, the lay leadership have a right to have a good working relationship with the pastor, and to get some clear signals regarding educational goals.

Pastors have a key role, also, because generally they possess information not readily available to others. They have been trained in theology, education, and other disciplines to a degree beyond most of the members of their parishes. Furthermore, they "get the mail" and are constantly supplied with information not available to most. It is a pastor's responsibility to exercise a strong leadership role in helping congregations set challenging but realistic educational goals.

How does the pastor do it? Here a word must be said about individuality. Obviously, no two pastors operate exactly alike, and no two situations are the same. But there are some tasks in the area of goal-setting about which the pastor should be excited.

Envisioning and Pointing to Large Possibilities

Pastors have the unique opportunity to be chief dreamers of dreams. Granted, this opens them to criticism and even scorn for being "dreamers." However, this is not cause for discouragement. Dreams and visions are the stuff of which progress is born. If the pastor is not a dreamer, it is hard for the people in the parish to overcome their reluctance to envision the future. It is difficult to maintain an excited, forward-looking parish if the pastor does not lead the way.

Participating in Formulating Specific Goals

Here the pastor is very important. If the members of a congregation know they have both the green light and the support to think large thoughts and make specific plans, they are generally capable of doing so. However, the pastor should participate with them, as much as seems appropriate, in setting some definite goals. Pastors should have the information and skill to help a group move along in its planning efforts. But while pastors may be key persons, they are not the only ones to set goals. If there is to be any chance that the goals will be achieved, they must be the goals of the people.

The pastor, as dreamer, may have to reconsider possibilities without rejecting the larger vision. To become reality, dreams must be achievable and realistic. In the give-and-take of honest discussion in a group, the goals are more likely to be realistic and reflect the feelings and intent of the group. Who "owns" the goals is verv important. If the group doesn't own them, they probably won't nurture them into fruition. Motivation is a critical factor.

Training Groups in Goal-Setting

Even though groups generally have the capacity to turn dreams into realistic goals, they may need help in doing this more effectively. Here the pastor can perform a valuable function as trainer. Training may seem to be time consuming, and not directly related to the task, but it will soon pay off. The time spent in training persons in goal-setting is likely to produce many dividends.

The Joint ALC/LCA Parish Life and Ministry Pilot Test Project involves a plan whereby congregations work toward developing goals and forward them, together with a Profile Report Form, to the appropriate churchwide agencies. See the sample goal sheet on page 207. On the basis of these working documents, optional program resources will be recommended.

A good goal-setting exercise is included in Robert Bacher's helpful booklet, *Developing Action Groups.*[2] These and other helps can be used by the pastor both in setting goals in the parish and in training people how to set goals.

2. Decision-Making

Few things are as crucial to the life and health of the parish as the way decisions are made. Each decision is sort of a "Y" in the road.

In a volunteer organization such as the church, it's important that decisions be made appropriately, involving the people concerned sufficiently so that they actually go along willingly and gladly, instead of having to be cajoled or scolded. Here we want to give special attention to the pastor's role in the decision-making process.

Initiative and Power

The diagram on page 233 describes the various participatory actions of the pastor in the decision-making process. The form the actions take is dependent on the degree to which the pastor's initiative and power are blended with the congregation's initiative and power.

Initiative and power are not to be thought of negatively. These are descriptive words, indicating that decision generally means power. Power is the ability to influence, to cause a person or group to take a new direction. The term *congregation* refers either to the whole congregation or to various groups within it.

Note that there is a continuum of pastoral actions from total control to total subservience. It is not assumed that a pastor takes any one of the positions as a standard way of operating. It may be appropriate to use any of these styles, depending upon the situation. Sometimes there is need for the pastor to take more or less unilateral and decisive action, as on the left. At other times the pastor does well to take the almost servant-like role, on the right in the diagram. Generally pastors will use several of the styles between the extremes. It might be revealing and very helpful for pastors and the groups they are working with (such as the education committee) to discuss openly their predominant leadership style in the light of the chart. Do they use a number of styles? Are the groups comfortable with the predominant styles? Are the pastors? What could be done to change, if change is called for? A word of warning! This kind of open exchange could be difficult and even threatening to both the pastor and the group. It could also open the way to improved understanding and better working relationships. It's worth the risk.

3. Enlistment/Involvement

Many fine decisions offer hope of some exciting, worthwhile programs, only to turn into flops with the attendant disillusionment for the decision-makers. The reason is that while the decision seemed good, people just did not participate or get involved. It doesn't take too many experiences of failure to cast a pall over any attempts at

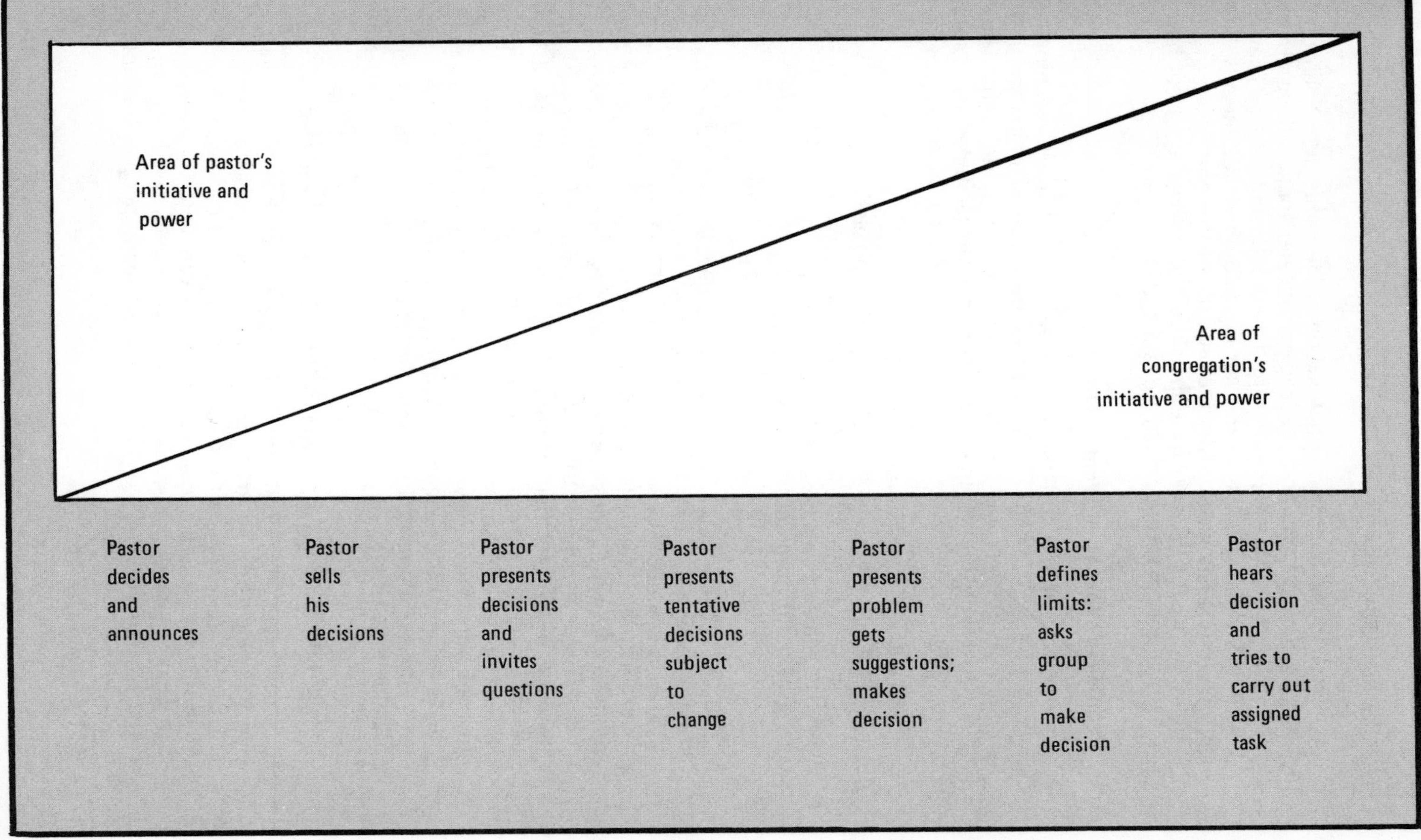

Area of pastor's initiative and power
Area of congregation's initiative and power
Pastor decides and announces
Pastor sells his decisions
Pastor presents decisions and invites questions
Pastor presents tentative decisions subject to change
Pastor presents problem gets suggestions; makes decision
Pastor defines limits: asks group to make decision
Pastor hears decision and tries to carry out assigned task

renewal, and to keep the congregation at the status quo. You don't have to have pastors and lay leaders together long, talking about the program of the church, before the complaining starts: "They're not interested." "You just can't get the people to volunteer." "It's always the very few who carry the big bulk of the load."

The causes for this may have their roots in many places, but here we point only to several which are rather general.

People Do What They Want to Do

That is, people will participate in the things that are meaningful and satisfying to them. They want to be involved in things they feel are important, and they avoid the trivial and irrelevant. Thus the activity must touch their lives, their problems, hopes, joys, sorrows, plans for the future. It must meet some need, such as:

- The desire for meaningful information;
- The satisfaction of having helped someone else;
- The exhilaration of having learned some new skill;
- The relief of having solved some problem;
- The gratification of having self-image built up;
- The feeling that God is being served and glorified.

This has several implications. First, the decisions and plans made should be tested against these criteria. For whom is the program or process intended? Who says it is good for them? What needs will it meet? Second, when attempting to enlist and involve persons, the moment of enlistment is crucial. The attitude and point of view of the recruiter has much to do with the decision of persons to get involved, as well as their performance once they are involved. For instance, the harried Sunday School Superintendent is in trouble if he approaches a person with the attitude, "We've tried to get people to help out. We're down to the bottom of the barrel, won't you please help?" If the program is worth it, it should honestly meet the needs of the congregation, and the efforts at involvement must breathe this attitude.

People Take Hold in Proportion to Their Opportunity to Decide

People generally are not moved to go out of their way to carry out someone else's program. They will, however, work to carry out *their* programs. It is their program if somehow they have helped to make decisions. Obviously, not everyone can vote on everything, but decision-makers must make an effort to gather and honor opinions, and develop ways to involve a great many people in shaping directions and having a voice in the decisions which affect them. If parents are to be concerned about and involved in the educational ministry program, ways must be developed to hear from them—their hopes and dreams for their children, their expectations of the educational program.

The Pastor's Contributions

As in other facets of the life of the congregation, the pastor has a key role in enlistment/involvement. Probably this would not mean to serve as the chief recruiter. That would be contrary to the participative kind of decision-making and involvement we have been discussing. But there are some things which pastors can contribute by virtue of their position and training, which they should acknowledge and use.

Status factors may seem to be an uncomfortable topic in the church. But this is a reality to be reckoned with. Status has to do with the relative importance an activity has for a person. If the pastor feels a person is needed, generally this carries weight. A way should be found to make use of this factor without loading all the recruitment responsibility directly onto the pastor.

Pastors are informed. Generally, the pastor is or should be the person with the most pertinent information about persons and tasks to be performed. The challenge is to have this information made available to decision-making groups, and still have them make their own decisions and actually do the work of enlistment. Perhaps if there were agreement openly arrived at regarding the kind of information input that the pastor should give, the group could take advantage of his counsel without being unduly bound.

Pastors can provide theological and theoretical insights. The pastor can perform a valuable role by training groups for their task. Recruiters need help understanding the theological implications of participating in the life of the body of Christ. This pastors can provide. Pastors can also offer some skill training in some of the appropriate ways to approach people when enlisting them in the life and mission of the congregation. An interesting example of this training function is found in 2 Corinthians 8 and 9, where Paul interweaves some powerful theological insight into his appeal for funds.

4. Leadership Development

Another key role for the pastor as organizer and administrator for educational ministry is leadership development. This does not mean doing all or even most of the actual training or educating needed.

Resources from both inside and outside the congregation should be used for this important task. But in considering the best personal use of time and abilities, the pastor should think seriously of functioning as an enabler, a person who helps release and develop the potential leadership abilities of others. An hour spent in good leadership development may be ten hours saved in matters the pastor has been doing alone.

There are four major "growth areas" in which leaders want or need development. These are: skills, self-image, information, and inspiration.

Each area may require some special helps or procedures so that persons may actually grow and change. Yet the areas are interrelated. Learning a new skill usually implies acquiring new information, and is a very good way to build self-image.

Skills

Teaching is an art, involving skill—the ability to do things and to handle tools. For teachers this generally requires:

- Mastery of subject matter;
- The art of relating to people;
- The use of a variety of procedures;
- Ability to set and strive toward objectives;
- Ability to evaluate and adjust both procedures and objectives accordingly.

Self-Image

A teacher's self-image is an extremely important ingredient in individual growth. It is closely linked with:

- The concept of the teacher's role;
- Personal abilities and skills;
- Relationships with others;
- Perceptions of how others view him.

A low self-image inhibits growth. A renewed self-image opens the doors to growth.

Information

The business of teaching is the business of handling information. To have adequate information, to know where to get information, and to know how to handle information are crucial to effective teaching.

Inspiration

One of the most intangible of the categories in which teacher growth takes place is inspiration or attitude. When it is high it can stimulate the desire for growth and change, and when it is low it can blunt the effectiveness of the teaching art. It is closely related to skills, self-image, and knowledge, but includes some other intangibles such as faith, hope, and love.

What is said here specifically about teachers' development needs can be translated in terms of other leaders in educational ministry. The need categories remain the same. The "teacher growth pyramid" on page 239 is an attempt to illustrate some of the factors involved in leadership development. The pastor as chief leadership developer should give disciplined thought to how this development can be done most successfully and efficiently.

Note that four categories of growth are not entirely separate and discrete, nor is it easy to identify how one grows and improves in them. But the pyramid suggests that some kinds of experiences foster their growth better than others do. Generally the type of experience which will demand the most personal involvement and take the greatest investment of time and energy is the one which will produce the most learning and change. For example, a Bible study group for SCS teachers which is helping them learn to *do* exegisis will be more demanding personally than a lecture on Bible exegesis.

Types of Experiences

It is dangerous to categorize such complicated and intangible things as learning experiences. But the categories identified on the pyramid may suggest some ways to evaluate various kinds of experiences for helping teachers grow. In general it can be said that:

Experiences toward the top of the pyramid tend to—

- Demand less involvement;
- Take less time;
- Foster less interpersonal involvement;
- Threaten less;
- Satisfy less;
- Produce fewer results;
- Be more temporary in their effect.

Experiences toward the bottom of the pyramid tend to—

- Demand a great deal of involvement;
- Take a lot of time and energy;

- Foster interpersonal involvement;
- Have more potential to threaten and upset;
- Satisfy more;
- Produce tangible results and change;
- Last much longer in their effect.

Each type of growth experience has certain characteristics. Starting from the top of the pyramid these are:

Inspirational talk
- Often offers admonition, expectation, promise, challenge;
- Usually is relatively brief, "one-shot" effort;
- Usually is the product of one person. May be augmented with audio visuals.

Lectures
- Are informational, perceptual, and perhaps anecdotal;
- Often are in a series on some general topics.

Study/discuss general topics
- Emphasizes principles, doctrine, or some other subject which is applicable to all (principles of teaching, teaching methods, doctrine, and the like);
- Involves lecture, study material, discussion, and may include audio visuals.

Study/discuss specific topics
- Emphasizes topics of special, usually practical, interest (discipline, use of audio visuals, interpretation of the Bible, use of dramatics, and the like);
- Involves lecture, study material, discussion, and possible involvement activities.

Study/discuss—age level
- Deals with specific classroom situations and problems (curriculum materials, use of facilities, use of Bible with specific age, specific methods, and the like).

Observation—study/discuss (two-way)
- Trainee group has a common experience observing a class. Discussion follows, often under direction of supervisor or trainer. Focus is on specific events, situations, and problems.

Observation—study/discuss (three-way)
- Characterized by observation of a class by trainees and supervisor, followed by a discussion involving trainees, supervisor, and the teacher of the observation class.
- May also include interview of pupils.
- Inspires a spirit of mutual ministering.

Simulated experience—study/discuss
- Trainees involved in a mutual experience. May take form of

THE TEACHER GROWTH PYRAMID

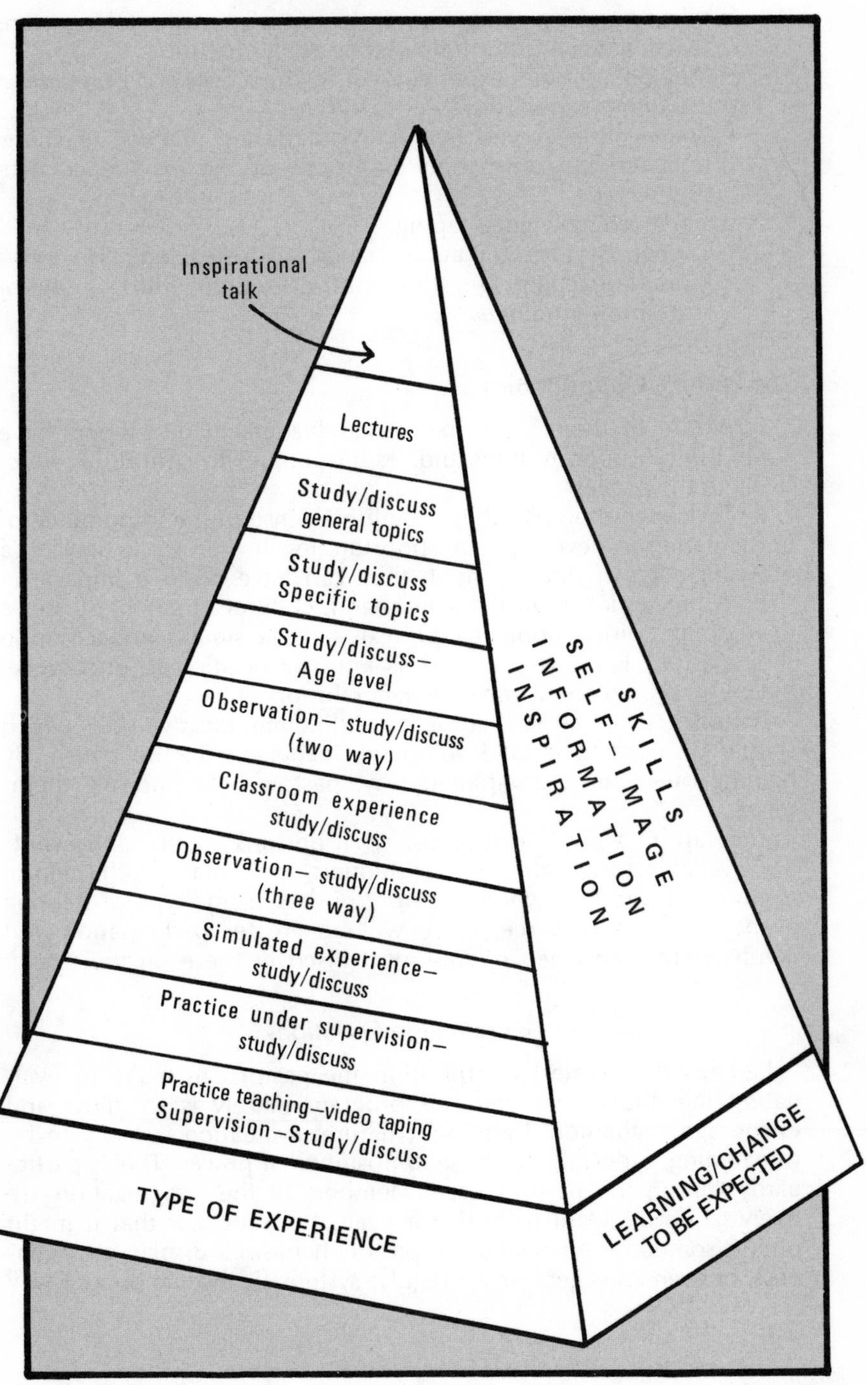
Inspirational talk
Lectures
Study/discuss general topics
Study/discuss Specific topics
Study/discuss– Age level
Observation– study/discuss (two way)
Classroom experience study/discuss
Observation– study/discuss (three way)
Simulated experience– study/discuss
Practice under supervision– study/discuss
Practice teaching–video taping Supervision–Study/discuss
TYPE OF EXPERIENCE
SKILLS
SELF–IMAGE
INFORMATION
INSPIRATION
LEARNING/CHANGE TO BE EXPECTED

micro-teaching with a small group of persons taking turns teaching each other followed by study/discuss.
- May be a mutual experience of learning a new skill together.

Practice under supervision—study/discuss
- Trainee is observed by supervisor during practice teaching, followed by some study/discussion of the experience with supervisor.

Practice teaching—video taping
- Trainee is video (or audio) taped while teaching. He views himself teaching and then has discussion with supervisor and/or other trainees.

The Pastor's Opportunities

By virtue of their office, pastors as leadership developers have some built-in opportunities and responsibilities to contribute effectively to the process.

By their own example, they establish a sense of the importance of participating in development opportunities. If they try to stay on a growing edge of development, they can have positive impact on their congregations. On the other hand, congregations that foster a developing spirit among leaders can have a similar impact upon their pastors. Furthermore, pastors are in a position to encourage, highlight, set direction, and give general support.

Pastors are trained in theological and communicative skills which should be used to help develop the leadership in the parish. By helping others in a disciplined way, pastors help improve themselves.

They are in a position to know what persons, media, and events are available, and can put parishioners in contact with helpful resources. Invariably, when a pastor "pushes" some type of training event or media resource, there will be greater participation and involvement than when people must discover these on their own.

5. Evaluation Questions

Perhaps the greatest contribution the pastor can make to evaluating the educational ministry program merely is to allow and encourage evaluation. By its very nature, evaluation is likely to be threatening, especially to those in positions of power. This is particularly true in the pastor's case. Members of the congregation are likely to be reluctant to push for evaluation, for fear that it might offend someone, especially the pastor. If pastors display an openness, or even an eagerness for regular systematic evaluation as a way of improving the educational ministry of the parish, then one of the largest barriers to evaluation will have been overcome.

Beyond this, pastors will want to participate actively in whatever evaluative procedures are used, and may also participate in developing appropriate tools and processes.

Typical Evaluation Questions

Some typical evaluation questions that are helpful are:

1. What are our efforts aiming to accomplish? Who is benefiting?
2. Who is determining the benefits? Are participants given a voice in expressing views? How is this done?
3. Is our program primarily aimed at helping people personally? At building the corporate body, the church? What evidence for each?
4. How are persons nurtured in the faith? What is the role of the worship services? The family? The whole life of the parish? The specifically educational program? Other experiences?
5. What evidence do we have that, as persons move through our educational program, it is assisting them in getting new information? Gaining appropriate skills? Developing hoped-for attitudes?

Evaluation procedures are developing in a variety of directions. Uthe's *Using Evaluation to Improve Teaching*[3] is a good place to start, but other resources include instruments for congregational analysis which denominational congregation development efforts are using.

NOTES

1. James D. Glasse, *Putting It Together in the Parish* (Nashville: Abingdon, 1972).

2. Robert Bacher, *Developing Action Groups* (Philadelphia: Division for Parish Services [Lutheran Church in America], 1973).

3. Edward Uthe, *Using Evaluation to Improve Teaching*, Consult Series no. 5 (Philadelphia: Lutheran Church Press, 1968).

5

CONTEMPORARY CLUES FOR EFFECTIVE EDUCATIONAL MINISTERING

The teacher who is attempting to teach
without inspiring the pupil
with a desire to learn
is hammering on cold iron.

—Horace Mann

It is in those situations, where good teachers can work with groups of pupils of such size that they can study each one individually and provide much small-group and individual instruction, that outstanding teaching is being done.

—Hollis L. Caswell

A Christian may be defined as a person who can listen.

—Emil Brunner

Media, by altering the environment,
evoke in us unique ratios of sense perceptions.
The extension of any one sense alters
the way we think and act—
the way we perceive the world.
When these ratios change,
men change.

—Marshall McLuhan

You are in the people business. You are paid to affect behavior, to produce information-gain, to induce attitude-change, and most importantly, to increase the learner's ability to learn without being taught.

—David K. Berlo

ON COMMUNICATING

The process of communication is of central importance to the educator. Frank Klos unpacks that process in his outline of communication theory, which provides insights for educational ministering. He suggests ways to look at our own communication, including criteria for evaluating communication acts. Recognizing how people "code" and "uncode" communications will help the pastor in his role as communicator, enabler, and educator.

There is much emphasis in educational circles on planning and objective-setting. Klos points out the values and perils in objective-setting in a critical and useful way linked to the communication model. To act without direction is folly, but to act in a legalistic, confining way may be likewise ludicrous.

Klos wades into Marshall McLuhan in discussing media. Recalling McLuhan's insights, Klos makes applications to the pastor-educator's responsibilities. Taking the point of view that "the more that learners are involved, the more likelihood that learning will take place," Klos shows how selecting educational media is a matter of matching purpose, people, and participation. Klos is insistent that mere electronic gadgetry will not *ipso facto* produce more learning. With these guidelines in mind, pastors are finding better ways of utilizing a variety of media for a variety of tasks.

Naturally, the purpose of educational ministry finally comes down to helping persons. Klos suggests helpful ways to look at the developing individual self. The material may be useful for teacher training or reflection on our own educational development.

ON COMMUNICATING

MAKING EDUCATIONAL MINISTRY COME ALIVE

Frank W. Klos

The essays in this volume provide a panorama of views of educational ministry. Educational ministry probes biblical and theological foundations as well as sociological and psychological ramifications. Educational ministry suggests new ways of developing parish life organization. Educational ministry challenges pastors and seminarians to investigate the many important facets of the clergy's teaching roles. Through all the essays, divergent as they may be on some points, there runs a common thread of conviction that educational ministry is a vital, integral part of the church's total ministry to people. But can we harness the energy in that concept to improve educational practices in the parish?

It would be wise to begin answering this question by settling on some working definitions. For several years The American Lutheran Church and the Lutheran Church in America have been working together to develop a joint program of educational ministry. As part of the documents outlining and proposing this common endeavor, both education and educational ministry were defined in operational terms:[1]

> *Education.* Education may be defined as the conscious effort to help persons to change in those understandings, attitudes, and patterns of action which are believed to be of value. It is distinguished from accidental or incidental learning by the deliberate focusing of attention on desired outcomes.
>
> *Educational Ministry.* Educational ministry is the conscious efforts of the church to help persons, through the learning process, to know and confess as their own the Christian faith and to assume responsible roles as Christians in the world.

Further, some of the salient characteristics of educational ministry were listed by the program builders:

- Educational ministry is *conscious*—intentional, guided by objectives.
- Educational ministry works *through the learning process*—dealing with conscious efforts to develop understandings, attitudes, and skills which are considered to be related to Christian faith. It is not everything in congregational life, but is rather limited to those activities consciously designed to be "educational" or learning experiences.
- Educational ministry is *broadly based*—encompassing all the educational activities of the congregation, not limited to specific ages (e.g., children) or specific settings (e.g., classes). It deals with the full range of life involvements faced by Christians as they live out their roles in the world.

Definitions, although illuminating, can become sterile, verbal prisons for ideas unless they are used as guidelines for action. Let's look at some ways of moving educational ministry vigorously from concept to reality, of making it come alive. That dynamic, anticipatory word *come* could serve as a useful acronymn to highlight four significant areas of consideration. C-O-M-E—each letter in turn could stand for one of these areas: *C*ommunication, *O*bjectives, *M*edia, and *E*ach Person.

COMMUNICATION

"What we got here," says Paul Newman as Cool Hand Luke in the film of the same name, "is a problem of communication." That is a convict's rejoinder to a prison guard. However, this keen assessment of human difficulties could very well be the summary evaluation of a great many of the tensions and turmoils in modern life. Is it possible that neat, categorical clichés, such as generation gaps and credibility gaps, are really part of a larger communication gap?

Words, Words, Words

An anonymous wag commented that, "There are only three races in the world—men, women, and children—and they all speak different languages." Language is, of course, a primary and critical factor in communication. Presumably, the nation's schools, with their almost neurotic emphasis on grammar, composition, and literature, would breed a citizenry solidly equipped to use the common language. That this assumption is patently untrue becomes readily apparent to anyone involved in the process of communication. The crisis-challenge of a previous generation, "Why can't

Johnny read?" has become transformed to a more frustrating "Why can't Johnny communicate?" Yet the fault cannot be assigned to the failure of the schools in accomplishing their practical goals. Few schools, if any, are capable of staying abreast of dynamic language changes emerging through the myriad facets of a changing society.

New technologies hatch new vocabularies; marketing campaigns invent or manipulate words to create instant reception for new products; evolving psychological and sociological concepts often degenerate into catchwords for frozen thoughts. Add to this the subtle ways in which each business, profession, and form of human endeavor devises its own "in-language" for the initiated. "Show Biz" shop-talk, Washingtonese, and the "God-talk" of theologians are obvious examples. Then there is the phenomenal way language develops slanguage. Who knows why exactly? Slang may emerge to meet the need for password privacy of an age group, a region, a special segment of society. On the other hand, slang may appear through careless enunciation or an attempt to shortcut long-winded phrases. But it happens, and one of slang's amazing features is that while much becomes rapidly dated, many terms achieve respectability. So, dictionaries are always marching toward their next editions.

Language is important in the communication process and, especially, as part of the church's ministry. Much of Christianity is based on the Word. From the theological idea of the living Word of God incarnate in Jesus Christ to the printed witness by that Word through scriptural pages, congregations are inspired to pass on the gospel message. Perhaps, it is an oversimplification to claim that most of the church's proclamation through the centuries has been oral-aural-verbal. Yet, the evidence of creeds, catechisms, and hymnals, for instance, suggests the high regard for precise, definitive terminology. Theologies often hinge on concise verbal expressions to encompass vast mysteries of the faith. Think of one of Martin Luther's landmark ideas, such as "justification by grace through faith," which is far easier to repeat verbatim than it is to explain in more common parlance.

Pastors are well aware of language-communication problems. Easily they can match old chestnuts, such as the boy who thought he was praying ". . . lead us not into Penn Station" as part of the Lord's Prayer, with equally garbled understandings from their own experiences. Is there a pastor who doesn't approach the pulpit with some worry and concern about how that day's sermon will be heard, or comprehended, or translated into life changes?

A sermon is an easy communication form to analyze. But everything pastors do involves some kind of communication: counseling, visiting, leading worship, teaching, conducting meetings, and don't forget personal study, meditation, and prayer. And in all relationships with parishioners and community, pastors are also communicating non-verbally through gestures, facial expressions, and various bodily movements accompanying the words they use. Whether they like it or not, pastors live in a spotlight with their lifestyle details expressing something of the faith they serve. That old adage, "What you do speaks so loudly that I cannot hear what you say," often sits in haunting challenge like the Ancient Mariner's albatross on the pastor's shoulder.

Communication Explosion

The twentieth century may someday be labeled as the time when communication exploded. The vast variety of communication forms that so permeate contemporary culture as to seem commonplace were born and grew to adolescence in the last hundred years. Radio, telegraph, telephone, television, records, satellites, motion pictures, computers, tape recorders—the list appears endless. Almost all of the recent communication inventions are electronic. According to Marshall McLuhan, the development of electronics is paralleled only by the development of movable type as a profound shaper and changer of society to such an extent that it is never again the same. He is fond of quoting Alfred North Whitehead's caustic comment, "The major advances in civilization are processes that all but wreck the societies in which they occur."[2]

When these new communication media are added to the older communication forms such as newspaper, books, magazines, and the multitudinous types of advertising display, the results are overwhelming. Short of moving into a wilderness cave, there is no escape from the communication explosion.

Maybe it is more useful to talk about a communication implosion, that is, the disruptive effect within persons. Almost everyone suffers with some form of information overload. Bombarded as they are with multisensory experiences, people control to some extent which forms of communication are allowed to register on their consciousness. Inveterate television viewers, for example, have a way of shifting their brains into neutral and allowing their minds to idle during chronic sieges of spectatoritis. Children and adults alike who fall into this category have a hard time remembering just what it was they saw and heard. Communication-supersaturation is a modern disease. Trying to sort out images, symbols, sounds for meaning, and value is part of the predicament in feeling at home in this world.

Pastors, like all other communicators, have some hard choices to make. They can put their major emphasis on the explosion side, seeking ways of utilizing the newer media to communicate the gospel. Or they can put their major emphasis on the implosion side, searching for ways of helping persons appropriate and internally structure the gospel message as part of their own value systems. The first choice is the way of proclamation; the second, the way of education. Hopefully, and ideally, pastors will choose to steer a middle course with the twin emphases peaking rhythmically as opportunities and situations permit.

Communication Theory

The vast area of communication can be overpowering unless some handholds are developed to bring the various forms under control. That is the primary function of communication theory. Properly, one should say theories, for there are many. For our purposes, one theory in particular offers a series of helpful insights. The Shannon-Weaver Communication Model has become a classic chart-form interpretation of what happens essentially when communication takes place.[3] Developed by Claude E. Shannon of Bell Telephone Laboratories and Warren Weaver, the theoretical model was first published in 1949, and since then has spawned a number of modifications. We shall be no exception to the practice and will suggest some modifications. But first, let's look at the springboard Shannon and Weaver provide.

SHANNON-WEAVER COMMUNICATION MODEL

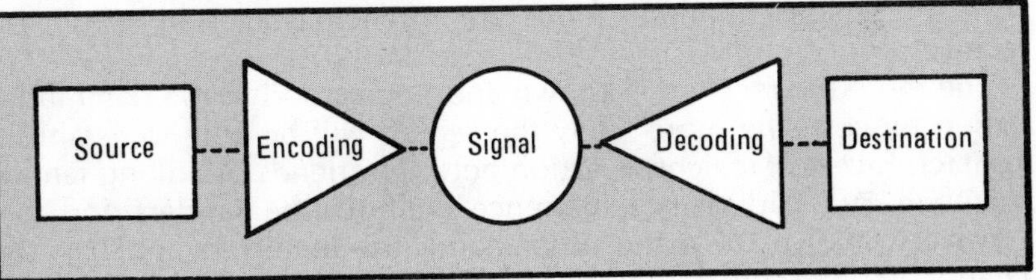

Basically, the Shannon-Weaver diagram deals with the way information is communicated. It originates with a source, is encoded in some form and then is transmitted through a signal. The signal means little until, again in some form, the message is decoded and ultimately reaches its destination. The model is as applicable to conversing with friends or painting a picture as it is to writing a letter or televising the six o'clock news.

Sender-Receiver

Let's start with our modifications by personalizing the two ends of the diagram. Someone, the sender, decides to send the message. The advertising layout artist at a drawing board, the sportscaster in a stadium broadcast booth, the pastor in the pulpit, the teacher in a classroom—all are persons trying to communicate with someone else. They choose the codes they will use—art, music, language, gestures. They also have some idea of the eventual receiver of the message. On a person-to-person basis, knowing the receiver presents few difficulties. Mass communication forms, by comparison,

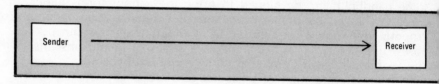

can be addressed only "to whom it may concern." Naturally, this creates a problem of identifying current audiences. Publications take periodic reader samples to find out who is reading what; television surveys of the number of viewers who watch certain programs are an integral part of the industry. But the problem persists because mass audiences are fickle and unpredictable. Many a well-made motion picture with critical acclaim has confounded its producers by turning out to be a box office dud. Publishers vainly search their crystal balls to determine which of their forthcoming books will catch the public fancy and vault to the top of the best-seller list. In reality, mass communications are often messages in search of receivers.

The more the receiver is known and understood in the communication process, the more likely the sender will be able to establish contact. Face-to-face conversation between friends or among family members is a fairly easy experience for both the senders and the receivers involved. On the other hand, the inanity of much party chatter among semi-strangers can be tedious for everyone.

As teachers, preachers, counselors, and visitors, pastors are involved with sending messages throughout their activities with their congregations. And the effectiveness of that communication process may indeed hinge on how well pastors know those for whom the messages are intended. Those clergy who find themselves so caught up in administrative and other worthwhile duties that they feel compelled to offer excuses for no longer visiting their parishioners regularly, simply don't understand the process of communication.

Whether they realize it or not, they are moving into the area of mass communications and losing the opportunity to individualize their messages to those whom they are serving. Not knowing the receivers is even more disastrous in the classroom for the teacher-sender who feels the importance of the message is all that matters. It can easily lead to the dead-end street of answering questions that have not been asked; it can build a house of knowledge on shaky foundations, leaving the teacher profoundly puzzled when that house collapses without apparent reason. The thinking teacher who answers, "I teach seventh graders or high school seniors or young adults," when asked "What do you do?" is well on the way towards utilizing communication effectively. Those who respond with the specific subject matter being emphasized are in for big trouble.

Codes

In place of the Shannon-Weaver *signal*, let's substitute the concept of *code*. While the transmission of a signal is important, even

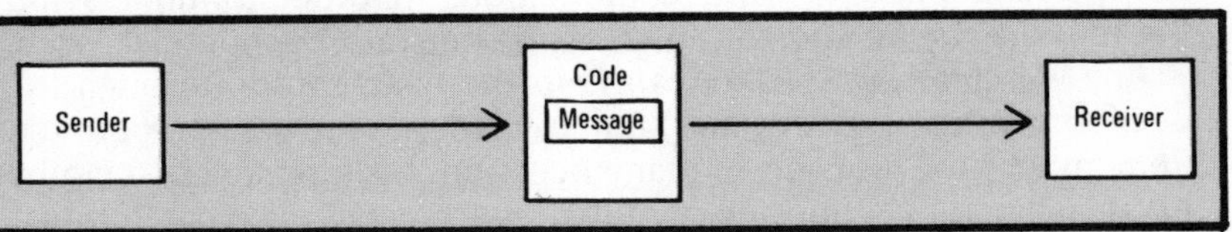

more significant is the code being carried. When you think of codes, you probably think about the Morse Code and semaphore and the devious systems used by spies. However, every communication uses some form of code. And every code is a secret, unfathomable language to the uninitiated. In fact, language itself is a code. So are films, pictures, radio sound effects, body movements, and facial gestures. Part of education consists simply of learning the codes to be used. You can't drive an automobile anywhere legally until you know the codes of the road signs, the traffic lights, as well as the signals of other drivers and traffic control officers.

The church has many distinctive codes of its own in liturgies and hymnody, in its creeds, and in confessions of faith. But teaching the codes to members of a congregation is only a small part of educational ministry. Being able to appropriate those codes on a personal level for their own growth in grace is a difficult task for even the most dedicated parishioners. They, like all other church members, need to be involved in person-centered educational processes that help them translate Christian codes into life. This is an important function of educational ministry. It may be that building new codes or revising older ones is as important as interpretation. Using contemporary language rather than 400-year-old King James English, for instance, offers a better chance of reaching people where they are with the biblical witness. Codes as carriers of message ideas are too crucial in the communication process to take for granted.

So far, the communication model with a sender, a receiver, and a code is inert. The twin activities of encoding and decoding release

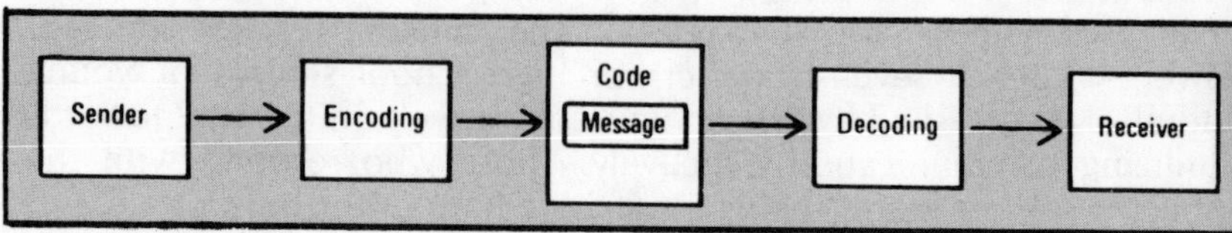

its dynamics. Now the sender manipulates the code according to some purpose and sends it on its way. A speaker puts words together in certain patterns and pronounces them. The hearer of those words has to listen to the pronouncements, comprehend the patterns, and define the word combinations in order to understand the message being spoken. In short, hearers are decoders at work.

Any way that the speaker can help the hearer wade through the decoding process is a giant step towards aiding comprehension. Remember how Jesus on so many occasions used parables to clothe his teaching. By choosing familiar events and everyday objects woven into story, Jesus provided an easy method of reaching his hearers where they were. Those who really heard what he said were astonished at the powerful spiritual teachings that flowed into their minds on the simple parable carriers. On the other hand, consider the directions for filling out income tax returns. Surely, those who devised that guidance had no clear idea of who the receivers were or how the decoding process could be expedited. Even tax experts find many ambiguous points for argumentative interpretation. Encoding is one thing; decoding is usually something else and maybe far removed from what the sender intended.

Sermon writing and sermon delivery are also two different things. Ideally, they are part of the same encoding process. Actually, they do not necessarily coincide; sometimes they war with each other. Teaching plans and what really takes place in the teacher-learner relationships similarly can diverge. No one would insist that either preparation of a communication or the execution of that communication is more significant than the other in helping the hearer decode the conveyed message. But it is important to understand that each form of encoding carries with it its own potentialities and its own weaknesses.

Static

Now is the time to start gumming up this useful communication model by introducing *static*. Static is a good term, borrowed from AM radio, to stand for anything that interferes with the communication process. While you can hear the electrical disturbances that intrude on or drown out a broadcast, you are not always aware of

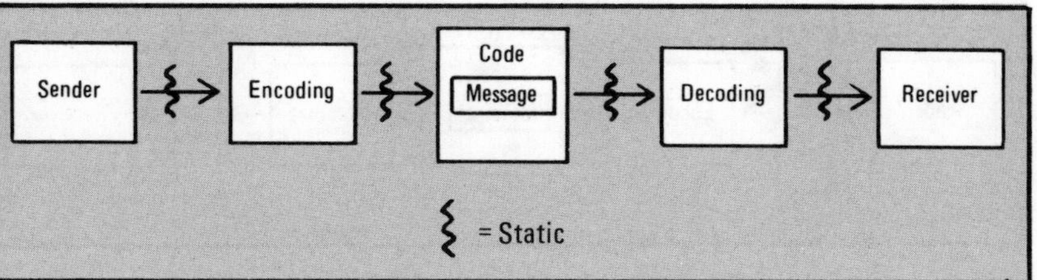

the static that can block communication at various points. A fuzzily focused filmstrip frame on the screen—static. A mumbling speaker—static. A misuse of any code selected—static. A receiver with his mind a million miles away—static. Like the devils that inhabited the Gadarene swine, legion is the name for static. Static results in misinformation, misinterpretation, and a gross mishandling of the whole communication process. Just think of the mischief that misprints can cause. One program for youth offered this enticing invitation in a stage direction: "During the fourth verse of the hymn, have the young people stand and sin softly." Not even Bibles escape the static of printing errors. A classic case was the so-called Sinful Bible in Merrie Olde England, in which the omission of one little word provided among the Ten Commandments, "Thou shalt commit adultery."

When you consider the things that can go wrong with the communication process, it is amazing that it works as well as it does. The specter of static looming over every part should motivate would-be communicators to make each part as effective as possible. It is an easy matter to fix the blame for faulty communication on atmospheric conditions, inoperative equipment or inattentive receivers. Yet it is the communicator's job to counteract the atmospheric interference, to check equipment for good running order before using, to capture the attention of those for whom the messages are intended. There is an old Chinese saying, "If the pupil goes wrong, punish the teacher," which suggests that the communicator does have responsibility for what happens.

Filters

One way to begin in dealing with potential static along the communication process line is to recognize that every human being operates with a set of filters. Filters are personal ways of looking at the world; they are mind-set strainers reshaping experiences that flow through them. For instance, let's take a certain male pastor who

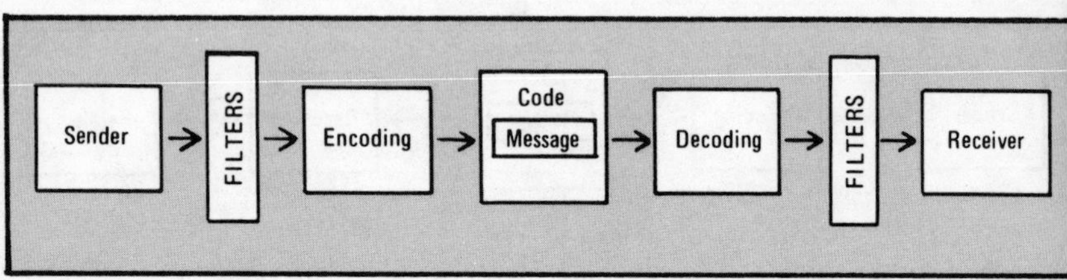

is a husband, a father, a Democrat, a Miami Dolphin fan, a Civil War buff, a model railroad enthusiast, a hunter, a golfer, a Kiwanian, an Old Testament scholar, a PTA member, a bridge player, a classical music devotee. And this pastor is trying to communicate with a fifteen-year-old girl who is a daughter, a sister, a tenth-grader, a tennis player, a hard rock fan, a budding fashion designer, a water skier, a stamp collector, a political liberal, a cheer leader, an old bottle collector, a reader of Gothic mysteries, a steady dater, a part-time actress. Unless the pastor knows something about this girl and her operating filters through which she will receive his communication, he may have a difficult time reaching her. Also, in all honesty, he has to know himself and be painfully aware of the personal filters through which he sends out his message.

There is no substitute for knowing people to improve the communication process. To know people is to understand and accept their filters which are even more complicated than we have suggested so far. For people are influenced by many sociological, economic, and psychological factors that are not always readily apparent. To shape communication as much as possible in terms of the uniqueness of the receiver is a good rule of thumb for any sender to follow.

Feedback

There is one more aspect of the communication model that needs to be added: The concept of feedback. Originally this term came from ballistics. Feedback referred to the radar information sent back from a missile's cone to the mechanism guiding the flight pattern. This feedback communication served to correct errors and to increase the possibilities of the missile hitting its target. Taken over into the area of communication, feedback means simply having the receivers report and interpret the messages that have gotten through to them.

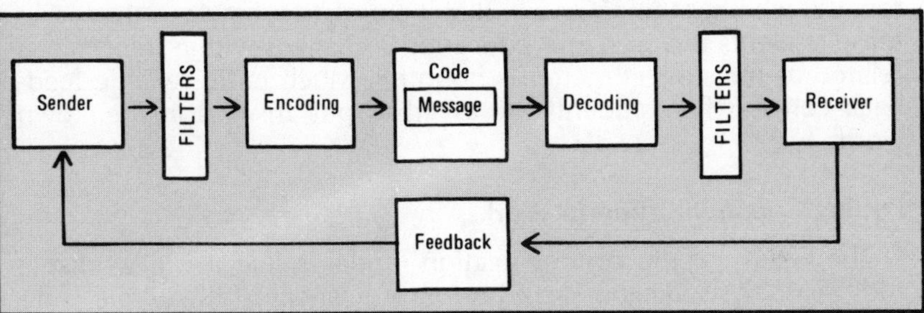

Everyone is familiar with the way rumors are spread, embellished, and jumbled at each step of the journey around the neighborhood. The reason is usually that few people take the time to check out the information they have received, to question, to repeat carefully, to make sure they heard clearly and correctly. More importantly, however, the one sending the message should determine that the receivers have it right. How? By listening to their description of what they heard and by noting their comments and questions for clarification. Too frequently, the communicator is so busy concentrating on getting the message across that he gives little attention to how it is being received. And then communication becomes "munication," which is about as effective as singing to yourself in the shower.

While the diagram, for the sake of simplicity, shows the feedback arrow reaching back to the sender, in reality, the situation is more complex. Like any form of code-message, feedback has to go through filters, the encoding-decoding processes and run the risk of various kinds of static. However, without feedback, the sender of a message has little idea of whether or not the message reached its destination. And feedback need not be verbal. A classroom full of pupils dropping pencils, noisily shifting around in their seats, or staring vacantly out the window has a lot to say to the teacher about the communicative effectiveness of whatever is taking place.

One caution: some feedback is not a very reliable index of how well a message is understood. Verbatim feedback is just repeating as exactly as possible that which was received. All it really indicates is the degree of successfulness of reproduction abilities; by no means does it provide information about comprehension. Just about everyone has had teachers who relied heavily on examinations for feedback information and who insisted that answers to questions be as precise as the textbooks' (or the teachers') explanation. For those students with good memorization skills, it was easy to get an *A*. Those who were able to "psych out" their teachers and anticipate a high percentage of the questions to be asked usually did very well too. But whether there was any direct correlation between the marks these students received and educational changes within their minds related to the subject matter is doubtful. Much more reliable feedback comes when students are asked to put answers in their own words.

Putting Communication to Work

The beauty of the communication model is that it is a workable tool for analysis, diagnosis, and for improvement of the whole communication process. Try putting it in front of you the next time you are getting ready to teach a group of persons or to prepare a sermon or to plan an agenda for a meeting. The model will challenge you to develop active, positive forms of communication that are most likely to bring results. And this is the way to define communication itself.

Purposely, a definition of communication has been postponed in the discussion until now. Rather than starting with a scientific or literary description of what communication is all about, we have allowed the concept to grow in personal terms, in a personal interaction between the sender and the receiver. Merrill Abbey best delineated communication on this transaction basis: "Communication is an ongoing process, in which the meanings of the sender make a creative contact with the meanings of a receiver, leading to action within a mutually responsive relationship."[4]

Sift Abbey's choice of words carefully. There is no room here for an egocentric sender and a passive receiver. There is instead "creative contact," and "leading to action" through an interrelationship of meanings. With these fluid concepts in mind, Abbey went on in his little book, *Man, Media and the Message*, to provide a series of criteria for guiding and testing communication.

1. Is there in the source integrity of purpose, full respect for persons, some healthy self-understanding, trust in his message and openness to the message of others?
2. Has the message been encoded in terms or symbols not only faithful to the intention of the source but sufficiently famil-

iar to the receiver to allow him to make reasonably open responses?

3. Has the message been fed into a channel or channels that provide maximum efficiency for the task? Are these channels sufficiently available to the persons to be served? Are they appropriate to the subject matter and purpose of the message?
4. Has the message been encoded in terms the receiver can accurately decode? Have we made it probable that he can arrive at a responsive understanding of the original meaning? Have we so entered into the other's experience that we can make ourselves understood at the depths where the reconciliation of differences take place and new patterns of life are tried?
5. Has the sender so succeeded in seeing the matter under discussion from the receiver's viewpoint as to enlist his active participation on the side of true understanding? Has the sender done all he could to present his message in ways the receiver can respond to with a minimum of subjective bias?
6. Has a sensitive response to feedback supported such mutual understanding as will advance not only communication of the message but communication between persons?[5]

Unsettling criteria such as these are a sure cure for complacency. In the context of educational ministry these probing questions can be revolutionary.

OBJECTIVES

The *O* in C-O-M-E stands for *objectives.* Objectives in education are simply signposts indicating the directions for changes in learners. Or to use Robert Mager's more precise statement, "An objective is an intent communicated by a statement describing a proposed change in a learner—a statement of what the learner is to be like when he has successfully completed a learning experience."[6] On the surface, the concept seems reasonable: it basically suggests that objectives indicate what learners are able to do following some form of educational involvement. However, educators are divided on the value of objectives stated so clearly and behaviorally. Some see objectives as useful tools in shaping the educational process to serve those involved more efficiently, while others consider objectives to be straitjackets inhibiting free and independent personal growth.

Without getting into the debate of whether objectives are the saviors or the saboteurs of the educational endeavor, let us say that both extreme points of view are right. Objectives can be useful tools; they also can be restrictive inhibitors. The difference lies in how the educator utilizes them. Objectives do not exist in a vacuum but are part of a larger purpose—in our case, educational ministry. Keeping that concern for the growth, development, and well-being of persons in mind (which is what ministry is all about), let us put the notion of objectives into the communication process. Then it becomes easier to accept them as workable ways for both leaders and learners to determine directions, evaluate experiences, and measure educational changes.

Why Objectives?

As one of Walt Kelly's cartoon characters in his comic strip *Pogo* said, "If you don't know where you are going, you're liable to end up someplace else." What more apt warning for a pastor-educator? To go into a teaching-learning situation without a clear-cut sense of direction is to play Russian roulette with apathy and boredom. Learners and leaders alike need to know where they are going in a particular session or course, and why, and what going in that direction will do for them.

Objectives enable a teacher to establish concisely what behavioral changes are desirable in students as a result of instruction. This information provides a perspective for what takes place in the learning environment. Objectives aid in the selection of appropirate learning experiences, in the sequencing of topics, in adapting churchwide programs for local use, in making the educational experience relevant for each participant.

Further, objectives offer a practical three-way evaluation system:

1. *On-the-way evaluation*—on the basis of feedback from the students, the teacher can assess how things are going. Modification of objectives may be needed or substitute learning experiences provided. The teacher who waits until the end of course to discover how well the educational-communication has gotten through to students has failed those students completely. If any *F*'s are given out, this teacher deserves every one of them. On-the-way evaluation prompts exploration and experimentation as alternate methods and learning resources are tested for those particular students involved.

2. *End-of-the-road evaluation*—objectives offer a form of measuring to what degree the students accomplished the tasks assigned. More importantly, students can examine their own rate of progress. Sometimes teachers play diabolical games with their learners by giving final exams steeped in esoterica. Testing, then, becomes a farce. What is really being tested is an unwritten objective, "to help

the students outguess the teacher." No one wins in this battle of wits. If a terminal test has any value it should be clearly and carefully designed in the light of the objectives. Maybe it should be given out the first day of class to communicate to everyone what is significant throughout the sessions to come. This would help cut through the adiaphora that often creep like fog into educational endeavors, dulling everyone's senses to priorities and purposes.

End-of-the-road evaluations according to objectives also offer clues for improving a course of study or a program or a series of discussion sessions for another group. Naturally, every group being made up of individuals is different from every other group. Yet there are enough similarities among groups on the same age level that some generalities can be made. Each group has something to teach the teacher about better ways of dealing with similar groups.

3. *Teacher evaluation*—objectives do indeed teach the teacher. As objective builders, as learning situation designers, as careers for the persons they teach, teachers need frequent opportunities to check their own performances. Having a qualified observer in a classroom to report on the effectiveness of the teaching and the quality of the learning is helpful. But self-evaluation can be helpful too if it is done humbly and honestly. Though maintaining impartiality and keeping the ego in check is a hard task, a dedicated educator constantly uses objectives to measure his own contribution to the learning process. By examining what happened in each session, the teacher can gain insights for improving educational strategies and personal ways of working with people. Objectives are the principal method of spotlighting that form of examination because they provide specific parameters to be measured. Self-evaluation by objectives tends to build self-reliance and a greater openness to the needs and interests of those being taught.

Two great contributions of objectives, according to Kibler, Barker, and Miles, are increased clarity of educational purpose and communication of that purpose.[7] Robert Gagne underscored that second purpose and put it in first place: "Statements describing instructional objectives have the primary purpose of communicating."[8] Remembering that communication means building two-way bridges, these ideas suggest that objectives make clear to everyone interested in the educational act exactly what should be happening.

Characteristics of Good Objectives

Good objectives are useful objectives; useful objectives tend to be effective objectives. With that in mind, let's identify some prominent characteristics of good objectives with six working adjectives.

Good objectives are:

- *Personal*—stated in terms of the learner, his interests, abilities and needs.
- *Directional*—indicative of desired changes in the learner's understandings, attitudes, or patterns of actions.
- *Accomplishable*—descriptive of what educational changes realistically can take place within a specified time.
- *Valuable*—worth the expenditure of the learner's time, interest, and energy.
- *Measurable*—evaluative of the learner's accomplishments, learning resources' and teacher's role.
- *Communicable*—clear, concise, understandable statements.

These characteristics summarize much of what objectives can contribute to the learning process. At the same time, the six adjectives are a handy checklist to consult whether you are developing objectives of your own or adapting those provided by another source.

Warning Flags

Before we get too carried away with glowing accounts of value of objectives, we have to notice several warning flags flapping in the breeze. Relying on objectives as the be-all and end-all of education is like skating past the warning flags to some mighty thin ice.

Too rigid a use of behavioral objectives can result in behavior manipulation. The teacher then becomes a puppet master pulling strings according to his whims. Or, to try another metaphor, the objectives are used like cookie cutters to turn all students out looking alike. From a Christian point of view, the sameness of persons within a homogenous groupings can never be more important than each person's uniqueness. Nor does one person have the right to exercise thought control over another. Thought control is not education by any stretch of the imagination.

Elliot Eisner, in his writings, stressed his conviction that education is much more than manipulating behavior. Teachers, he felt, had to allow learners to respond creatively and to experience the joy of discovery. Good teachers, in his opinion, should be dynamic rather than mechanical, utilizing changes of pace and tempo in the classroom setting to capitalize on the changing interests of their students.[9] George Kneller pointed out that objectives can easily become reductionistic and deterministic, stifling rather than encouraging students, while ignoring the fact that "real learning is self-directed, unstructured, and to a large part unpredictable."[10] Perhaps behavioral objectives are appropriate for specific training experiences, Robert Ebel concluded, but they are inappropriate for enabling the learner to make independent and responsible choices or "to respond adaptively and effectively to unique future problem situations."[11]

These warnings are well expressed. In effect they are saying that the compass should not sail the boat. But a wise sailor depends on the compass to help chart the course.

Using Objectives Wisely

To avoid using objectives altogether may be one way of avoiding the dangers of misusing them. However, this opens the trap of a far greater danger, aptly described by a reporter who commented on a political speaker, "He aimed at nothing and hit it squarely on target." Objectives are really an integral part of any teaching-learning enterprise of any value. They describe and clarify intentions to help learners understand and apply facts, master skills, reshape attitudes, and develop desirable action patterns.

Maybe it would be helpful to use two different kinds of objectives. One kind would be the traditional behavioristic variety designed to specify precisely what learnings are anticipated. The other kind of objective could be used to encourage and support self-motivated learnings far beyond the basics. It seems to me that the term "expressive objectives" coined by Eisner[12] is useful to describe open-ended and flexible objectives following more heuristic models. Expressive objectives are non-predictive, dependent on the learner's personal involvement with a given set of learnings, and lead to create responses. This is how persons learn to think for themselves and to develop inner resources for coping with personal and societal problems.

Educational ministry is concerned that every person understand the facts of the faith, the claim of Christ upon his life, and the nurturing strength realized in the Christian community. But over and beyond the facts, every Christian needs to forge his own interrelationship with the impulse of the gospel with a built-in sense of discipleship. Objectives are practical tools in helping persons meet both concerns and needs. As tools, objectives need regular evaluation and reshaping to remain useful.

MEDIA

The *M* in C-O-M-E stands for *media*. A medium is whatever is used to transmit a message: oral and written language, pictures, symbols, film, television, radio, computer language. The list seems endless. Right over the horizon new forms of media are appearing in laboratories and test facilities. Most of them will be electronic. Direct access to computer banks from personal touch-tone telephones, Dick Tracy's two-way wrist TV, copies of printed and pictorial materials electrostatically produced by the living room television set and supplied at the flick of a switch—these and other developments are more than possibilities right now. Since we cannot escape from media, we might as well learn to live with them.

In the communication model, we put the message inside a larger block called the code. In a certain sense, the terms *media* and *code* are interchangeable. Each medium also has its own grammar, syntax, and language, which are clues to understanding the code it conveys. And then, to add another dimension, Marshall McLuhan insists that the medium is the message itself.

McLuhan's Insights

Like the comet Kahoutek, Marshall McLuhan streaked across the intellectual skies of the late sixties and left a dazzling tail of implications for everyone concerned with communication and education. Alternately praised and damned, he startled the complacent with his notion that the Gutenberg world of printing was waning and a shiny new electronic world was coming into being. Soon his terms, such as *hot and cool media* and *the global village*, became by-words. Often misinterpreted and frequently misquoted, McLuhan still forced those who dealt with media in any way to think seriously about the phenomena which they were manipulating and, more often, were manipulating them.

McLuhan is not consistent, systematic, or easy to read. His happy use of puns coupled with obtuse reasoning at times make his books hard going. Yet, every pastor-educator should be familiar with his insights. *Understanding Media* deserves to be high up on a "must" reading list.

To assert that the medium is the message is to recognize that this is action terminology. Media seek involvement of some form or another of those who use them. A film in a can is nothing more than a dust catcher until it is put on a projector and shown to someone. Then the film exerts its magic, but only to people who comprehend film language. Quick cuts, dissolves, close-ups turn film into gibberish for primitives who are unfamiliar with cinema techniques. Once film language becomes second nature, the viewer enters a new dimension of reality in which pictures move and talk. The medium is the message means, according to McLuhan, "in terms of the electronic age, that a totally new environment has been created."[13]

If you have ever seen the same film in a movie theater and on television, you know that you have had two different viewing experiences because you have participated in two different viewing environments. With its rapid scanning of electronic impulses, the TV picture is much less defined. In fact, it is your eye that puts the picture together on the screen. Therefore, you have to be more involved with watching the television version. And the more a medium demands your involvement, the "cooler" it is, to use McLuhan's phrase. In other words, a "hot" medium supplies so much detail for one or more senses that the participant has little to do beyond the medium. A "cool" medium, on the other hand, requires resolution and filling in the gaps. Thus film is hot and television is cool. A lecture is hot while a discussion group is cool. Radio is hot but a telephone conversation is cool.

So McLuhan roamed through the fields of media with his classifications and analyses dealing with everything from advertising to automation. We need not follow his probes in detail here, but we should understand his point that all media are extensions of the human senses offering varied ways of seeing, of hearing and speaking, of touching and smelling. The more all of the senses get into the act, the more involved we are.

The electronic revolution, according to McLuhan, increases the chances for all of the senses to get into the act simultaneously. We can see, hear, and experience things while they are happening. The whole world could tune in and take part in the funeral of a martyred president or meditate on the Christmas greetings sent by a team of astronauts circling the moon. McLuhan feels that simultaneous participation possibilities are turning the world into a "global village." Information is no longer released in an orderly, linear fashion alone, as it was during the print-oriented centuries. News explodes through many media to everyone at once. It took days before the results of Custer's battle with the Sioux and the Cheyenne on the Little Big Horn could reach the headlines of metropolitan dailies. But film-clips of one day's action in Vietnamese rice paddies could be shown on the eleven o'clock news (along with headache commercials and the weather report).

Like the monster created by Baron Frankenstein, media can get out of hand so that they control their users. With a play on words, McLuhan says in the title of another of his provocative studies, *The Medium Is the Massage*, media have the capacity to massage, to manipulate, to control the unwary. This is not particularly a new threat. Legalists have used lawbooks like weapons to force obedience to the letter of the law, thereby crushing the spirit of the law which usually made it much more humane. Textbooks have become prisons, and even the Bible has been turned by others into a "paper Pope." The only solution is to understand the uniqueness of each medium, what it can and cannot do, and then to use it carefully to accomplish the objectives of a communication-education process.

The Incarnation Medium

Biblically, much of what McLuhan has to say makes sense to pastor-educators. The incarnation of God in Christ is a classic demonstration of the message-medium configuration. As John wrote, "So the Word became flesh; he came to dwell among us, and we saw his glory, such glory as befits the Father's only Son full of grace and truth" (John 1:14, New English Bible). Gospel accounts of Jesus' ministry detail the many ways he offered himself as a living exposition of what God was like.

Those who knew Jesus during his earthly days were impressed by his healing methods which often turned out to be parables-in-action. And they were caught up in wonder as he related great truths in homey parables which were more calls to new lifestyles than they were intellectual explanations of theology. Directly or indirectly, he challenged all with whom he came in contact to get involved with God. So the church grew as an extension of his body through time, as a continuance of his ministry of involving people with God. Running like a silver thread through the tapestry of church history has been the conviction of the part of God's people that there is, indeed, a global village and that it is called the Christian church.

The medium is the message even applied to the church itself. Its architecture, its liturgies, its form of government—all speak emphatically about its purpose. Often these aspects of church life have spoken so loudly that the message they were designed to further was all but drowned out. Look at another example. The composition and conduct of a congregation at any given time—the medium is the message. The preacher explaining the day's text, the teacher leading a class, the counselor listening to personal woes—in these and all other clergy roles, the pastor is the medium is the message. And how does Jesus Christ, the Word incarnate, come through these forms? That questions should head the evaluation agenda of every service and every act of church life.

Thus it becomes imperative that the design of educational ministry, as well as all other forms of communication experiences within the family of God, utilize media effectively. And using media effectively is more than just knowing what a certain medium can and cannot do—it is determining how a specific medium can command the respect and involvement of those for whom it is intended.

Media and Learning

When choosing educational media, the key word is involvement. The more that learners are involved, the more likelihood that learning will take place.

A decade before McLuhan's blockbuster, *Understanding Media*, was published, Edgar Dale wrestled with the effectiveness of various media in a passive to active learner participation continuum. He developed what he called the "cone of experience," which graphically displayed the results of his studies of possible learning experiences useful for the classroom.[14]

DALE'S CONE OF EXPERIENCE

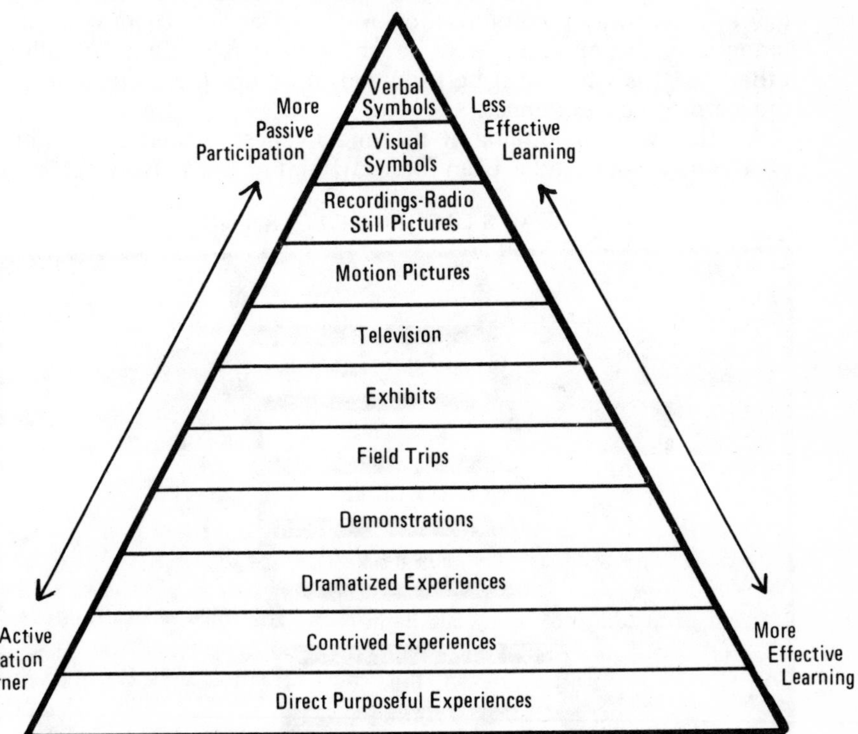

While the cone's demarcations are perhaps too discrete, allowing no estimate of multimedia combinations, Dale's analysis is a very useful focusing guide for determining what may be expected if learning experiences are coupled with certain media. Notice how the media at the tip of the cone instill more passive learner participation and thus produce less effective learning. As the bands become broader moving toward the base, more and more active participation is demanded of the learner and consequently, more effective learning occurs.

One of the striking features of Dale's contribution to understanding some of the dynamics of the teaching-learning process is the way his findings support many of McLuhan's insights. The cooler the medium, the more users have to get involved with its message; the more involvement, the more possibilities for learnings to take.

You can easily see why the lecture method is so ineffective. Of course, note-taking can provide some learner involvement, but notes are generally just condensed repetitions of ideas transmitted basically in a one-way communication form. Regardless of how scintillating their presentations may be, those who rely solely on telling others what is what must be prepared to accept the inefficiency of the learning consequences.

Another way of looking at the effectiveness of learning experiences and media used is from the viewpoint of the sensory activities

HOAG'S LADDER OF LEARNING

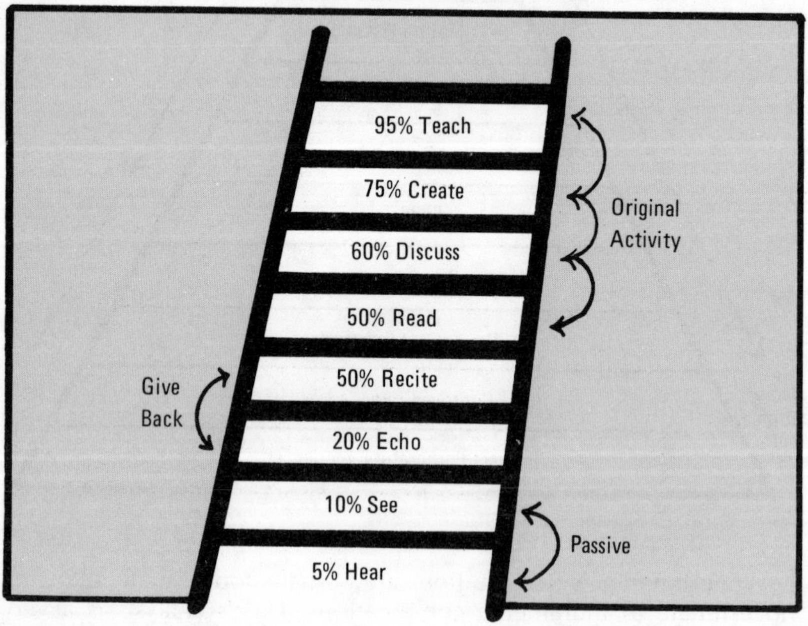

95% Teach
75% Create
Original Activity
60% Discuss
50% Read
Give Back
50% Recite
20% Echo
10% See
Passive
5% Hear

of the learners. In *The Ladder of Learning,* Victor Hoag suggested a ladder-like chart to indicate the average person's ability to remember what he has experienced.[15] Each step of the ladder represents a percentage of what an individual may remember for long periods of time following the use of one or more of his senses:

According to Hoag, hearing offers only a five percent effectiveness rating. This is bad news for preachers as well as lecturers. It also gives little solace to those parents who think that once they have told their children something, memory will take over and keep that information readily available. That old saying, "in one ear and out the other," has a basis in reality.

Since Hoag's ladder is based on learner activity, it establishes another series of checkpoints for evaluating media potentialities. For instance, recordings and radio come further down the bands of Dale's cone than the verbal symbols at the top. Yet just listening to a tape recording can be as ineffective as listening to a lecture. Switching to more sophisticated media does not necessarily mean that more effective learning follows—quite the contrary, if the switch does not include additional sensory involvement. There may be a flare-up of interest because of the gadgetry employed, but soon the novelty loses its impact. Tape cassettes have turned out to be boring when they are used to can straight informational data in modern guise. If the medium becomes tedium, then that is exactly the message it conveys.

On the other hand, suppose that learners have a part in developing creative tape scripts and recording these on cassettes. What happens then, according to Hoag, is a skyrocketing of memory retention of the contents manipulated in this form. Creative original activity pays off with 75 percent memory factor. Or go on further, and motivate these learners to develop this tape presentation for use with another group of learners. As they work through the educational demands of the task, they can increase their memory percentage another 20 points. Maybe this is why teachers usually learn so much more than their students; if they don't, it probably means that they have been unwilling to commit themselves fully to their education responsibilities.

Let's look at one more resource for guidance in media selection. James Campbell felt that sensory involvement is only one of four qualities that could assist in the communication-educational process. The other three are: individual/psychic involvement (profound learnings on the emotional level); the concrete/abstract spectrum (every form of medium used lies somewhere on a continuum between the very concrete and the very abstract); and the ambiguity level (each specific form of medium has a greater or lesser degree of ambiguity for users dependent on associations triggered in their minds).[16] Each of these qualities Campbell identified deserves careful study by every pastor-educator, for each possesses many implications for more successful forms of educational ministry.

Due to space limitations, we can only here reproduce Campbell's summary of these qualities in chart form weighing each against a typical media list. For each medium, he rated the qualities as "hi," "med," and "lo."[17]

CAMPBELL'S MEDIA GRADING ACCORDING TO FOUR QUALITIES

Media	sensory involvement			individual psychic involvement			concrete/ abstract			ambiguity		
	hi	med	lo	hi	med	lo	hi	med	lo	hi	med	lo
1. planned experiences	x			x			x				x	x
2. role play	x			x			x	x	x	x		
3. demonstration	x				x		x					x
4. realia	x			x	x		x				x	
5. motion pictures		x		x	x	x	x	x	x	x	x	x
6. sound filmstrips		x			x	x	x	x	x	x	x	x
7. recordings		x		x	x	x		x		x		
pictures		x			x	x		x		x	x	
8. visual symbols			x			x			x			x
9. verbal symbols			x			x			x	x		x

From *Communication-Learning for Churchmen*, edited by B. F. Jackson, Jr.

Naturally, Campbell is dealing in generalities. He insisted that his classifications and gradings be considered rough attempts to evaluate the qualities he felt were important. Actually, each specific form of a medium should be graded independently. One sound filmstrip may have a highly abstract level of presentation while another sound filmstrip may be much more concrete. The effects will be different. Therefore, the chart shows the range of possibilities that exist.

The lasting value of the chart is its challenge to be alert to what each medium can offer so that we make our media choices for substantially valid reasons. Notice, by the way, that Campbell is using items from Dale's cone of experience in reverse order.

When you put together the insights of McLuhan, Dale, Hoag, and

Campbell, some functional guidelines for choosing and using media begin to emerge:

- Match educational tasks with appropriate media according to their potential for learner involvement.
- Utilize the message of the media themselves to further the accomplishment of these tasks.
- Select and sequence learning experiences built around media in such a way that the educational event has an integrity and that each part is complementary to the whole.
- Arrange learning experiences so that learners move from the concrete to the abstract, from the simple to the complex.
- Plan a variety of media usages within a given educational event because individual differences preclude everyone's getting involved with a given medium in the same way.
- Choose media forms that enable learners to use all of their senses as well as their individualized creativity while learning.
- Test media choices against the communication model to enhance sender-receiver interrelationships.

These guidelines may seem to make choosing and using media a difficult task. It is, and no apologies are needed. No one has ever claimed that educational ministry and all that it entails is an easy operation. But helping persons appropriate the gospel for themselves and apply its guidance to real life situations is worthy of the greatest investment of energy and time.

EACH PERSON

That previous sentence brings us to the *E* of C-O-M-E: *Each Person*. It's too bad that *person* doesn't start with an *E*; the system would be neater. But maybe *each* is a better word to emphasize. It stresses individuality and personhood, the uniqueness of one human being. Educationally, this is sound, for each person learns for himself. As good communication focuses on the receiver, good education focuses on the learner, indicating once again how closely the two processes are related.

The Learning Self

To say that each person learns individually suggests a syndrome of implications. For example, everyone has a personal rate of learning, a certain amount of time needed to assimilate new ideas and reshape old ones. Everyone has a different intensity of response to different forms of media.

Everyone also has a tendency to learn more effectively through one form of sensory involvement than another. It is possible, therefore, to talk about "eye learners" and "ear learners," about "thinkers" and "doers." These categories are far from scientific, but they do stress personalized and preferential learning abilities. While almost everyone has a mixture of these categories available, usually he favors one above the rest.

Theories of learning abound and merit attention. Yet they are only theories; no investigator yet has produced a universally accepted explanation of the mysteries of learning. But most educators are convinced that learning is a private task. To "learn" is to grow, develop, change, perceive, experience; all interiorly-oriented verbs. Learning is what each person can only do for himself. In this light, the teaching function simply stated is to help each person learn. Good teaching begins with respect for individuality.

By examining the nature of the thinking self, it is easier to understand why learning is such a private matter. In an unpublished paper, William Koppe traced four basic systems within each person linked with the process of thinking. He described these systems as: the memory system, the belief and value system, the ego system, and the behavioral system.[18] Koppe could just as well have applied his systems to all of learning. The memory systems refer to the build-up, both consciously and unconsciously, of a "memory bank," which both collects and classifies individual perceptions and experiences. Here, intellectual understandings, emotions, and remembrances of past actions color the way any person views himself, God, others, and any part of his world environment. If someone says he "knows" something, he is really saying, "This is the way it seems to me." Kurt Lewin, the Gestalt learning psychologist, talked about "cognitive maps" to explain the internal phenomena of organizing data into some kind of useful configurations for ready reference. To learn is to change, reshape, alter, replace, and expand these maps.

The belief and value system describes a person's attitudes towards things, persons, and events and helps determine whether or not the memory bank (or the cognitive map) is changed in any way. The old saw that "beliefs are better caught than taught" is true up to a point. Many of our values and subsequent beliefs are absorbed from others. However, unquestioned values and undigested beliefs can foster a host of internal contradictions leading to uncertainty and confusion. Part of maturing (at any age!) is testing, critically examining one's value hierarchies in the light of experiences. Educational ministry can and must create a supportive climate in which each person can check and build his attitudes in the light of his communion with Christ. The whole person is one who has gone through the agonies of affective change and formed his own freely chosen system of beliefs. This is what Paul had in mind when he wrote to fledgling Christians in imperial Rome, "Adapt yourselves no longer to the pattern of this present world, but let your minds be remade and your whole nature thus transformed. Then you will be able to discern the will of God, and to know what is good, acceptable, and perfect" (Romans 12:2 NEB).

The ego system, in Koppe's model, refers to the self, one's conscious awareness of who he is. The search for valid self-identity so strong in adolescence, never really ends. As people grow and change in a shifting, changing society, the same questions, "Who am I," and "Why am I living?" must be pursued endlessly like variations on a music theme. It is the ego that does the learning, the changing, the modifying of values, the adjusting of memory bank contents. But the ego is vulnerable. So identity searching is risky, and to some extent threatening. Therefore, defense mechanisms, to use the Freudian concept, are erected for protecting and buttressing the ego against change. As Arthur Jersild explained the task, "To gain in knowledge of self, one must have the courage to seek it and the humility to accept what one may find."[19] Here is where educational ministry can live up to the ministry part of its name—in its willing acceptance of persons so that they can accept themselves, and then to go beyond this plateau to see themselves as the kind of persons they can become through their partnership with God.

The fourth component in Koppe's model is the behavioral system. Overt actions are included in behavior as well as thought processes such as problem-solving and creative imagining. While many actions become the products of habit which short-circuits deliberate thinking, most of our activities are directed by the thinking self. And the self must bear the responsibility for its actions. Here again, educational ministry seeks to serve individuals by helping them develop patterns, both mental and physical, as suitable, viable expressions of their faith-value systems and as indicators of their emerging selves.

Koppe related his four thinking systems to education:

> From the viewpoint of Christian education, our interest in each of these systems must never be taken in isolation. We may teach content in order to provide a rich memory system, or we may give individuals practice in assigning religious values to experiences and in organizing their belief systems. Still, these are meaningless unless we help individuals to develop a strong positive ego structure supported by adequate theological thinking habits.[20]

The Developing Self

One primary characteristic of selfhood already mentioned briefly is its dynamic. Throughout infancy, childhood, adolescence, young adulthood, and adulthood, the self is always in a state of coming-into-being. At each developmental stage, the self possesses certain capacities and certain limitations. It can be no other than what it is.

A common failing of many traditional catechetical courses was the insistence of providing junior high youth with adult answers to adult questions concerning Christian faith and life. Underlying this procedure was probably the conviction that once young persons knew "the truth," they would never depart from it. However, junior high boys and girls can only be Christians aged 12 or 13 or 14; they cannot be, think, or function as adults.

In both The American Lutheran Church and the Lutheran Church in America, educators on the churchwide staff charged with responsibility for designing parish education curricula have stressed matching content and learning experience to individuals at their particular stage of maturation. But the churchwide curricula can only deal in generalities. In each parish the programs and courses produced must be adapted to local needs. While genetic and other biological factors are critical in development, environmental and sociological factors also play a major role. Each individual, each homogeneous group of persons on a common age level, must be considered in terms of his or her needs, capacities, and interests. Resources and teaching plans have educational value for the most part only when they are modified to fit people where they are.

The developmental studies of scholars such as Jean Piaget, Erik Erikson, and Ronald Goldman can aid the pastor-educator in understanding how people of different ages in the parish can learn. However, general observations are immeasurably enriched by personal knowledge of the real human beings concerned. Going back to the communication model, for instance, we remember how significantly personal "filters" and individually generated "static" can interfere with reception of a message. Only as you live and work with people, listen to them, allow them to express their interests and concerns, and permit their participation in shaping objectives can you help them change educationally or can you build more effective two-way communication with them. What Jesus said about himself as the good shepherd, "I know my own sheep and my sheep know me" (John 10:1b, NEB), should be said humbly by all other shepherd-educators who serve in his name. "The basic stuff of the teacher's craft," Ralph Heim wrote, "is not some social inheritance, such as a book or an institution, but the growing life of a pupil."[21]

COME ALIVE

Making educational ministry come alive is putting together what we know about communication, objectives, media, and the nature of individuals, checking frequently for assurance that each ingredient in the mixture is receiving adequate attention. These four areas of investigation are intertwined to such a degree that it doesn't matter much on which area you focus attention. You can hardly proceed without considering the other areas to an intensive degree. However, some sequencing of these considerations is desirable to avoid circular ramblings. Let's construct a rough chart to demonstrate (see p. 276).

By starting with "Understand Persons," we keep reminding ourselves that it is for human beings that we accept a teaching role, to promote their growth and well-being, to stimulate their ability to think for themselves, and to believe in the gospel for themselves. As pastor-educators, then, we can conceive of teaching in only one way: as facilitating the learning of others. All of the other blocks in the chart should be understood in this context.

One of Carl Rogers' cogent comments about the goal of education is just as applicable to Christian education as it is to any other form:

> We are, in my view, faced with an entirely new situation in education where the goal of education, if we are to survive, is the facilitation of change and learning. The only man who is educated is the man who has learned how to adapt and change; the man who realized that no knowledge is secure, that only the process of seeking knowledge gives a basis for security. Changingness, a reliance on process rather than upon static knowledge, is the only thing that makes any sense as a goal for education in the modern world.[22]

But educational ministry goes further than other kinds of education because it is powered by the impulse of the gospel. The abiding presence of the living Christ calls people to join together in a fellowship with him and with each other. While religious faith does have its personal side, it reaches its fullest expression in fellowship, a sense of community forged through common devotion. This commonality, through root-word structure, welds together some significant terms, such as communion, community, and communication. All three are valid dimensions of the people of God as they live and grow, worship and serve in a common sense of discipleship. Pastor-educators, therefore, can see their teaching roles more sharply defined as they take the concept of educational ministry seriously. All their efforts geared toward facilitating individual changes in

A WAY OF MINISTERING EDUCATIONALLY

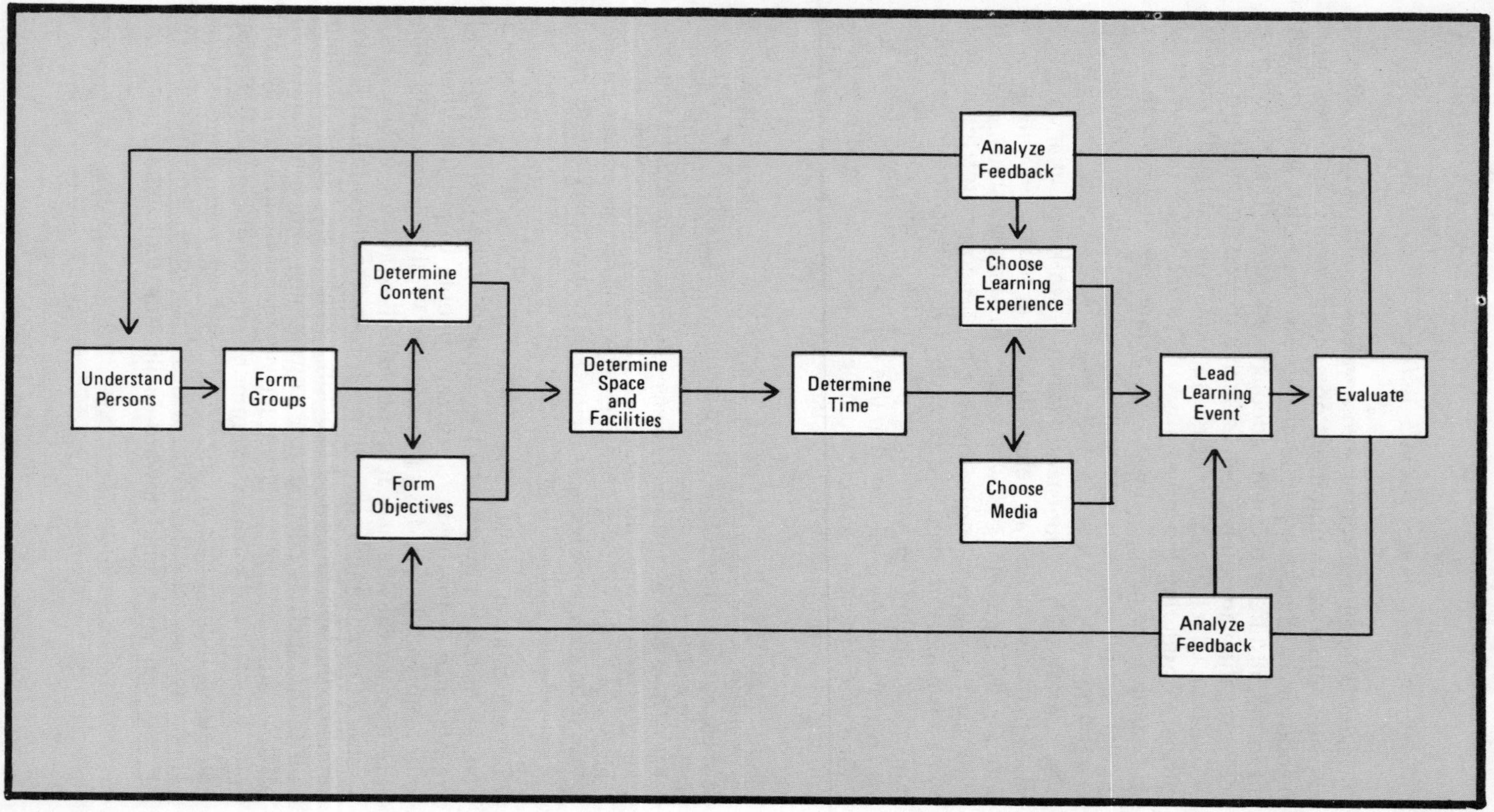

understandings, attitudes, and action patterns are designed to enable persons, as the definition of educational ministry states, "to know and confess as their own the Christian faith and to assume responsible roles as Christians in the world."

NOTES

1. *Design for Developing Educational Ministry in the Parish, ALC/LCA*, vol. 1 (Philadelphia: The American Lutheran Church and the Lutheran Church in America, 1972), p. 21.

2. Cited in Marshall McLuhan and Quentin Fiore, *The Medium Is The Massage* (New York: Bantam Books, 1967), pp. 6-7.

3. Wilbur Schramm, "How Communication Works," in *The Process and Effects of Mass Communication*, ed. Wilbur Schramm (Urbana, Illinois: University of Illinois Press, 1954), p. 4.

4. Merrill R. Abbey, *Man, Media and the Message* (New York: Friendship Press, 1960), p. 47.

5. *Ibid.*, pp. 48-58.

6. Robert F. Mager, *Preparing Instructional Objectives* (Palo Alto, Calif.: Fearon Publishers, 1962), p. 3.

7. Robert J. Kibler, Larry L. Barker, and David T. Miles, *Behavioral Objectives and Instruction* (Boston: Allyn and Bacon, 1970), p. 1.

8. Robert M. Gagne, "Behavioral Objectives? Yes!" *Educational Leadership*, February, 1972, p. 394.

9. Elliot W. Eisner, "Educational Objectives, Help or Hindrance?" *The School Review*, Autumn, 1967, pp. 252-253.

10. George F. Kneller, "Behavioral Objectives? No!" *Educational Leadership*, February, 1972, p. 397.

11. Robert L. Ebel, "Behavioral Objectives, A Close Look," *Phi Delta Kappan*, November, 1970, p. 172.

12. Elliot W. Eisner, "Instructional and Expressive Educational Objectives: Their Formulation and Use in Curriculum," in *Instructional Objectives*, ed. W. James Popham, American Research Education Association, Monograph Series on Curriculum Evaluation, no. 3 (Chicago: Rand-McNally & Co., 1969), p. 15.

13. Marshall McLuhan, *Understanding Media* (New York: Signet Books, 1964), p. ix.

14. Edgar Dale, *Audio Visual Methods in Teaching, Revised* (New York: Holt, Rinehart, and Winston, 1954). Chapter 4 develops this idea in detail around the cone chart.

15. Victor Hoag, *The Ladder of Learning* (Greenwich, Conn.: The Seabury Press, 1960), p. 114.

16. James C. Campbell, "Using Audiovisual Resources," in *Communication-Learning for Churchmen*, ed. B. F. Jackson, Jr., vol. 1, (Nashville: Abingdon, 1968), pp. 250-255.

17. *Ibid.*, p. 290.

18. William A. Koppe, "The Process of Thinking and Its Implications for Christian Education," 1967 (unpublished paper), pp. 4-12.

19. Arthur T. Jersild, "The Search for Meaning," in *The Self in Growth, Teaching and Learning*, ed. Don E. Hamachek, (Englewood Cliffs, N.J.: Prentice-Hall, Inc., 1965), p. 542.

20. Koppe, "The Process of Thinking," p. 12.

21. Ralph D. Heim, *Leading a Church School*, (Philadelphia: Fortress Press, 1968), p. 172.

22. Carl R. Rogers, *Freedom to Learn* (Columbus, Ohio: Charles E. Merrill Publishing Company, 1969), p. 104.

CONTRIBUTORS

Robert Newell Bacher, M.Ed.
Project Manager for Action Research, Division for Parish Services, LCA; previously a pastor in Wheat Ridge, Colorado, and Associate Director of the LCA Commission on Youth Ministry.

John R. Cochran
Pastor, Emanuel Lutheran Church, Center City Lutheran Parish in Philadelphia; served as pastor of the Lilly-Gallitzin Lutheran Parish in Central Pennsylvania; president of the Queens Village Housing, Inc., and the United Communities of Southeast Philadelphia.

Richard Simon Hanson, M.Th., Ph.D.
Associate Professor of Religion, Luther College, Decorah, Iowa; formerly an instructor at Harvard University and at Luther Theological Seminary, St. Paul, Minn.; author of *The Psalms in Modern Speech* and *The Future of the Great Planet Earth*.

Frank William Klos, S.T.M., M.Ed.
Senior Editor for Adult Program Resources, Division for Parish Services, LCA; formerly a pastor in Martinsburg, W. Va., and an educational consultant for the *Davey and Goliath* TV Series; presently serving on the Upper Dublin, Pa., School Board; author of *Confirmation and First Communion* and *A Companion for Reading and Studying the Good News* (Lutheran Study Edition of *Good News for Modern Man*).

William Aram Koppe, Ph.D.
Associate Director for Analysis and Evaluation, Department for Research and Planning, Division for Parish Services, LCA; formerly a professor of parent education at the University of Minnesota; author of *How Persons Grow in Christian Community*, Yearbooks in Christian Education, IV.

Calvin D. Kuder
Pastor, First Lutheran Church, Tiffin, Ohio; formerly served pastorates in Centralia and Chicago, Illinois, and as Audio-Visuals Editor for the LCA Board of Parish Education.

Richard Henry Luecke, Ph.D.
Professor of Rhetoric and Philosophy, Valparaiso University, Indiana; formerly served as pastor in Princeton, N.J. and as Director of Studies, Urban Training Center for Christian Mission in Chicago; author of *Violent Sleep* and *Perchings: Reflections on Society and Ministry.*

John O. Lundin
Pastor, West Nidaros Lutheran Church, Crooks, South Dakota; presently a chaplain in the United States Army Air Force Reserve and a member of the Tri-Valley School Board.

Richard Allan Olson, Ed.D.
Assistant Professor of Christian Education, Lutheran Theological Seminary at Philadelphia; formerly a public school educator and a teacher at Union Theological Seminary in New York City and at Drew University Theological School in Madison, N.J.; served as consultant for the Department of Ministry, National Council of Churches.

Richard I. Preis, M.A.
Senior Pastor, Trinity Lutheran Church, Ann Arbor, Mich.; formerly served as a counselor for Lutheran students at the University of Kansas and as a pastor in Springfield, Ohio.

Richard Rehfeldt, S.T.M.

Pastor, Windsor Heights Lutheran Church, Des Moines, Iowa; served as a pastor in Waverly, Iowa, and as a student minister at Yosemite National Park.

Norman Wegmeyer

Administrative Assistant, Division for Life and Mission in the Congregation, ALC; previously served pastorates in Formersville, Columbus, and Toledo, Ohio, and in Butler, Pa.; was Director of Leadership Development for the ALC Division of Parish Education; author of *The Art of Christian Relationships* and *Rejoice with Us*.

Andrew John White, Th.M., Ph.D.

Associate Professor of Practical Theology, Lutheran Theological Seminary at Philadelphia; served pastorates in Cicero, Illinois and E. Cleveland, Ohio; presently the Coordinator of the Urban Church Institute and a Democratic Committeeman in Philadelphia's 22nd Ward.

HELPFUL BOOKS AND RESOURCES

A very wise teacher always told his students, "Responsible persons should have in their libraries on every subject in which they are interested, at least two books that present differing points of view. Generally in this way they will be forced to think for themselves."

Thus, the following books and resources are recommended. Selections were made on the basis of: usefulness, stimulation for thinking, and suggestions for action. The authors do not reflect one theological stance or one educational perspective. Each has contributions to make to the growth of pastor-educators.

For convenience, the items are listed according to the topics considered in the specific parts of this volume. To avoid unnecessary duplication, each item appears only once even though it may be equally appropriate in other categories.

ON VISIONING

Apps, Jerold W. *How to Improve Adult Education in Your Church*. Minneapolis: Augsburg Publishing House, 1972.

Evenson, C. Richard, ed. *Foundations for Educational Ministry*. Yearbooks in Christian Education, vol. III. Philadelphia: Fortress Press, 1971.

Heim, Ralph D. *Leading a Church School*. Philadelphia: Fortress Press, 1968.

Jahsmann, Allan Hart. *Power Beyond Words*. St. Louis: Concordia Press, 1969.

Nelson, C. Ellis. *Where Faith Begins*. Richmond: John Knox Press, 1967.

Westerhoff, John H. *Values for Tomorrow's Children*. Philadelphia: Pilgrim Press, 1970.

ON THEOLOGIZING

Bible

Anderson, Bernhard W. *Understanding the Old Testament*. Englewood Cliffs, N.J.: Prentice-Hall, 1966.

Bright, John A. *A History of Israel*. 2d ed. Philadelphia: Westminster, 1972.

Daniel-Rops, Henri. *Daily Life in the Time of Jesus.* New York: New American Library, 1964.

deVaux, Roland. *Ancient Israel.* New York: McGraw-Hill, 1965.

Klos, Frank W. *A Companion for Reading and Understanding the Good News,* in the Lutheran Study Edition of *Good News for Modern Man.* Minneapolis: Augsburg Publishing House and Philadelphia: Fortress Press, 1972.

Price, James L. *Interpreting the New Testament.* New York: Holt, Rinehart, and Winston, 1961.

Tenny, Merrill C. *New Testament Times.* Grand Rapids: William B. Eerdmans, 1965.

Theology

Benne, Robert. *Wandering in the Wilderness.* Philadelphia: Fortress Press, 1972.

Gritsch, Eric W. *The Continuing Reformation.* Philadelphia: Lutheran Church Press, 1971.

Heinecken, Martin J. *Christian Teachings: Affirmations of Faith for Lay People.* Philadelphia: Fortress Press, 1967.

Uthe, Edward W. *Theology: An Assessment of Current Trends.* Philadelphia: Fortress Press, 1968.

ON CARING

Psychological Concerns

Erikson, Erik H. *Childhood and Society.* New York: W. W. Norton, 1950.

Erikson, Erik H. *Youth: Change and Challenge.* New York: Basic Books, 1963.

Goldman, Ronald. *Readiness in Religion.* New York: Seabury Press, 1965.

Koppe, William A. *How Persons Grow in Christian Community.* Yearbooks in Christian Education, vol. IV. Philadelphia: Fortress Press, 1972.

Rood, Wayne. *On Nurturing Christians.* Nashville: Abingdon, 1972.

Strommen, Merton P.; Brekke, Milo L.; Underwager, Ralph C.; and Johnson, Arthur L. *A Study of Generations.* Minneapolis: Augsburg Publishing House, 1972.

Seifert, Harvey, and Clinebell, Howard J., Jr. *Personal Growth and Social Change.* Philadelphia: Westminster, 1969.

Pichaske, Donald R. *A Study Book on The Manifesto.* Philadelphia: Board of Publication of the Lutheran Church in America, 1967.

Schaller, Lyle E. *Community Organization: Conflict and Reconciliation.* Nashville: Abingdon, 1966.

Uthe, Edward W., ed. *Social Change: An Assessment of Current Trends.* Philadelphia: Fortress Press, 1968.

ON ORGANIZING

Organization Development

Addison-Wesley Series on Organization Development. (Reading, Mass.: Addison-Wesley Publishing Co.).

- Bennis. *Organization Development: Its Structure, Origins, and Prospects.*
- Beckhard. *Organization Development: Strategies and Models.*
- Blake and Mouton. *Building a Dynamic Corporation Through Grid Organization Development.*
- Lawrence and Lorsch. *Developing Organizations: Diagnosis and Action.*
- Schein. *Process Consultation: Its Role in Organization Development.*

- Walton. *Interpersonal Peacemaking: Confrontations and Third Party Consultation.*

Bennis, Warren G.; Benne, Kenneth; and Chin, Robert. *The Planning of Change.* 2d ed. New York: Holt, Rinehart, and Winston, 1969.

Blake, Robert R., and Mouton, Jane Srygley. *Corporate Excellence Through Grid Organization Development.* Houston, Texas: Gulf Publishing Co., 1968.

Fordyce, Jack K., and Weil, Raymond. *Managing with People.* Reading, Mass.: Addison-Wesley Publishing Co., 1971.

Rudge, Peter F. *Ministry and Management.* London: Tavistock, 1968.

Schaller, Lyle E. *Parish Planning.* Nashville: Abingdon, 1971.

Worley, Robert C. *Change in the Church: A Source of Hope.* Philadelphia: Westminster, 1971.

Leadership Development

Blake, Robert, and Mouton, Jane. *The Managerial Grid.* Houston, Texas: Gulf Publishing Company, 1964.

Eddy, W.; Burke, W.; Dupre, V.; and Smith, O., eds. *Behavioral Science and the Manager's Role.* Washington, D.C.: NTL, 1969.

Flynn, Elizabeth, and LaFaso, John. *Group Discussion as a Learning Process.* Paramus, N.J.: Paulist Press, 1972.

Reid, Clyde. *Groups Alive—Church Alive.* New York: Harper & Row, 1969.

Schaller, Lyle E. *Change Agent.* Nashville: Abingdon, 1972.

Schindler-Rainman, Eva, and Lippitt, Ronald. *The Volunteer Community: Creative Use of Human Resources.* Washington, D.C.: NTL, 1971.

ON COMMUNICATING

Communication

Bach, Robert O., ed. *Communication: The Art of Understanding and Being Understood.* New York: Hastings House, 1963.

Berlo, David K. *The Process of Communication: An Introduction to Theory and Practice.* New York: Holt, Rinehart, and Winston, 1960.

Hayakawa, S. I. *Language in Thought and Action.* New York: Harcourt, Brace and World, 1964.

Jackson, B. F., Jr., ed. *Communication-Learning for Churchmen.* Communication for Churchmen Series, vol. 1. Nashville: Abingdon, 1968. (Four parts in this basic study deal with: communication, learning, print as a resource for learning, using audio-visual resources.)

Objectives

Kibler, Robert J.; Barker, Larry L.; and Miles, David T. *Behavioral Objectives and Instruction.* Boston: Allyn and Bacon, 1970.

Mager, Robert F. *Preparing Instructional Objectives.* Palo Alto, Calif.: Fearon Publishers, 1962.

Media

Abbey, Merrill R. *Man, Media and the Message.* New York: Friendship Press, 1969.

Babin, Pierre, ed. *The Audio-Visual Man, Media and Religious Education.* Dayton, Ohio: Pflaum, 1970.

Jackson, B. F., Jr. *Audiovisual Facilities and Equipment for Churchmen.* Communication for Churchmen Series, vol. 3. Nashville: Abingdon, 1970.

Jackson, B. F., Jr. *Television-Radio-Film for Churchmen.* Communication for Churchmen Series, vol. 2. Nashville: Abingdon, 1969.

Kemp, Jerrold E. *Planning and Producing Audiovisual Materials.* 2d ed. San Francisco: Chandler, 1968.

Kuhns, William. *Environmental Man.* New York: Harper & Row, 1969.

McLuhan, Marshall. *Understanding Media: The Extensions of Man.* New York: Signet Books, 1964.

Development and Learning

Borton, Terry. *Reach, Touch and Teach: Student Concerns and Process Education.* New York: McGraw-Hill, 1970.

Gagne, Robert M. *The Conditions of Learning.* 2d ed. New York: Holt, Rinehart, and Winston, 1970.

Goldman, Ronald. *Religious Thinking from Childhood to Adolescence.* New York: The Seabury Press, 1964.

Havighurst, Robert J. *Developmental Tasks and Education.* 3d ed. New York: David McKay & Co., 1972.

Leypoldt, Martha M. *Learning Is Change: Adult Education in the Church.* Valley Forge, Pa.: Judson Press, 1971.